THE CAPTURE OF ATTU

A World War II Battle
as Told by the Men Who Fought There

Compiled by Lt. Robert J. Mitchell, 32nd Infantry

with contributions by

Sewell T. Tyng and
Capt. Nelson L. Drummond Jr.,
Field Artillery

Introduction to the Bison Books Edition
by Gregory J. W. Urwin

UNIVERSITY OF NEBRASKA PRESS
LINCOLN AND LONDON

Library of Congress Cataloging-in-Publication Data
The capture of Attu: a World War II battle as told by the men who fought there /
compiled by Robert J. Mitchell, with Sewell T. Tyng and Nelson L. Drummond Jr.;
introduction to the Bison Books edition by Gregory J. W. Urwin.
p.   cm.
Originally published: Washington, D.C.: Infantry Journal, 1944. 1st ed.
Prepared by the U.S. War Dept.
Includes Bibliographical references and index.
ISBN 0-8032-9557-X (pbk.: alk. paper)
1. Attu Island (Alaska), Battle of, 1943—Personal narratives, American.
I. Mitchell, Robert J., Lieutenant.   II. Tyng, Sewell T. (Sewell Tappan), 1895–
1946.   III. Drummond, Nelson L.   IV. United States. War Dept.
D769.87.A4A5   2000
940.54′28—dc21
99-058662

CONTENTS

CONTENTS — *Continued*

CONTENTS — *Continued*

IV: COUNTERATTACK AND CLEANUP

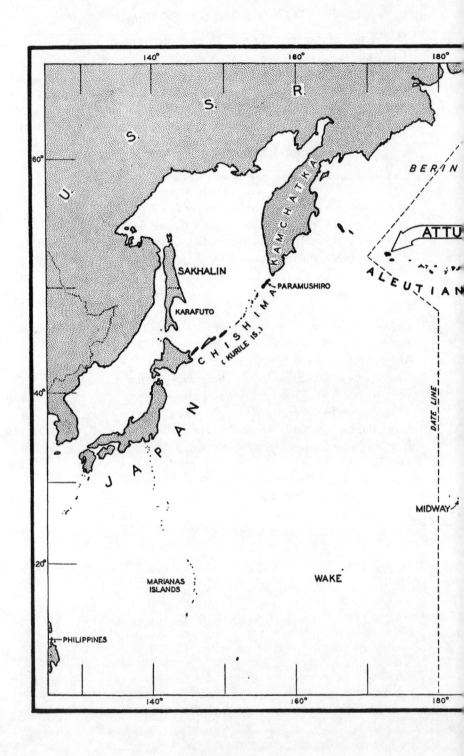

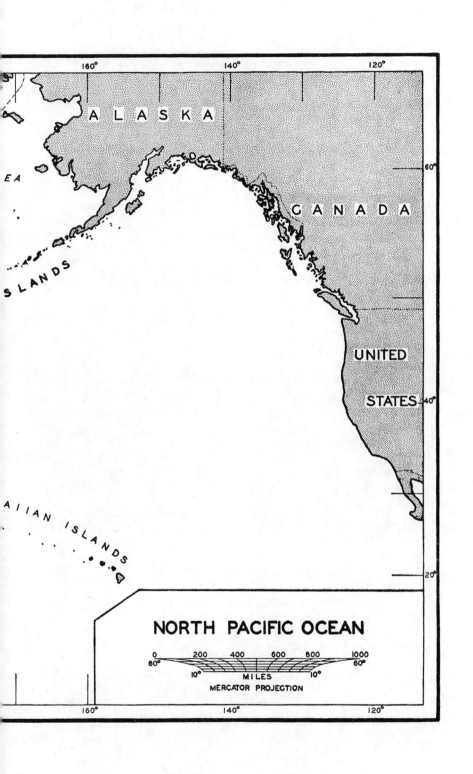

S

A L A S K A

E A

S L A N D S

I S L A N D S

C A N A D A

UNITED

STATES — 40°

A I I A N I S L A N D S

NORTH PACIFIC OCEAN

| 0 | 200 | 400 | 600 | 800 | 1000 |

MILES

MERCATOR PROJECTION

160° 140° 120°

60°

20°

PREFACE

This book attempts to put the reader on the battlefield with the ground soldier. Men who fought on Attu, officers and enlisted men, told their stories to Lieutenant Robert J. Mitchell of the 32d Infantry, one of the regiments engaged. Lieutenant Mitchell was wounded during the latter stage of the battle and while convalescing wrote the accounts which are now published as Part Two of the book. These stories tell of the discomforts and perils, the failures and successes, the fear and courage, the many fights between small groups and the occasional humor, of which battle consists. In preparing these accounts for publication, every effort has been made to keep them as nearly as possible in the exact form in which they were written down by Lieutenant Mitchell; consequently, a minimum of editorial changes has been made.

Part One, written by Sewell T. Tyng, is an introduction in the form of a connected narrative of events leading up to the invasion of the Aleutian island of Attu and a detailed account of the battle which resulted in the capture of Attu by American forces. This narrative is based on official sources and on material collected by Captain Nelson L. Drummond, Jr., Field Artillery, formerly of the Alaska Defense Command. Captain Drummond visited Attu shortly after the battle, studied the terrain, and interviewed participants of all ranks.

The volume has been prepared in the War Department under the supervision of the Military Intelligence Division. Aerial photographs are by the 11th Air Force; battle photographs are by the U. S. Army Signal Corps; and terrain feature photographs are by Captain Drummond, assisted by Private First Class A. E. Johnson, 50th Engineer Regiment. The panoramic sketch is based on an original by the 50th Engineer Regiment.

The publication of the volume in its present form has been made possible by the coöperation of Colonel Joseph I. Greene, Editor of *The Infantry Journal*, and his staff.

Introduction

Gregory J. W. Urwin

During the great Pacific War of 1941–45, some of the most godforsaken spots on this planet became invested with strategic importance. Thousands of young Japanese and Americans journeyed to the furthest corners of the world's largest ocean to fight and die for places they would have otherwise shunned. The war's literature brims with tales of nightmarish slugging matches through steaming jungles on Guadalcanal and New Guinea, across the coral reefs and sand of Tarawa and other misshapen atolls, and amid the volcanic ash of Iwo Jima. Interestingly enough, one of the most hellish campaigns in the Pacific Theater, the American conquest of Attu, was also the coldest. Attu was as dramatic, bloody, and miserable as any other clash between Japanese and American forces, but its story remains as obscure as its setting.

Attu is the westernmost point in the Aleutians, the bleak island chain that stretches in a graceful arc from Alaska to within easy reach of the Soviet Union and the northern limits of Japan. A jumble of sheer snowcapped peaks, barren valleys of brown tundra, and narrow beaches, Attu measures roughly thirty-five miles in length and fifteen miles in width. It hardly seems the kind of place for which sensible men would give their lives—unless compelled by the inexorable dictates of war. The adjective historians invariably use to describe Attu is "forbidding." Even as American and Japanese forces grappled in combat there, the *New York Times* characterized Attu as "the loneliest spot on earth," and an official at the U.S. Navy Department sniffed that it looked "from the air like a picture of a frozen sea." Observers who experienced Attu firsthand confirmed these negative impressions. The U.S. Army's official history of the campaign did not exaggerate when it stated, "To the soldiers who had to fight not only the Japanese but the weather and terrain of the island, it must have seemed that the Creator of the universe was an unskilled apprentice when He brought Attu into existence."[1]

Attu's weather alone presented a formidable obstacle to the tactic that the American military honed to a fine edge during World War II—the massive application of high-tech firepower by combined arms from the sea, air, and land. "Modern armies had never fought before on *any* field that was like the Aleutians," explained Dashiell Hammett, the famed mystery writer who spent eighteen months on Adak as a corporal in the U.S. Army. "We could borrow no knowledge from the past. We would have to learn as we went along, how to live and fight and win in this land, the least-known part of our America."[2]

Hanson W. Baldwin, the long-time military editor and analyst for the *New York Times*, admirably summarized the tactical challenges that confronted the American soldiers and sailors who came in May 1943 to evict the twenty-four hundred Japanese troops holding Attu: "Williwaws, or sudden fierce squalls, rage around Attu; the holding ground for ships is dangerous, in fact almost impossible; fog is almost always prevalent, and the clinging white mist is so thick that soldiers advancing in skirmish lines across the rocky hills lose sight of each other; the supporting fire of naval vessels cannot be observed; planes cannot bomb."[3]

It is no wonder that Samuel Eliot Morison, the author of the U.S. Navy's official history of World War II, dubbed Attu and the rest of the Aleutians the "Theater of Military Frustration." "Sailors, soldiers and aviators alike," Morison revealed, "regarded an assignment to this region of almost perpetual mist and snow as little better than penal servitude." In fact, Morison went so far as to argue that both the Japanese and Americans "would have done well to have left the Aleutians to the Aleuts for the course of the war."[4]

Attu's rendezvous with destiny began as a diversion intended to win Japan a much more valuable prize far to the south in the Central Pacific. When Adm. Isoroku Yamamoto massed the bulk of Japan's Combined Fleet to seize Midway, he dispatched two aircraft carriers to raid Dutch Harbor, the only American naval base in the Aleutians, on or shortly after 1 June 1942. Yamamoto hoped this northward lunge would prompt an outnumbered U.S. Pacific Fleet to divide its strength, setting the stage for a decisive Japanese naval victory off Midway. Yamamoto had no way of knowing that American code breakers had uncovered his plan in time for Adm. Chester W. Nimitz to deploy the Pacific Fleet's flattops for an ambush. A humbled Combined Fleet would end up limping away from Midway after losing four of its best carriers.[5]

While Yamamoto's main effort ended in disaster, the Japanese Navy established a foothold in the Aleutians. Following two air strikes on Dutch Harbor, Vice Adm. Moshiro Hosogaya's Northern Area Fleet landed troops on a pair of undefended islands, Attu and Kiska. This proved a poor trade for the carriers sunk at Midway. The occupation of Attu and Kiska did set off an invasion scare in the Pacific Northwest that spread as far south as Seattle, but the Japanese envisioned a purely defensive role for their new American bases.[6]

Had Attu not been part of Alaska, the American military probably would have bypassed it like so many other Japanese strongholds that lay off the main road to Tokyo. But the fact that the Japanese had set foot on American soil— even such a worthless patch of it—made possession of Attu a matter of national pride. Something also had to be done to appease those Americans who kept demanding revenge for Pearl Harbor and a greater allocation of military resources to the Pacific front. The American Joint Chiefs of Staff believed this political pressure could be relieved without a heavy expenditure in men and materiel by authorizing an offensive against Attu.[7]

The U.S. Navy and Army still had much to learn about the art of amphibious warfare in the spring of 1943, and that showed in their conduct of the Attu operation. The staff officers who planned the invasion knew precious little about their objective. The only map available to them, a Coast and Geodetic Survey chart, contained no information on the island's terrain more than a thousand yards beyond the shoreline. Day after day of pea-soup fog inhibited aerial reconnaissance, which kept the Americans ignorant of much of Attu's topography—not to mention the location of enemy defenses.[8]

The dirty job of going ashore and digging the Japanese out of their foxholes, trenches, and bunkers fell to the U.S. Seventh Infantry Division. It was a curious decision. At the time of its selection, the Seventh Division was in Nevada training for motorized warfare in the deserts of North Africa. The division was abruptly demotorized and whisked off to Fort Ord, California, for retraining in amphibious techniques. The Seventh's personnel practiced their new specialty under the tutelage of the world's top authority on the subject, Marine Maj. Gen. Holland M. "Howlin' Mad" Smith, but the beaches near Monterey hardly resembled what awaited them on Attu.[9]

The Seventh Division did not even receive proper winter clothing to shield its members from Attu's vicious climate. The American high command recognized this deficiency, but did not think the troops would suffer very much. After all, the planning staffs predicted that Attu would fall in three days. As it turned out, the Japanese, who met the chilled invaders garbed in fur-lined uniforms, goatskin moccasins, fur caps, and thick, tightly woven mittens, maintained organized resistance for two and a half weeks.[10]

In the meantime, the Seventh Division floundered through an alien world where the ground was so spongy it often gave way beneath the weight of a single man and everything one touched was wet. Russell Annabel, a correspondent for the United Press, shared this ordeal with the troops, and he conveyed their sufferings to the readers of the *Saturday Evening Post*:

Your outfit would move into a position under cover of fog and darkness, and you would dig a foxhole and put up a breastwork of cut sod and rocks. You were already wet from fording streams and falling into sinkholes in the dark, and now seepage began trickling into the foxhole, so that presently you were standing in a foot or more of bitterly cold water. You couldn't search for a drier place, because by this time the Jap snipers and mortar crews had spotted you. So you crouched there, returning their fire, and after a while, strangely, your feet and legs no longer ached.[11]

Robert Sherrod, a gifted combat correspondent employed by *Time* and *Life*, offered this word portrait of the penalty common GIs paid for the shortsightedness of their superiors: "They were gaunt and haggard. Not one of them had shaved in the 16 days they had been fighting. Red beards and black beards and dirty blond beards covered their grimy faces. Each wore two pairs of long wool drawers, two or three pairs of heavy socks under their soaked leather boots, a wool shirt or two, a sweater and a parka. But no amount of clothing seemed enough on this Attu mountainside. Most of the men were shivering as the icy wind pierced to their bones. Their feet were wet and probably black with cold, as are most feet on Attu."[12]

In addition to Annabel and Sherrod, seven other American journalists covered the fighting on Attu. All nine of them received high praise from their side's high command. Lt. Col. Robert G. Fergusson, the landing force's intelligence chief, declared that the Attu press corps earned the "respect of all the officers and men" in the Seventh Division. "The stories written were the result of first hand information received under fire," Fergusson pointed out. Frigid winds so severely numbed the correspondents' fingers that note taking was often impossible. "To write a story," *Time* disclosed, "reporters had to climb down to the beach, board a ship, thaw out, borrow a typewriter." An admiring Colonel Fergusson opined that the reporters' willingness to endure the same hardships as the combatants "contributed in some measure to the realism of their writing."[13]

Most press dispatches from Attu were delayed for security reasons, but they eventually provided the American people with graphic accounts of what *Time* considered "one of the hardest battles U.S. soldiers ever fought." The best stories to come out of Attu featured interviews with the troops who took the island, allowing them to narrate their own experiences.[14] The year after the Attu campaign, the U.S. Army's *Infantry Journal* published a rich treasury of such soldier testimony as part of its Fighting Forces series. Titled *The Capture of Attu: As Told by the Men Who Fought There*, this remarkable book could be purchased by American servicemen for twenty-five cents in a small paperback edition. It is obvious that *The Capture of Attu* was intended to build the confidence of the American soldier and familiarize him with Japanese tactics. This work was so well constructed, however, that its value as a historical source has outlived its wartime purpose. In 1951 Samuel Eliot Morison announced that *The Capture of Attu* was "the best account of the ground fighting that has yet appeared." Thirty-three years later, another critic compared the book to the writings of Ernie Pyle, America's most celebrated combat correspondent of World War II.[15]

In common with Pyle's dispatches, *The Capture of Attu* immerses the reader in what it felt like to be at the front. Though published while wartime passions and censorship were at their height, the first-person accounts that make up this book have the ring of authenticity. There is no effort to hide the anxiety and terror men experienced in combat or the horrors they beheld. Most of the interviews that follow tend to show American forces in a positive light, but some contain refreshingly candid admissions. These include incidents of friendly fire, getting surprised by enemy counterattacks, and at least one GI's taste for Japanese pornography.[16]

The 1980s and 1990s witnessed the release of several fine oral histories that illuminated important aspects of America's involvement in World War II. *The Capture of Attu* compares favorably to any of these newer titles. Moreover, it has the added advantage of containing interviews recorded weeks after the event, rather than decades. This is combat history in the raw, uncorrupted by the strictures of political correctness or memories faded by time.[17]

Despite its riveting immediacy, *The Capture of Attu* does suffer from certain shortcomings. The most conspicuous is a lack of balance. Although the book offers an intimate portrait of the men who conquered the island, those who defended it remain shadowy figures. Considering the circumstances under which *The Capture of Attu* was written, that is understandable. After all, this was a project sponsored by the U.S. Army. Yet even if the book's compilers had been interested in the enemy's point of view, they would have been hard-pressed to obtain material. Only twenty-eight members of the Japanese garrison survived the campaign.[18]

The absence of any reminiscences from Attu's defenders should not obscure the fact that they performed their duty with as much valor and greater ingenuity than their assailants did. Lacking the numbers required to hold the entire island, Col. Yasuya Yamazaki, the garrison commander, instructed his troops to man prepared positions on the high ground overlooking the valleys leading to the main Japanese base at Chichagof Harbor. The elaborate nature of many of these strongpoints showed that Yamazaki's troops had put their months on Attu to good use. "Their foxholes were large and dry, and were well supplied with food, clothing, bedding and ammunition," marveled Russell Annabel. "In some cases they had dug underground chambers large enough for a dozen or more men." The strength and location of these defenses made an even stronger impression on the Americans who stumbled across them in battle. "The Japanese had dug in well," admitted Associated Press correspondent Eugene Burns. "Their mountainside positions were prepared so that they offered the maximum protection and the best field of fire through which troops had to go."[19]

On 14 May 1943, the day on which American planners originally expected Japanese resistance to cease, Maj. Gen. Albert E. Brown, the commander of the landing force, filed this disheartening assessment:

Reconnaissance and experience . . . indicates Japanese tactics comprise fighting with machine guns and snipers concealed in rain washes or in holes or trenches dug in each side and at varying heights of hill along narrow passes leading through mountain masses. These positions are difficult to locate and almost impossible to shoot out with artillery. They produce casualties in excess of casualties which can be returned. Number of machine gun positions out of proportion to estimated enemy strength. In addition, small infantry groups are dug in high up on sides of pass parallel to axis of approach through pass as well as all commanding terrain features in passes. . . . Progress through passes will, unless we are extremely lucky, be slow and costly, and will require troops in excess to those now available to my command.[20]

The Japanese also exercised wise restraint in firing their weapons. They realized that promiscuous shooting would waste ammunition and enable the Americans to locate what Russell Annabel termed "their camouflaged trenches and interconnected foxholes despite the fog." Thanks to thorough preparation

and savvy tactics, the Japanese succeeded in pinning down the main American landing force in Massacre Valley during the waning hours of its first day
ashore. The standoff in this quarter of the battlefield dragged on for the better
part of the week. General Brown alienated his superiors with his repeated
pleas for reinforcements and pessimistic pronouncements. In one moment of
exasperation, he was heard to exclaim that it would take six months to pacify
Attu. On 16 May the high command relieved Brown and named Maj. Gen.
Eugene M. Landrum to replace him.[21]

Right after Landrum took charge of operations, superior American numbers—aided by close-air support, naval gunfire, and land-based artillery whenever visibility permitted—broke the stalemate in Massacre Valley. Taking care
to sound upbeat, Landrum assured reporters: "The Jap force will be given no
time to recoup. Continued pressure will be exerted to capture or destroy him."
This was just the kind of language the general's superiors wanted to hear. In a
repetition of history, Landrum would relieve the commander of the faltering
Ninetieth Division thirteen months later in Normandy.[22]

The certainty of defeat failed to reverse the Attu garrison's resolve to kill as
many Americans as possible. Tokyo radio told the truth when it asserted on 18
May that Yamazaki's soldiers "have been carrying on, with the determination
to fight to the last man." All but a handful of Attu's defenders chose death over
surrender—even when they found themselves cut off and completely surrounded. When the Americans finally breached the defenses screening
Chichagof Harbor and all hope was lost, Yamazaki gathered seven hundred to
one thousand of his surviving troops in the predawn hours of 29 May and
launched one of the war's largest banzai charges. As seen in the dramatic
interviews that follow, this final, desperate effort overran two American command posts and a medical aid station, creating tremendous havoc in areas the
invaders considered safe and secure. The Japanese were finally blasted to a
halt by a dogged detachment of U.S. Army engineers. Even then, surrender
remained an unthinkable option. In one last act of devotion to their country's
warrior culture, those Japanese left alive committed suicide with hand grenades.[23]

Afterward, Robert Sherrod picked his way over the two miles of ground
covered by Yamazaki's wild charge. He counted eight hundred enemy corpses.
In an article published in *Time*, he sketched the scene in gruesome detail:

The results of the Jap fanaticism stagger the imagination. The very violence of the
scene is incomprehensible to the Western mind. Here groups of men had met their
self-imposed obligation, to die rather than accept capture, by blowing themselves to
bits. I saw one Jap sitting impaled on a bayonet which was stuck through his back,
evidently by a friend. All the other suicides had chosen the grenade. Most of them
simply held grenades against their stomachs or chests. The explosive charge blasted
away their vital organs. Probably one in four held a grenade against his head. There

were many headless Jap bodies between Massacre [Bay] and Chichagof. Sometimes the grenade split the head in half, leaving the right face on one shoulder, the left face on the other. . .

In a burned tent about two miles from Massacre, I found eight grotesque little Japanese bodies, clothes burned off, arms reaching outward or upward—where there were arms. Two bodies were burned to crisps, one atop the other, fused into one charred hump.

Within a hundred yards there were 45 more Japanese bodies. Four were in one foxhole; in death the Japs seemed to seek companionship wherever they could. Another body, its red and yellow and blue entrails spilling out like yeasty dough, lay atop the mound beside the hole. Twenty yards from this foxhole there was a little brown-skinned hand, blown there after it pressed a grenade against the stomach. The glove encasing the hand was only slightly torn.[24]

Throughout the war years, American journalists and filmmakers celebrated such last-ditch courage as it was reputedly displayed by their countrymen at the Alamo, Little Bighorn, Wake Island, and Bataan. Confronted by similar behavior on the part of the Japanese, however, the American press generally reacted with expressions of contempt. "The ordinary, unreasoning Jap is ignorant," commented Robert Sherrod. "Perhaps he is human. Nothing on Attu indicates it." Russell Annabel chimed in with identical sentiments: "After a while you began to get the conviction that these Japs were not quite human, or at least that they were not quite sane. It was in some respects more like a mad-dog hunt than a battle." Safe and warm on the home front, an editorialist for the *New York Times* echoed the theme: "The Japanese are aboriginal savages who will fight to the death and to the last man, and in that respect are even tougher enemies than the Germans."[25]

To their credit, many of the American troops on Attu developed a grudging respect for their foes, referring to them as "little yellow bastards" with a mixture of hostility and awe. "They're tough cookies, every way you look at it," spat Capt. William H. Willoughby, commander of the crack Seventh Scout Company, the unit that spearheaded the landings on the north side of Attu. A hollow-faced private sporting red stubble on his cheeks blurted this disturbing anecdote to Robert Sherrod: "I thought I was going to capture one of the sons of bitches the other day. I was standing over his foxhole and he was badly wounded. But he reached for his gun and I had to shoot him. I don't care if you call it fanaticism or just plain guts, they fight to the last man. They are tough bastards."[26]

Perhaps the most objective tribute to Yamazaki's garrison lies in the statistics of the Attu campaign. Out of the more than 15,000 American soldiers to participate in the assault, 549 died in action and 1,148 sustained wounds. Exposure, disease, and nonbattle injuries incapacitated another 2,100 Yanks. The victors buried 2,351 Japanese corpses, although an undetermined number of enemy dead were probably disposed of by their own comrades in the course of the fighting. From the American perspective, Attu represented one of the worst casualty exchange rates in the entire Pacific Theater. As the Army's official history put it: "In terms of numbers engaged, Attu ranks as one of the most costly assaults in the Pacific. In terms of Japanese destroyed, the cost of taking Attu was second only to Iwo Jima: for every hundred of the enemy on the island, about seventy-one Americans were killed or wounded."[27]

The slaughter and misery at Attu did produce a few benefits. The American military learned valuable lessons about loading and unloading transports, naval gunfire support, and how to campaign in foul weather and in mountain country. This knowledge would save American lives in other Pacific battles and as far away as Italy. What it cost in human terms to prod America's massive war machine into upgrading its doctrine, uniforms, and tactical procedures is not so easily cataloged. Readers desiring to delve deeper into that issue will be well advised to read *The Capture of Attu*.[28]

NOTES

1. Samuel Eliot Morison, *Aleutians, Gilberts and Marshalls, June 1942–April 1944*, vol. 7 of *History of United States Naval Operations in World War II* (Boston: Little, Brown and Company, 1951), 19, 41, 45; *New York Times*, 15 and 23 May 1943; and Stetson Conn, Rose C. Engleman, and Byron Fairchild, *Guarding the United States and Its Outposts*, United States Army in World War II: The Western Hemisphere (Washington DC: Office of the Chief of Military History, Department of the Army, 1964), 257, 280, 281, 288.

2. Dashiell Hammett and Robert Colodny, "The Battle of the Aleutians 1942–1943," in *The Capture of Attu: Tales of World War II in Alaska as Told by the Men Who Fought There* (Anchorage: Alaska Northwest Publishing Company, 1984), 9.

3. *New York Times*, 26 May 1943.

4. Morison, *Aleutians, Gilberts and Marshalls*, 3–4.

5. The fullest account in English of Japanese planning for Midway and the Aleutians diversion is Gordon W. Prange, Donald M. Goldstein, and Katherine V. Dillon, *Miracle at Midway* (New York: McGraw-Hill Book Company, 1982).

6. George L. MacGarrigle, *Aleutian Islands*, The U.S. Army Campaigns of World War II (Washington DC: Center of Military History, United States Army, 1992), 4, 9; Morison, *Aleutians, Gilberts and Marshalls*, 4, 6, 8, 14–15; Prange et al., *Miracle at Midway*, 22–24, 335; Conn et al., *Guarding the United States*, 259, 263; George C. Marshall, *Biennial Reports of the Chief of Staff of the United States Army to the Secretary of War, 1 July 1939–30 June 1945* (Washington DC: Center of Military History, United States Army, 1996), 67; and *New York Times*, 16 and 23 May 1943. A detailed examination of the successful American defense of Dutch Harbor may be found in Donald M. Goldstein and Katherine V. Dillon, *The Williwaw War: The Arkansas National Guard in the Aleutians in World War II* (Fayetteville: University of Arkansas Press, 1992).

7. Morison, *Aleutians, Gilberts and Marshalls*, 8; MacGarrigle, *Aleutian Islands*, 8–9; and *New York Times*, 16 May 1943.

8. Morison, *Aleutians, Gilberts and Marshalls*, 37; and Conn et al., *Guarding the United States*, 281, 283.

9. Frustrated over not having a combat command of his own, General Smith would go along as an observer when the Seventh Division landed at Attu. Conn et al., *Guarding the United States*, 277–78; Morison, *Aleutians, Gilberts and Marshalls*, 38; MacGarrigle, *Aleutian Islands*, 13, 16; and Harry A. Gailey, *Howlin' Mad vs. the Army: Conflict in Command, Saipan 1944* (Novato, CA: Presidio Press, 1986), 26–27.

10. MacGarrigle, *Aleutian Islands*, 16–17; Conn et al., *Guarding the United States*, 284; *New York Times*, 30 May 1943; and Russell Annabel, "Mad-Dog Hunt on Attu," *Saturday Evening Post*, 14 August 1943, 67.

11. Annabel, "Mad-Dog Hunt," 25.

12. Robert Sherrod, "Company X on Attu," *Life*, 21 June 1943, 33.

13. "Reporters on Attu," *Time*, 28 June 1943, 40.

14. Robert Sherrod, "Burial in the Aleutians," *Time*, 28 June 1943, 62.

15. Morison, *Aleutians, Gilberts and Marshalls*, 45; Terrence Cole, "Foreword" in *Capture of Attu*, 6.

16. Many of the interviews that originally appeared in *The Capture of Attu: As Told by the Men Who Fought There* were reprinted in the similarly titled *The Capture of Attu: Tales of World War II in Alaska as Told by the Men Who Fought There* (Anchorage: Alaska Northwest Publishing Company, 1984).

17. Among the best of these recent oral histories are Studs Terkel, *The Good War: An Oral History of World War II* (New York: New Press, 1991); Donald Knox, *Death March: The Survivors of Bataan* (New York: Harcourt Brace Jovanovich, Publishers, 1981); Robert S. La Forte and Ronald E. Marcello, eds., *Remembering Pearl Harbor: Eyewitness Accounts by U.S. Military Men and Women* (Wilmington DE: Scholarly Resources Inc., 1991); and Robert S. La Forte, Ronald E. Marcello, and Richard L. Himmel, eds., *With Only the Will to Live: Accounts of Americans in Japanese Prison Camps, 1941–1945* (Wilmington DE: Scholarly Resources Inc., 1994).

18. Morison, *Aleutians, Gilberts and Marshalls*, 50.

19. Conn et al., *Guarding the United States*, 282, 287–88; McGarrigle, *Aleutian Islands*, 18; Morison, *Aleutians, Gilberts and Marshalls*, 43; Annabel, "Mad-Dog Hunt," 65; *New York Times*, 30 May 1943.

20. Conn et al., *Guarding the United States*, 292.

21. Massacre Valley and the adjoining Massacre Bay were named long before World War II. Russian fur hunters slaughtered fifteen Aleut natives in that area in 1745. Annabel, "Mad-Dog Hunt," 25; and *New York Times*, 19 May 1943.

22. MacGarrigle, *Aleutian Islands*, 22; Conn et al., *Guarding the United States*, 294; *New York Times*, 30 May 1943; and Russell F. Weigley, *Eisenhower's Lieutenants: The Campaign of France and Germany, 1944–1945* (Bloomington: Indiana University Press, 1981), 99.

23. *New York Times*, 19 May 1943; Annabel, "Mad-Dog Hunt," 67, 70; Morison, *Aleutians, Gilberts and Marshalls*, 50; and Conn et al., *Guarding the United States*, 294–95.

24. Robert Sherrod, "Perhaps He Is Human," *Time*, 5 July 1943, 28–29.

25. Gregory J. W. Urwin, *Facing Fearful Odds: The Siege of Wake Island* (Lincoln: University of Nebraska Press, 1997), 5–12, 527; Sherrod, "Perhaps He Is Human," 29; Annabel, "Mad-Dog Hunt," 67; and *New York Times*, 19 May 1943. See also John W.

Dower, *War without Mercy: Race and Power in the Pacific War* (New York: Pantheon Books, 1986).

26. *New York Times*, 30 May 1943; Sherrod, "Company X," 34.

27. Morison, *Aleutians, Gilberts and Marshalls*, 50; and Conn et al., *Guarding the United States*, 295.

28. In addition to the works cited in the preceding notes, readers interested in the Attu campaign should consult the following: Brian Garfield, *The Thousand Mile War* (New York: Doubleday and Co., 1969); *The Aleutians Campaign, June 1942–August 1943* (Washington DC: Office of Naval Intelligence, United States Navy, 1945; and Ronald H. Spector, *Eagle against the Sun: The American War with Japan* (New York: Free Press, 1985).

PART ONE
THE BATTLE OF ATTU

The battle of Attu was essentially an infantry battle. The climate greatly limited the use of air power, for almost every day the island was shrouded in fog and swept by high winds. The terrain—steep jagged crags, knifelike ridges, boggy tundra—made impracticable any extensive use of mechanized equipment and, indeed, of all motor vehicles. Thus deprived of the most important accessories of modern war, the Doughboy, moving only on foot, had to blast his way to victory with the weapons he could carry with him.

The job was far from easy. In fact it proved much harder than had been expected. For American troops that were inexperienced in combat, fighting under the toughest conditions, found themselves faced by a vigorous enemy, fully equipped, thoroughly acclimated, and fanatically determined to hold their strong, well-chosen defensive positions.

But the men who fought on Attu added a memorable page to the story of the United States Infantry.

THE ISLAND OF ATTU

The Aleutian Islands, discovered in 1741 by Vitus Bering, a Danish navigator employed by Russia, were acquired by the United States in 1867 as a part of the Alaska Purchase. Extending for more than 1,000 miles westward from the Alaskan mainland, the chain ends with Attu, which is some 600 miles from Siberia and 650 miles from the Japanese base at Paramushiro in the Kurile Islands, the most northerly bastion of the main defenses of Japan.

Unsuited to agriculture, devoid of mineral resources, and with no other possibility of commercial exploitation, Attu received slight attention from the United States after its acquisition. However, a chart of the coast line was prepared by the United States Coast and Geodetic Survey, and a stock of blue foxes was placed on the island to provide its native inhabitants with a means of livelihood.

At the time of the Japanese occupation in June 1942 the population of the island consisted of forty-five native Aleuts, a branch of the Eskimos, and two Americans: Foster Jones, a sixty-year-old schoolteacher, and his wife. All lived in a little hamlet of frame houses around Chichagof Harbor, maintaining a precarious existence by fishing, trapping foxes, and weaving baskets. Occasional visits from missionaries, explorers, government patrol boats, and small fishing craft provided the inhabitants with their only direct contact with the outside world, except for a small radio operated by Mr. Jones. One writer has called Attu "the lonesomest spot this side of hell."

Though the temperature on the island rarely attains arctic severity, Attu is beset through most of the year by a cold, damp fog, often accompanied by snow or icy rain. Even the high winds, which reach a velocity of more than 100 miles per hour, are not able to dispel the continuous fog. Fine days on Attu are rare indeed, and there are many days when the weather prevents any possibility of outside work.

Only a short distance from the shore line and throughout the interior of the island, steep mountains rise abruptly to a height of some 3,000 feet—rugged peaks

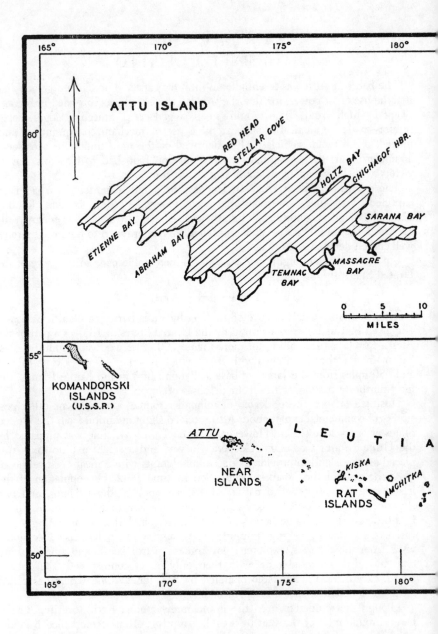

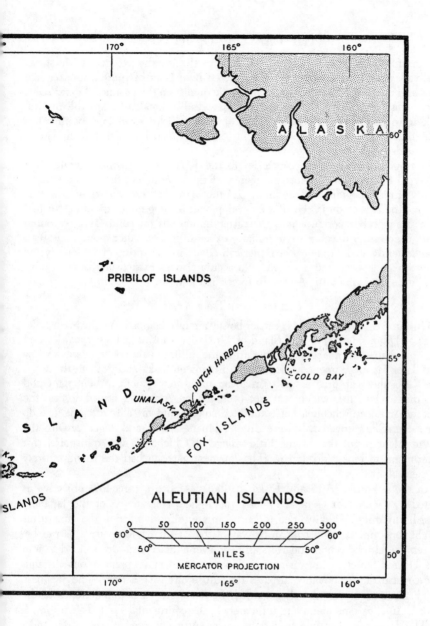

ALASKA

PRIBILOF ISLANDS

DUTCH HARBOR

UNALASKA

COLD BAY

S L A N D S

FOX ISLANDS

KA

SLANDS

ALEUTIAN ISLANDS

0   50   100   150   200   250   300

MILES

MERCATOR PROJECTION

and narrow, knife-sharp ridges without growth, usually covered with snow. The valleys and the lower slopes are covered by a layer of tundra, muskeg-like moss and coarse grass, which gives an elastic quality to the ground. Water seeps under this layer. Even a man on foot may readily break through the tundra, sinking in watery mud up to his knees. Motor vehicles, even those with caterpillar treads, quickly churn the tundra into a muddy mass in which sunken wheels and treads spin uselessly.

During the seventy-five years prior to the Japanese occupation, while Attu belonged to the United States, no agency of the government made any detailed survey of the topography of the interior of the island and no military installations of any kind existed on it. Until the development of long-range aircraft Attu had little strategical importance and thereafter limitations on funds and personnel made it necessary to concentrate military expenditures on other more vital areas. Consequently at the time of the American attack in the spring of 1943 only the shore line was accurately mapped. No accurate maps existed of the mountains and passes over which the American forces had to fight.

The Japanese Take Attu

On June 3, 1942, Japanese carrier-borne aircraft bombed American installations at Dutch Harbor on the island of Unalaska, causing a few casualties and minor damage, but not seriously impairing the military value of the base. A few days later Japanese troops landed on the islands of Kiska and Attu to the west. On Kiska they captured a small American naval detachment, a lieutenant and ten men. On Attu, which was not occupied by American armed forces, the elderly American schoolteacher committed suicide and his wife attempted to do the same. She recovered, however, under Japanese care, and, together with the entire Aleut population of the little village of Chichagof, was transported for internment to Hokkaido, Japan. The Japanese garrison had the island entirely to themselves.

In the seizure of Attu and Kiska the Japanese had a three-fold objective as stated by Lieutenant General Hideichiro Higuda, commander of the Japanese Northern Army. They wanted to break up any offensive action the Americans might contemplate against Japan by way of the Aleutians, to set up a barrier between the United States and Russia in the event that Russia determined to join the United States in its war against Japan, and to make preparations through the construction of advance airbases for future offensive action. The Japanese High Command undoubtedly regarded the Aleutians as stepping stones to the North American mainland and ultimately to the continental United States itself.

The Japanese force which initially seized Attu consisted of the 301st Independent Infantry Battalion which landed at Chichagof Harbor. But the harbor, though well protected, is small, with a narrow, rockbound entrance studded with reefs which renders it unsuitable for the landing of supplies in any quantity. Accordingly, the Japanese established their principal base at the end of the west arm of Holtz Bay, a wider and better harbor, leaving Chichagof merely as a subsidiary base held by a skeleton force. No important installations were established in the Sarana Bay area or at Massacre Bay, where the main American force later landed.

In the latter part of September, for reasons which are not plain, the garrison of Attu was transferred to Kiska and for about a month after that the island was unoccupied. Although this evacuation of Attu did not escape the vigilance of the Alaska Defense Command, American forces made no attempt to occupy the island. Our Alaskan defenses at this period were not yet complete, and troops and naval units in sufficient strength were not available. The American High Command limited itself to keeping Attu under observation, for it had no wish to undertake the seizure of so remote an island with an inadequate force, and preferred to wait until it could feel assured that Attu, once taken, could be firmly and permanently held.

On October 29, 1942, a Japanese mixed force from Paramushiro, commanded by Lieutenant Colonel Hiroshi Yanekawa, landed on Attu and reëstablished the base at Holtz Bay, installing beach defenses and dual-purpose antiaircraft guns. These were not first-line troops, but were composed in the main of older men recalled to the colors and recruits who, after a summary training period, had been sent on active duty under officers and noncommissioned officers drawn from the regular army.

The principal duty of this force was apparently to build an airfield to supplement the one already under construction on Kiska, but the work went slowly. In the worst weather months of the year the mere mechanics of living absorbed much of the men's time. On many days work was impossible, and it does not appear that living conditions in the Aleutians were any more attractive to the Japanese soldier than to the American. Though the survey for the airfield was completed in December, construction did not start until two months later. The field had not been finished when American troops landed in May.

The Attu garrison, which numbered about 500 at the outset, received a series of reinforcements until it was about 2,300 strong, when the last transport arrived on March 10. From that time on, owing to the activity of the United States Navy and the 11th Air Force, only submarines carrying limited quantities of supplies at irregular intervals, were able to reach Attu.

Although the airfield was still incomplete when the American landing force arrived on May 11, 1943, by that time the Japanese had established strong, shrewdly chosen defensive positions at strategic points throughout the area they occupied. They were well provided with weapons, munitions, and equipment, and had numerous caches of arms, ammunition, and food at different points on the island, thus giving greater mobility to small units operating independently and avoiding the need to establish and keep up a continuous supply line from a central base. These dispositions stood them in good stead in the scattered defensive fighting that followed.

PRELIMINARY OPERATIONS AGAINST ATTU

The Japanese had scarcely landed before the American High Command began to lay its plans to retake both Kiska and Attu. As an initial step, on August 30, 1942, a task force of the Alaska Defense Command occupied the island of

Adak and the neighboring island of Atka. Situated some 275 miles east of Kiska and 450 miles east of Attu, Adak was an excellent station from which activities on the two islands could be kept under air observation. It was also a potential base for offensive operations and a barrier against any farther eastward advance by the enemy.

A few months later, on January 13, 1943, American forces likewise seized Amchitka, approximately 75 miles southeast of Kiska and 275 miles southeast of Attu. On both Adak and Amchitka, the Army engineers rapidly constructed airfields. With such bases established within ready bomber range of Attu and Kiska, it became possible for planes of the 11th Air Force to harass the enemy and bomb his installations on both islands whenever opportunity offered and the weather permitted.

In the closing days of March 1943 a United States naval force operating west of Attu encountered a Japanese convoy—two transports escorted by cruisers and destroyers—apparently bringing reinforcements and supplies to the Attu garrison. After a short, inconclusive engagement, the Japanese turned back toward their bases in the Kurile Islands, doubtless fearing the appearance of American land-based bombers, while the American vessels broke off the pursuit and retired to the east. From then on the Japanese made no further effort to support their troops on Attu by surface craft.

American Preparations for Invasion

The size and composition of the American force required to recapture Attu and Kiska received long consideration and study by the American High Command. In the latter part of December a force composed of units of the 7th Infantry Division, then commanded by Major General Albert E. Brown, was finally selected. The main force consisted of the 17th and 32d Infantry regiments, two battalions of Field Artillery (105mm.), and the 50th Engineers, to which were added suitable numbers of medical units and other supporting and service troops. In addition, the Alaska Defense Command arranged to organize a reserve on the island of Adak, consisting of one battalion of the 4th Infantry and additional troops.

The 7th Division, which had not previously seen action, had been training as a motorized unit in the desert at Camp San Luis Obispo, California, under conditions which suggested that it might ultimately fight in the North African theater. Its selection for duty in the Aleutians, where the use of mechanized equipment was impossible, thus represented a big change from its previous training experience. Early in January 1943 the division was transferred to Fort Ord, near Monterey, where it had about three months of additional instruction, including amphibious training under the direction of the commander of the amphibious force of the Pacific Fleet. This training laid emphasis upon basic infantry tactics and upon amphibious work. A number of practice landings were made, though of necessity upon terrain very different from the tundra-covered, mud valleys of Attu. A group of officers from the Alaska Defense Command were temporarily assigned to the 7th Division to advise and instruct its officers and men about the special conditions and problems it would meet in the Aleutians.

Few men in the 7th Division had previous Alaskan experience or any familiarity with the harsh weather and terrain that would confront them. As events proved, most of the men suffered hardship after the landing until they became used to the severe conditions. In recognition of this fact, when another expedition was organized some time later to capture Kiska, a substantial part of the training period was spent in the Aleutian area.

In amphibious operations the simultaneous or almost simultaneous landing of troops and supplies is of the utmost importance. But in the landing tests executed by the 7th Division, although the men themselves went ashore, only simulated unloading was carried out with a small part of the load of supplies and heavy equipment that actual battle would require.

The clothing issued to the 7th Division for the Attu campaign proved unsatisfactory for the extremely rigorous conditions of Aleutian warfare. The clothing was neither warm enough to withstand the biting Attu winds nor waterproof enough to keep out the icy rain and the water that seeped into every foxhole. The boots supplied were the all-leather, high-laced blucher type of the sort often worn by loggers and hunters in the northern woods of the United States. They were good for tramping through damp underbrush when facilities for drying them existed. But they were unsuitable for men who had to stand for hours in deep pools of almost freezing water. The troops were not initially provided with the rubber-bottomed, leather-topped shoepac, sometimes called lumbermen's rubbers, which have proved well-suited to Alaskan conditions. On the arrival of the division in Alaska, these defects in equipment were recognized. A hasty effort was made to remedy them, but though some progress was made, there was not enough time to eliminate them entirely. As a result, the Attu landing force suffered heavily from exposure, particularly with trench foot resulting from immersion.

On April 24, 1943, the landing force sailed from San Francisco in five transports with a strong naval escort, and arrived at Cold Bay on the southwest Alaskan peninsula, on April 30.

THE ADVANCE ON ATTU

Until the latter part of March the American High Command had considered Kiska as the primary objective and had intended to make the assault on the more westerly island of Attu at a later date. Instead, however, it was determined to attack Attu first in the hope that the taking of Attu might make Kiska untenable and compel the Japanese to leave it. This is in fact what happened. The result of the Attu battle demonstrated the strategical soundness of this conclusion.

The landing on Attu had been fixed for May 7, but bad weather compelled the convoy to stay at Cold Bay until the 4th, with the result that the landing date had to be postponed until the 8th. Protected by a naval force, including battleships, cruisers, and destroyers under command of Rear Admiral F. W. Rockwell, the convoy put to sea and arrived off Attu after an uneventful trip. But its movement had not gone unobserved for the Japanese radio on Kiska warned the garrison on Attu of its coming. For a week, from May 3 to May 9, inclusive, the Japanese on Attu stayed on the alert, occupying their combat positions. But when the attack did not materialize, they apparently decided that the expedition was headed for Kiska or somewhere else, and returned to their routine duties, leaving the Attu beaches relatively unguarded.

When the convoy first arrived off Attu on May 7, it became evident that the strong unfavorable winds then blowing would make an immediate landing extremely hazardous, especially an opposed landing. It was accordingly decided to postpone the attack until the 10th. The convoy steamed northward far into the Bering Sea in order to avoid detection while it killed time. On its return a dense fog caused a further postponement until the 11th. The delay, though irritating at the time, proved a piece of luck for the American force. The Japanese did not discover the convoy's return and by May 9 had given up all expectation of an attack.

A number of plans of operations were drafted for the landing on Attu, each with several variations. The plan as finally approved called for four landings— two main landings and two subsidiary landings. The main body, known as the Southern Force, was to land on the beach of Massacre Bay. It consisted of the 2d and 3d Battalions of the 17th Infantry; the 2d Battalion of the 32d Infantry; and three batteries of field artillery (105mm.) with auxiliary troops, all under command of Colonel Edward P. Earle, commanding officer of the 17th Infantry. The mission of this force was to advance rapidly up Massacre Valley, seize Jarmin Pass (Massacre-Holtz Pass) and Clevesy Pass (Massacre-Sarana Pass), and move into the Holtz Bay area to join up with the Northern Force. The combined forces were first to hold and finally to destroy the enemy in the Chichagof Harbor area.

The Northern Force was to land on Red Beach, some three miles north of the main Japanese camp at the end of the west arm of Holtz Bay. This force, commanded by Lieutenant Colonel Albert V. Hartl, consisted of the 1st Battalion of the 17th Infantry and a battery of field artillery, together with auxiliary troops. After landing, the Northern Force was to attack and clear the west arm of Holtz Bay, securing the high ground, later known as Moore Ridge, between the west and east arms of the Bay. After effecting a junction with the Southern Force moving north over Jarmin Pass, the Northern Force was to complete the capture of the Holtz Bay area and the valley to the southwest. Two battalions of the 32d Infantry, the 1st and 3d, under Colonel Frank L. Culin, commanding officer of the regiment, with two batteries of field artillery, were to stay on shipboard in reserve.

A subsidiary landing was to be made at Austin Cove by a provisional battalion consisting of the 7th Scout Company and the 7th Reconnaissance Troop, less one platoon, Captain William Willoughby commanding. This force, which sailed from Dutch Harbor in a destroyer and two submarines, and arrived at Attu independently of the main convoy, had the mission of moving into the west end of the valley opposite the west arm of Holtz Bay, attacking to the east toward the enemy battery position at the head of the west arm of Holtz Bay, containing the maximum enemy force, and compelling it to fight facing to the west. The Provisional Battalion was to assist the attack of the 1st Battalion of the 17th by fire action, and to join it as part of the Northern Force as soon as Moore Ridge could be taken and held.

Another subsidiary landing was to be made by one platoon of the 7th Reconnaissance Troop on Alexei Point, east of Massacre Bay. Its mission was to cover the rear of the forces landing at Massacre Bay by establishing an outpost across the peninsula to the north, to reconnoiter to the west and north in the area between Lake Nicholas and Massacre Bay, and thereafter to reconnoiter the peninsula itself, destroying enemy detachments and installations. It was expected that this platoon would promptly pass on any information it obtained to the Landing Force Command Post, and that it would eventually make contact with the 17th Infantry in Clevesy Pass.

This was the plan finally decided upon as the American task force converged on Attu and prepared to land on the morning of May 11, 1943. It involved four landings by independent forces with little direct liaison. It proved harder to carry out than was expected. The battle as it developed may for convenience be treated in four principal phases:

(1) The landing at Massacre Bay and the operations of the Southern Force until the capture of Jarmin and Clevesy passes on May 19-20 cleared Massacre Valley;

(2) The landing at Red Beach and the operations of the Northern Force in the Holtz Bay area, including the operations of the Provisional Battalion;

(3) The advance of the combined forces toward the Chichagof Harbor area after the capture of Clevesy Pass;

(4) The final Japanese counterattack and the mopping up that followed.

MASSACRE BAY

In the early morning of May 11, 1943, the transports carrying the Southern Force with their naval escort approached through a dense fog within landing distance of Massacre Bay. The time of landing—H-hour—was originally fixed for 0740, but the time schedule followed the pattern familiar to soldiers the world over, a series of hour-to-hour postponements. The fog, which had caused a collision between two destroyers, compelled the time to be advanced to 1040 and continued fog caused another postponement to 1530. The first troops finally landed on the Attu beach at 1620. A strip of shale and small rocks, extending for several hundred yards along the end of Massacre Bay, presented no difficulty for the landing and there was no sign of the enemy.

After a short delay for organization on the beach, the main body started its advance up the valley in the direction of Jarmin Pass, the 2d Battalion of the 17th on the right moving along the ridge known as the Hogback, and the 3d Battalion on the left along the floor of the valley. Behind them the tractors and artillery were landing on the beach. The advance party of artillery observers had already disappeared into the fog when the lumbering "cats" began to tow the guns in the wake of the infantry. Slowly they moved for some seventy-five yards from the water's edge. And then the crews had their first experience of Aleutian terrain when the treads broke through the tundra, spinning helplessly in the thick, black mud beneath. For the moment any further advance became im-

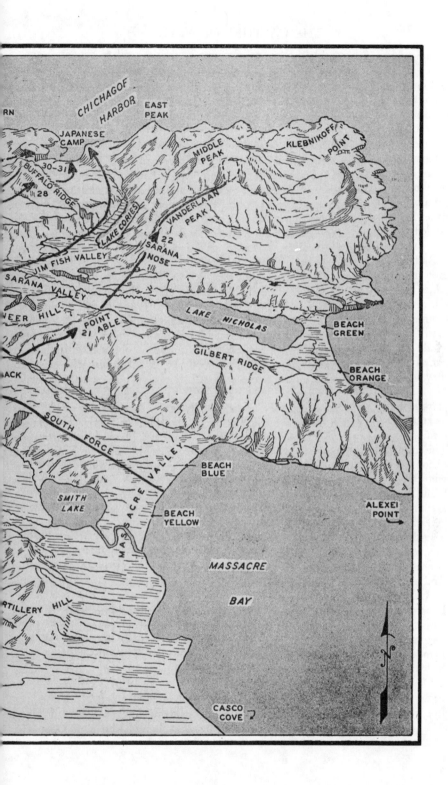

possible, but contact with the enemy was expected and artillery support was essential. The gun crews, working in feverish haste, swung their pieces around and set them up pointing up the valley in the general direction of the objective. More than half an hour passed before the observer's voice came over a portable radio reporting that he had located the position of a Japanese mortar. Speedily, then, the American artillery fired the opening gun of the Attu battle.

To cover the left flank of the landing, Company F of the 32d Infantry, under command of Captain Robert E. Goodfellow, was to land at Casco Cove (Purple Beach) west of Massacre Bay, move west to Temnac Bay, and clearing Temnac, then move independently to clear the enemy from the high ground west of Jarmin Pass, thus to aid the advance of the 3d Battalion of the 17th through the pass. In the dense fog Company F missed Casco Cove, and after some delay, landed intermingled with the first wave of the main body at Massacre beach. It then at once turned southwest to carry out its mission.

As the detachment climbed Artillery Hill four Japanese were seen hurrying away into the hills to the north. Behind them on Artillery Hill, in a position which enfiladed the landing beaches, they had left two undamaged 20mm. anti-aircraft pompom guns with a large supply of ammunition. Why these enemy gunners, who must have been able to watch the landing, never fired these guns is still a mystery. If they had done so, there can be no doubt that the landing would have been badly hindered, and accomplished only with heavy losses. Company F found no other enemy troops or installations except a deserted tent which they destroyed.

The left-flank protection for the main body consisted of one platoon of Company I of the 17th under command of Lieutenant Odus E. Long. His platoon had the mission of clearing the high ground to the left of Massacre beach and continuing on up Henderson Ridge, which formed the southwest rim of the valley. The unfamiliar tundra underfoot and growing darkness made progress slow and tedious. From time to time the platoon drew fire from invisible enemy snipers who fell back into the fog as the Americans approached. In a small ravine they found a smoking Japanese camp, which its occupants had deserted and burned. Darkness had fallen and Lieutenant Long decided to bivouac for the night some 500 yards from the smouldering camp.

Early next morning the advance squad of the platoon ran into a patrol of four Japanese, one of them an officer, with a light machine gun. After a brief exchange of fire at less than 200 yards, all four of the enemy were killed without loss to the American platoon.

But a short further advance along the slopes of Henderson Ridge brought Long's detachment under machine-gun and rifle fire which pinned them down. This time the enemy did not fall back. Further advance became impossible and, digging in defensively, the platoon held its position as rear flank guard along Henderson Ridge northwest of Elwood Lake until ordered to rejoin the main body on May 18.

On the right flank of the main body a platoon of Company F of the 17th commanded by Lieutenant Charles K. Paulson had a similar mission—to protect the right flank of the battalion, block the pass through the mountains from

Sarana Bay, move up Sarana Valley, and join the main body at a point near Clevesy Pass. This platoon, reinforced by a section of light machine guns and a 60mm. mortar squad, set out shortly after 1600 on the afternoon of May 11. The steep, snow-covered slopes made hard going. It was the next morning before they succeeded in crossing Gilbert Ridge into the Sarana Valley. Almost immediately the detachment came under enemy machine-gun fire from the opposite side of Lake Nicholas, beyond the range of the light mortar.

Leaving one squad and a machine gun to guard the pass, Paulson led the other two squads along the ridge in the direction of their objective. It soon became evident that the area was alive with enemy. All but surrounded, the platoon had to retreat. After much trouble and a number of casualties from Japanese bullets and exposure, it eventually made its way back to the base on Massacre beach. Lieutenant Paulson found, on the body of a dead Japanese officer, a map and accompanying order giving the detailed plan for the defense of Chichagof Harbor. This was the one positive result of the mission.

Meanwhile, two battalions of the 17th moved up Massacre Valley virtually without resistance. About 1900 the right-flank battalion, the 2d of the 17th, after it had advanced some 2,500 yards inland, received scattered Japanese rifle fire from the high ground on its right which temporarily halted its advance. Resuming its forward movement after about an hour's delay, the battalion met increasingly heavy fire from both front and flank. The 3d Battalion of the 17th on the left likewise found itself under enemy fire, fire that grew in intensity as the unit drove ahead, until it had to halt some 600 yards short of Jarmin Pass. A bombardment by the American artillery then in position near Massacre beach seemed to make little impression on the Japanese. Another American attempt to advance broke down under heavy fire from the fog-bound peaks surrounding Jarmin Pass.

Under cover of darkness the two battalions halted and reorganized, establishing all-round defensive perimeters. The 2d Battalion was on the Hogback, facing north and east, nearly level with Clevesy Pass. The 3d was facing north and west on lower ground approximately 600 yards from the entrance to Jarmin Pass. Except for a few slight gains on the left flank, the positions thus established were hardly changed at all from the night of May 11 to the evening of May 17.

STALEMATE IN MASSACRE VALLEY

On the morning of May 12, the day after the landing, the Southern Force in Massacre Valley found itself in an unenviable tactical position. Despite some confusion and many difficulties, the landing had been successfully carried out and the American force now held an important foothold on Attu. But they had not attained their objectives, and within a few hours it had become evident that they could not do so as easily as they had expected or as rapidly as they had planned. The two infantry battalions then in the valley faced the strongly manned and well-organized main Japanese defensive positions.

From the towering heights of Henderson Ridge on the left, from Black Mountain and Cold Mountain in front, and from Sarana Nose and Point Able (Nees Peak) on the right, the enemy had perfect points of observation from which he could take the American units under fire from three sides. The fog that hung along the tops and sides of the mountains gave the Japanese complete concealment, yet left the floor of the valley clear.

Held in cold, water-filled foxholes, our own troops were eager for action no matter how difficult the task before them. On the 12th the left-flank battalion managed to make a little progress until it was held up by heavy fire from Henderson Ridge. But this advance was not deep enough to affect the tactical situation substantially. Owing to confusion at the beach as well as to enemy action, and above all to the terrain, supplies moved up slowly and with great difficulty, and it was not until the afternoon of May 12 that certain units got food or ammunition. Communications between the front line and regimental headquarters temporarily broke down, and Colonel Earle, regimental commander of the 17th, went forward with an Alaskan Scout to check the position of the front-line units. Sometime later a searching party found the colonel's body with the scout lying near by, unconscious and severely wounded. Colonel (now Brigadier General) Wayne C. Zimmerman, up to that time General Brown's chief of staff, took over Colonel Earle's duties as commander of the 17th, and Colonel Stewart of the Alaska Defense Command took over the post of chief of staff of the 7th Division.

A general attack was now planned for the morning of the 13th, but the dense fog that hid the Japanese mountain positions compelled its postponement until that afternoon. In the late afternoon of May 13, the 3d Battalion of the 17th attacked. Their objective was Jarmin Pass, about 600 yards to their front across a stretch of tundra and low grass cut by small, ice-cold meandering streams.

The Japanese positions were on the slopes of Black Mountain, which separated Jarmin Pass on the right from Zwinge Pass (False Pass) on the left. These positions were linked with other entrenchments on the 100-foot plateau at the entrance of Jarmin Pass and with entrenchments on Robinson Ridge and Cold Mountain on the right. Their machine guns and rifles from the enemy lines completely dominated the floor of the valley. In the area over which the 3d Battalion had to pass there was no cover except for the twisting stream beds, that were rarely more than three feet below the level of the ground. To the southwest, Japanese machine-gun and sniper positions were scattered along the jagged height of Henderson Ridge, which constituted the western rim of the valley and commanded the left flank of the attacking force. A well-planned trench system 400 feet up the abrupt slope of Henderson Ridge and some 500 yards short of Zwinge Pass permitted the enemy to enfilade the entire floor of the valley in front of Jarmin Pass with plunging fire. Positions on Cold Mountain to the right of the pass dominated the American right flank.

But in spite of their unfavorable tactical situation, the 17th Infantry tried desperately to push ahead. And in the face of furious enemy fire from mortars, heavy machine guns, and rifles, some of the leading units succeeded in getting within 200 yards of the mouth of Jarmin Pass. But the resistance was too stiff. When darkness came the Americans fell back just about to their starting positions. On the 14th they tried again, this time with elements of the 2d Battalion of the 32d attacking simultaneously along the slopes of Henderson Ridge on the left, while on the right a platoon of the 17th advanced along the Hogback toward the enemy positions on Cold Mountain. But on this day the results were no more happy than on the day before.

In the course of the night of May 14, Colonel Zimmerman visited the command posts of both battalions of the 17th. The 3d Battalion, on the left, which had so far borne the brunt of the attacks, had suffered severely; its casualties had been heavy, including two company commanders killed and two evacuated. To give the battalion an opportunity to rest and reorganize, Colonel Zimmerman withdrew it in the darkness to more sheltered support positions and replaced it in the front line with the 2d Battalion of the 32d, which thus far had seen relatively little action. At noon on the 15th this battalion, supported by Company M of the 17th, tried to advance but was forced back under heavy fire. On the 16th another attack, again supported by Company M of the 17th, had the same discouraging result.

Between May 11 and May 16 the Southern Force had made five distinct attempts to capture Jarmin Pass by frontal attack, but it had not succeeded in making even a dent in the Japanese main line of defense. The American units had suffered heavily, not only at the hands of the enemy but also from exposure and lack of supplies. Yet the troops, though disappointed in their inability to carry out the mission assigned them, had suffered no loss of morale and no one doubted the final result.

Realizing the situation, General Brown ordered the 1st Battalion of the 32d (less Companies A and B), thus far held on shipboard as a floating reserve, to be moved by sea to Massacre Bay to strengthen the Southern Force. He also requested on May 14 the transfer of part of the Alaska Defense Command reserve from the island of Adak—the 1st Battalion of the 4th Infantry. This request, seconded by Admiral Rockwell, was approved, and on May 17 the 4th Infantry units left Adak for Massacre Bay and arrived the next day.

Thus the Southern Force was increased from its original three battalions to five. On May 17 Major General Eugene M. Landrum, formerly commanding on Adak, assumed command of all forces on Attu, relieving General Brown. Colonel Lawrence V. Castner, for two years G-2 of the Alaska Defense Command, became General Landrum's deputy chief of staff.

During the first five days of the battle no contact had existed between the Southern Force and the Northern Force. Each was preoccupied with its own immediate problems; each knew that the other had landed, but had no detailed information beyond that fact. In the afternoon of May 16 the Northern Force had seized and held the high ground dominating the west arm of Holtz Bay, the site of the main Japanese base. Foreseeing that this would mean its capture, the enemy withdrew to the east arm on the following day. This withdrawal left the Japanese forces opposing the American Southern Force in a precarious position and in imminent danger of being taken from the rear by the American Northern Force's advance. The Japanese commander then determined to break off the defensive battle he had thus far successfully waged against the Southern Force, withdraw from the positions on Henderson Ridge and immediately surround Jarmin Pass in the direction of Chichagof, and reinforce the defensive positions around Clevesy Pass. During the night of May 16-17 the Japanese successfully executed this movement, undisturbed and unobserved by the Americans in Massacre Valley. On the morning of May 17 the Jarmin Pass lay open and undefended.

The day of May 17 passed quietly for the American Southern Force, a welcome respite after five hard days of combat. Colonel Zimmerman, commander of the 17th, spent the day in an advance observation post watching intently for any sign of life in and around the pass. At length he concluded that the enemy might have withdrawn and ordered forward a patrol of Company K of the 17th to reconnoiter. The patrol reported no signs of the enemy and Colonel Zimmerman joined it in person to assure himself that the pass was in fact abandoned. Satisfied of the enemy's withdrawal, he directed Company I to advance and occupy the pass, and on its arrival pushed forward another patrol under command of Lieutenant Morris C. Wiberg to investigate the other side of the pass. Advancing cautiously along the heights that dominated the east arm of Holtz Bay, the patrol encountered no enemy and at last dropped down the steep slope that led to the main Japanese base on the valley floor of the west arm. There at 0230 on May 18 Wiberg's patrol met a platoon of the 7th Reconnaissance Troop. Junction had been effected between the Northern and Southern Forces and the struggle for Jarmin Pass was ended.

The Opening of Clevesy Pass

One outlet of Massacre Valley was in American hands and the enemy no longer separated the Northern and Southern Forces. But much was left to be done. The Japanese positions around Jarmin Pass had not been captured, they had been evacuated in an orderly manner; the enemy had not been destroyed. With Jarmin Pass in the hands of the Southern Force and the enemy installations at the end of the west arm of Holtz Bay in the hands of the Northern Force, it was a fair assumption that the Japanese had established a new principal base at Chichagof. It could also be assumed that the rugged heights and valleys leading to it would be tenaciously defended. The American plan of attack, based on these assumptions, provided that the Southern Force, pushing out of Massacre Valley by way of Clevesy Pass, would advance on Chichagof from the other side, capturing enemy-held heights and peaks on the way while the Northern Force, after cleaning out the area around the east arm of Holtz Bay, would advance toward Chichagof along the northern slope of Prendergast Ridge.

The Southern Force spent the day of May 18 in reorganizing and regrouping its forces for an attack on Clevesy Pass and the adjacent heights. The 3d Battalion of the 17th, which had suffered heavily in the fighting for Jarmin Pass, was placed in force reserve, leaving one reinforced company, Company K, to guard the pass. The 2d Battalion of the 32d moved into position near the command post of the 17th, and the 1st Battalion of the 4th moved about a mile up the Hogback, where it bivouacked for the night as the force reserve.

The main assault on Clevesy Pass was entrusted to the 2d Battalion of the 17th, with the 2d Battalion of the 32d in support. During the night of May 18-19, patrols went forward and at 0952 hours on the 19th the 17th Infantry launched its attack supported by artillery fire. By noon it had advanced some

750 yards into the pass and during the afternoon the 32d succeeded in clearing the high ground northeast of the pass. The fighting continued, however, on the southeast side of the pass, particularly around Point Able, a towering eminence where a Japanese platoon, strongly entrenched and skillfully led, resisted all efforts of two companies of the 32d to dislodge them. The Japanese lieutenant in command hurled derisive epithets in excellent English at the attackers.

During the night the fighting continued mainly on the high ground on the left side of the pass. In this area the 1st Battalion of the 4th Infantry, released from force reserve, took over from the 17th and soon after daylight proceeded through the pass up to Prendergast Ridge. Progress continued during the day of May 20 until in the late morning Clevesy Pass was cleared of the enemy. It was not until the early morning of May 21, however, that Company E of the 32d, aided by Company C, finally reduced the enemy strong point at Point Able, wiping out the Japanese garrison in a gallant attack which won official commendation and a unit citation for Company E.

On the left of the pass, fighting continued on the upper slopes of Cold Mountain even after the pass itself had been opened, but in the morning of May 20 all enemy positions had been reduced by Company F and Company H of the 17th.

By the close of the day of May 21, Clevesy Pass with all its dominating heights, Cold Mountain, Engineer Hill, and Point Able, was in American hands. The Southern Force controlled all of Massacre Valley, and the 4th Infantry, despite strong enemy resistance, had reached a point halfway along the slope of Prendergast Ridge on its way toward Chichagof.

THE LANDING AT RED BEACH

On May 11, the same day that the Southern Force landed at Massacre Bay, the Northern Force landed on Red Beach some three miles from the main Japanese camp at the end of the west arm of Holtz Bay. The force consisted of the 1st Battalion of the 17th Infantry under the command of Lieutenant Colonel Hartl, a battery of field artillery, and supporting troops. The 1st and 3d Battalions of the 32d Infantry and two batteries of field artillery were held on shipboard in reserve.

The selection of Red Beach as a landing site was a bold decision amply justified by the results. Half-submerged rocks at the approaches to the beach forced the landing craft to take a winding course to reach the shore, and only two could be landed side by side at any one place. The beach itself is not more than a hundred yards long, and though fairly level for some seventy-five yards inland, is surrounded by steep hills that rise abruptly 250 feet above the sea. Altogether it must have seemed to the Japanese a most unpromising and unlikely place for a landing, and to this fact is doubtless due their neglect to establish any defenses there or even to guard the beach.

Before the principal landing it was determined to make a thorough reconnaissance to find whether the beach was suitable for a landing and whether opposition would be encountered. For this purpose a detachment of Alaskan Scouts with a Navy beachmaster and Colonel Culin, commanding the 32d Infantry, put off in small boats, closely followed by Company A of the 17th. A destroyer protected the party to a point some eight hundred yards off shore after which the smaller craft proceeded alone.

On the transport the main body anxiously waited for news until shortly after 1100 when Colonel Culin reported by radio from the shore that the beach seemed adequate for landing and that the advance party had seen no signs of the enemy. The destroyer guided the empty landing boats back to the transport and the debarkation began immediately. The first wave reached the beach at 1530.

Owing to the difficulty of the terrain the landing proceeded slowly but was unhampered by enemy activity. At 1800 hours the battalion was ready to begin its advance in the direction of the end of the west arm of Holtz Bay, with the main body moving over the high ground back of the beach and one platoon going along the beach as a left-flank guard.

It was this platoon that first made contact with the enemy about an hour later. Four Japanese infantrymen were observed approaching along the beach apparently unaware of the American landing. The American platoon took cover, let the four Japanese come within 150 yards, and then opened fire. Two of the enemy were killed, but the other two escaped. Within half an hour the Japanese dual-purpose antiaircraft guns at Holtz Bay opened fire on the beach platoon, but the main force, back of the defilade offered by the high ground above the beach, remained undiscovered and undisturbed by the enemy.

The battalion moved ahead in column of companies over the rolling snow-patched hillocks. On their left was Holtz Bay; on their right a ridge of foothills stretched up to high peaks in the distance. The objective for the day was a group of heights known as Hill X, which dominated the enemy camp on Holtz Bay. Assuming that unseen units might open fire at any moment, the battalion moved forward cautiously, but no opposition developed. By 2200 it had advanced some two miles inland from Red Beach but was still 800 yards short of its objective. In the heavy fog and gathering darkness visibility had become extremely restricted. The outline of the terrain did not seem to agree with the map. Uncertain as to his exact position, Colonel Hartl ordered a halt and the battalion took up defensive positions where it remained until daylight.

In the circumstances this seemed a prudent decision. But the Japanese in Holtz Bay had become aware of the American force and during the night occupied positions on Hill X which they had already prepared but had not previously occupied. Consequently, in the morning the battalion was faced by enemy units strongly entrenched on ground that dominated its own positions. If the battalion had continued its advance, the evening before, the situation on the following day would have been reversed.

From dawn until 0900 on May 12 the whole area held by the American force was covered by almost impenetrable fog and no forward movement was attempted. Shortly after 0900 the fog lifted and it became evident that the enemy positions would have to be taken by assault. Colonel Hartl ordered a right-flank enveloping attack on Hill X by Company A. In making this attack, with high ground rising above its right flank, the company reached a deep ravine running diagonally across its front. Suddenly taken under heavy mortar, machine-gun, and rifle fire, the company sought shelter in the ravine, which was partly enfiladed from the heights on the right. Throughout the rest of the day Company A stayed pinned to the ground, unable to advance or withdraw, under an incessant fire that caused numerous casualties.

At the same time the main body of the battalion received harassing fire from snipers in concealed positions about 300 yards along the high ground to the right, but suffered no casualties. In midafternoon, with the support from field artillery on Red Beach and from the guns of the warships lying off the island, the battalion prepared a frontal attack on the enemy positions. At 1650 Navy aircraft effectively bombed and strafed the enemy positions on the forward face of Hill X. And ten minutes later, behind a barrage, the battalion advanced. In about an hour and a half it had taken the south side and the near peak of the group of hills without a single American casualty, though many of the enemy met death in their foxholes. It also repulsed a savage counterattack from the high northern knob still in Japanese hands, and the fighting ended with darkness.

During the night Company A was able to get out of its bad spot in the ravine, and in the morning, May 13, another attack gave the American units complete possession of Hill X. In full control of the high ground dominating the tundra slope which stretched for 1,000 yards down to the main Japanese camp behind the beach at the end of the west arm of Holtz Bay, the battalion halted to reorganize and consolidate its positions.

During the afternoon of May 13 it was decided to reinforce the 1st Battalion of the 17th with the 3d Battalion of the 32d, one of the two Infantry battalions which had so far been held in reserve on shipboard. Colonel Culin assumed command of the whole Northern Force, now almost doubled in strength. The first units of the reinforcing battalion reached the forward area at 2000, and by noon the next day the whole battalion was in position.

Colonel Culin, after conferring with Lieutenant Colonels Hartl and John ("Mickey") Finn, who commanded the 3d Battalion of the 32d, determined to launch a combined attack by both battalions against the Japanese camp, supported by artillery and naval fire. Throughout the afternoon enemy snipers harassed the 32d, and the enemy artillery in Holtz Bay kept up a heavy but inaccurate fire on the positions on Hill X and the rear areas of both battalions. The American attack, originally planned for the afternoon of the 14th, was postponed until the morning of the 15th.

THE PROVISIONAL BATTALION

During the period while the fighting for the possession of Hill X was going on, the Provisional Battalion, under Captain Willoughby, consisting of the 7th Scout Company and the 7th Reconnaissance Troop, had worked its way through the mountains to positions on high ground to the rear of the Japanese left flank. This force, which had landed on May 11 at Austin Cove from two submarines and a destroyer, had a particularly arduous task. Cut off from communication with the rest of the landing force except by a portable radio that operated only intermittently, and short of food and ammunition, it had pushed over the steep snow-covered slopes of the mountains. It had had to bivouac for the night on a wind-swept mountaintop in the midst of an icy fog, and the troops had suffered greatly from cold and exposure. Although the Army Air Forces made gallant efforts to drop food and supplies to Willoughby's command, the attempts were only partly successful because of the bad weather.

The battalion made its first contact with the Japanese when, after crossing the summit of the mountains, its leading units came down upon the enemy positions on the high ground west of Holtz Bay in the morning of May 12. For three days, until the enemy finally evacuated the Holtz Bay camp on the 15th, the Provisional Battalion was continuously engaged under the toughest conditions. Because the battalion was out of touch with the main force, an impression existed that it had lost its way in the mountains. But in fact, despite all handicaps, it reached the area designated in the general plan of operations on time. And it accomplished its assigned mission by compelling the enemy to fight facing west and by diverting a considerable fraction of the Japanese force which otherwise would have opposed the main body of our Northern Force. Thus the Provisional Battalion made a substantial contribution to the general operation and set a highly creditable example of courageous endurance and reliability in an independent operation.

The Capture of the Japanese Base

On the morning of May 15 fog limited visibility to a hundred yards and forced a postponement of the attack of the 1st Battalion of the 17th and the 3d Battalion of the 32d until shortly after 1100. When the two battalions advanced down the slope they found that the enemy had pulled out of the camp and withdrawn to Moore Ridge, which separates the west arm from the east arm of Holtz Bay. The Japanese had left behind them large stores of food, ammunition, and miscellaneous supplies, including a battery of six 70mm. dual-purpose guns and some machine guns and mortars.

During the night the Northern Force pushed its lines forward to the middle of the west-arm floor preparatory to an attack on Moore Ridge. With the coming of daylight, heavy enemy machine-gun fire from the ridge pinned the leading outfits of both battalions to the floor of the valley. But detachments of Companies B and C of the 17th found a covered approach to the ridge along the beach, and stealthily forced their way up the slopes on the Japanese right flank to a point which dominated the main enemy positions. For this exploit Company B, which took the lead, received a well-earned unit citation.

To avoid machine-gun fire, Colonel Culin ordered both battalions to make a coördinated night attack, which was launched at 0010 on May 17. By 0300 the attack had reached the crest of the ridge without a casualty only to find that the enemy had withdrawn in the darkness into the east-arm valley. The American force spent the rest of the night in consolidating its new positions. In the morning, patrols sent into the east-arm valley met only slight resistance and it became evident that the enemy had moved back still farther to the heights in the direction of Chichagof Harbor, leaving the whole Holtz Bay area in American hands. In the early morning of May 18 junction was made between the Northern and Southern Forces.

THE BATTLE FOR CHICHAGOF

In anticipation of the possible arrival of Japanese reinforcements, it seemed desirable to organize the Holtz Bay area strongly for defense and this task fell to the 1st Battalion of the 17th. One reinforced company of the 3d Battalion started on May 19 up the steep trail leading over the mountains to Chichagof, but almost immediately encountered opposition so strong as to make it evident that reinforcements were needed. The other companies of the battalion, plus two companies of the 17th, were successively sent up. Very slowly, almost yard by yard, this force made its way along the northern slope of Prendergast Ridge until on the 25th it reached the base of the steep and rugged semicircle of snow-covered mountains known as the Fish Hook. Constantly under fire from good enemy positions on higher ground, the force had to overcome and destroy numerous snipers and machine-gun positions as it went along.

Meanwhile, on May 21, the Southern Force that had cleared Massacre Valley and its surrounding heights prepared to move on Chichagof, with the strong enemy positions on Sarana Nose as its first objective. This mission was assigned to the 3d Battalion of the 17th, with three infantry heavy machine-gun companies, D and H of the 32d and H of the 17th, to give supporting fire from Engineer Hill on the opposite side of the valley. At 0640 on the 22d the fires of preparation started. Thirty-two heavy machine guns, eight light machine guns, fourteen 37s, twenty-three 81mm. mortars, a section of 75mm. pack howitzers, and four batteries of 105mm. howitzers—every powerful Infantry weapon available, opened up simultaneously on the target, covering every open inch of Sarana Nose with a rain of projectiles.

At 0700 the infantry moved forward over the flat, coverless valley, 800 yards wide, under this roof of fire. And when Company K reached and stormed up the slope of Sarana Nose, it found the first enemy emplacements entirely deserted. At the second line, as the company moved farther on up the hill, it found the Japanese defenders unwilling to surrender, but so badly dazed and shaken as to be incapable of serious resistance. Many were killed, and many ran away at top speed. By early afternoon the whole of Sarana Nose was in American hands and Companies I and L had joined Company K in consolidating defensive positions on the Nose. American casualties were very light. This action is a fine example of the results that can be obtained from carefully coördinated action by infantry and its heavy weapons and Field Artillery support.

While the battle for Sarana Nose drove forward, the 1st Battalion of the 4th Infantry was in action on the slope of Prendergast Ridge. Just at dawn, Company A saw troops coming over the crest of the ridge from the Holtz Bay side. Unable to distinguish in the fog whether they were friendly or Japanese troops, but thinking that they might be elements of the Northern Force, Company A withheld its fire. A quick call to headquarters brought out that the Northern Force had had to pull back during the night, and that accordingly the troops encountered must be Japanese.

With this information, Company A engaged the enemy along the ridge, but met such strong opposition that it made little progress even though reinforced by a platoon of Company B. At last convinced of his inability to dislodge the Japanese from their rocky position on the crest of the ridge with the weapons at his command, the company commander called for artillery support—this in spite of the poor visibility caused by fog. Within a few minutes shells from the 105mm. howitzers began to crash along the top of the ridge, driving the defenders out from behind the rocks that concealed them and permitting Company A to take them under rifle and machine-gun fire. Painfully, but steadily, the company pushed forward up the precipitous slope, firing as it went, and finally reached the summit of the ridge. Then the Japanese, driven from their shelters and disorganized by the artillery fire, disappeared into the fog, retreating down the reverse slope in the direction of Holtz Bay.

The capture of Sarana Nose and of Prendergast Ridge made possible a direct attack against the entrance to Jim Fish Valley (Chichagof Valley). The Southern Force had taken a long step on the road to Chichagof.

AID FROM JAPAN

From the beginning of the invasion the American commanders both of ground and naval units had kept in mind the possibility that an effort might be made from the enemy base at Paramushiro either to reinforce or rescue the Japanese troops on Attu. The Japanese commander had repeatedly assured his men that help in the form of heavy reinforcements was on the way. Whether this was merely a step taken on his own initiative to bolster the morale of his men, or whether he had in fact received assurances from the Japanese High Command that his force would be strengthened or extricated, may never be known. In any case, the expected reinforcements never arrived and so far as is known they never started. Nor was any effort made to take the Japanese garrison off the island by sea, as was later done at Kiska.

The only assistance the Japanese received came in the middle of the afternoon of May 22, the day of the attack on Sarana Nose, when a flight of ten low-flying planes suddenly appeared out of the mist and launched twelve torpedoes against the United States cruiser *Charleston* and the destroyer *Phelps,* which were lying off Massacre Bay. None of the torpedoes hit its mark. The planes circled briefly over Chichagof Harbor, dropping some white packages, and then disappeared westward. A few minutes later a "large flight of high-flying heavy bombers or many lights" was reported seventy-four miles south of Chichagof Harbor. Six American P-38s from Amchitka immediately took off to intercept them. When contact was made they were found to be sixteen heavy bombers, which jettisoned their bombs and fled. Nine were reported shot down into the sea. Except for these two brief and abortive air attacks, the Japanese forces defending Attu received no help.

THE TAKING OF THE FISH HOOK

The Japanese now occupied the inner perimeter of defense around their Chichagof Harbor base. Their positions in the south sector ran in a straight line from the steep ice-coated Fish Hook Ridge down to the plateau in Jim Fish Valley short of Lake Cories. An effort to push down the valley floor would bring an attacking force under flanking fire from the shelf below Buffalo Ridge as well as from the lower ground between the ridge and Lake Cories. Accordingly, sticking to the general tactics he had followed since assuming command—a policy of taking and dominating high ground before trying to move along the valleys—General Landrum decided to attack Fish Hook Ridge and initially gave this job to the 2d Battalion of the 17th, which relieved the 1st Battalion of the 4th on the morning of May 23. At 1700 the 2d Battalion launched its attack, but it was able to advance only 200 yards before concentrated machine-gun fire halted it. No further progress was made on that day.

On the Holtz Bay side of Prendergast Ridge, the 3d Battalion of the 32d, of the Northern Force, reinforced by two companies from the 1st Battalion of the 17th, after several days of hard fighting, had reached positions from which it could participate in the attack against the Fish Hook to the left of the 2d Battalion of the 17th. A coördinated attack by both battalions was launched at 1000 on the 24th. Some initial progress was made along the bare, ice-crusted slopes on opposite sides of the ridge line joining Prendergast Ridge to the Fish Hook, but heavy machine-gun and rifle fire sweeping the narrow approaches to the Japanese positions compelled the attackers to halt, and before nightfall forced them to withdraw substantially to their starting points. In the course of the day the attacking force was reinforced by Companies C and D of the 1st Battalion of the 32d, which went into action on the right of the 17th and made some progress. In the night the 1st Battalion of the 4th was moved into supporting positions behind the 17th.

The enemy, occupying a 200-yard trench which was deep-dug in snow and in places so covered over as to be virtually invisible, held the 3d Battalion of the 32d pinned down. On the morning of the 25th, Company E of the 17th cleaned out a section of the right end of this trench, advancing above it to a narrow ledge on the slopes of the Fish Hook where it held its position under heavy fire until the rest of the battalion came to its support. Company B of the 4th moved up behind the 17th, mopping up, but suffered numerous casualties from enemy snipers who had stayed in position below the 17th.

At daylight on May 26 the 2d Battalion of the 17th and Company B of the 4th firmly held their positions on the base of the Fish Hook. The 17th covered by fire the entrance to the narrow pass that led from the Holtz Bay side across the lower "shank" of the Fish Hook and down the precipitous bowl at the end of which was the Japanese Chichagof base. Company B's position dominated the interior slopes. To increase the effectiveness and range of this unit's fire, a 37mm. gun was laboriously dragged up from the valley floor.

The rest of the snow trench which had held up the advance of the Northern Force was destroyed by two platoons of Company A of the 4th. They descended on it from above while the Northern Force, consisting of the 3d Battalion of the 32d and Companies A and C of the 1st Battalion of the 17th, attacked the Holtz Bay side of the Fish Hook known as Bahai. This action, in which Companies I and K of the 32d particularly distinguished themselves and received unit citations, was entirely successful. The Northern Force was now established on

Fish Hook Ridge in positions that it held until the final assault on Chichagof on May 30.

Meantime, at the eastern end of the Fish Hook, the 1st Battalion of the 4th was finding heavy going among the high peaks and jagged knife-edged ridges. Theirs was an action of platoons, squads, and individuals against enemy machine-gun and sniper positions, well chosen, widely dispersed, and artfully concealed among the rocks and snowdrifts—a game of hide-and-seek, with death as the penalty for the loser. The principal units in this fight were Companies A, C, and D of the 4th. Company D, which had had the toughest work in the opening phase of the action, was temporarily placed in battalion reserve, only to return to the front on the closing day. It was May 28 before every part of the Fish Hook was in American hands.

While the attack against the Fish Hook was in progress, the 1st Battalion (less Companies A and B) and the 2d Battalion of the 32d began a series of attacks to capture Buffalo Ridge, which was lower than the Fish Hook and not so formidable. On the 27th, the 2d Battalion, with artillery support, attacked and reached a point some 200 yards short of the ridge. The attack on the ridge itself was delayed until 1830 on the 28th, waiting for the 4th Infantry to take the Fish Hook. Buffalo Ridge had been systematically pounded by our own artillery, mortars, and 37s throughout the afternoon, and this fire got heavier about an hour before the attack began. The advance up the ridge met some opposition, but the long, heavy bombardment had softened up the enemy, and by nightfall the 32d held an important part of Buffalo Ridge. It had not, however, been able to occupy the part that would have permitted observation of the whole plateau stretching toward Chichagof, where the Japanese counterattack later assembled.

At the same time that the attack on Buffalo Ridge started, 1830 on May 28, a force consisting of the 3d Battalion of the 17th with Company B of the 32d attached, began an advance in column of companies up the floor of Jim Fish Valley, proceeding to a point beyond the southern edge of Lake Cories where it halted for the night, establishing patrol contact with the 32d on Buffalo Ridge to the left.

The net had now closed around the enemy forces gathered at their base at Chichagof Harbor. The situation that existed in Massacre Valley in the early days of the battle was reversed. The Japanese, with the sea at their backs, were now crowded into a small, flat area hardly susceptible of defense. The American forces, in superior numbers, held the dominating heights around them. The Japanese position seemed tactically hopeless. It seemed to the Americans that the bitter struggle—it had been much harder and longer than at first expected—was finally about to come to a victorious conclusion. General Landrum determined to move in for the kill with an attack by his full force the following morning, May 29. In the night of May 28-29, for the first time since the beginning of the battle, no infantry was left in force reserve.

Yamasaki's Decision

In the evening of May 28 the Japanese commander, Colonel Yasuyo Yamasaki, found himself in a desperate situation. For eighteen days he had fought a stubborn and skillful delaying action, giving ground only under pressure, but in the process he had lost approximately seventy per cent of his force. He now had some 700 men, battle-weary, undernourished, and despondent over the failure of expected reinforcements to arrive. The loss of the Holtz Bay base had cost him a large proportion of his supplies and most of his artillery. He had abandoned any hope that help might come from Japan, and he had no illusions as to the tactical strength of his position. He knew that he was confronted by a powerful, confident enemy, greatly superior in numbers and tempered by the fire of battle. And he had to assume that this force would strike hard and without delay.

Four possible courses of action lay open to him: (1) to surrender, which was unthinkable under the Japanese military code; (2) to make a suicidal last stand at Chichagof, which would be useless and wholly unprofitable; (3) to attempt a further withdrawal into the hills in the direction of Klebnikoff Point and there carry on the fight; but this would delay matters only a few days at best, for he would eventually be cornered again and he lacked the means of carrying away any substantial quantity of food or ammunition; (4) to counterattack. Only in the last course did there seem any possibility of success.

Knowing that the main American forces were occupying the ridges of the Fish Hook, he reasoned that the weakest point in the ring that encircled him would be the floor of the valley. By a sudden, brutal assault, executed by his entire force and under cover of darkness which would neutralize flanking fire, he might be able to cut his way through to the American battery positions behind Engineer Hill. Once the American guns, even a few of them, were in his possession, the main American base at Massacre Bay could be captured or destroyed despite the American superiority in numbers. There was a chance that the situation might be reversed or that the invaders might be compelled to reëmbark and start over again at a later date. It was a desperate gamble, with a bare possibility of brilliant victory if it succeeded—but certain death if it failed. At 0030 on May 29 Yamasaki issued his order for the counterattack.

After advancing up Jim Fish Valley with the 3d Battalion of the 17th, Company B of the 32d took up a position for the night on the floor of the valley near the southern end of Lake Cories, with the lake on its right and Company L of the 17th on the rising ground to its left. At 0300 on May 29 Company B received an order to withdraw. The reasons for this order are obscure in the official records so far available, but apparently there was no expectation of enemy action during the night. It is said that the purpose was to permit the men to go back to the battalion kitchen, some distance to the rear, so that they could get a hot breakfast before going into the attack against Chichagof the following morning. At about 0330, while the Company was in the act of thus withdrawing, a horde of shrieking Japanese, bayonets fixed and grenades in hand, struck its rear guard. Taken completely by surprise and greatly outnumbered, the company was thrown into confusion and all hope of organized resistance quickly vanished. The American company poured back down the valley or sought safety on the higher ground, while the Japanese main body pushed swiftly in the direction of Clevesy Pass.

Apparently to prevent the possibility of flank attacks, the enemy main body detached small groups to either side as it advanced. Although because of the general surprise and resultant confusion these groups succeeded in causing numerous casualties at Sarana Nose and other points, they were in the main beaten off with loss. The Japanese main body, seriously reduced in strength by this dispersal of force, swept across Sarana Valley toward Clevesy Pass.

In this area the bulk of the divisional engineers and the 50th Engineers and various service units were bivouacked with no anticipation of any combat with the enemy. Though they heard the sound of small-arms and shell fire in Jim Fish Valley, they had paid no particular attention, for it was not unusual and they were far out of range. Infantry and medical soldiers streaming down the valley shouting that the enemy was coming gave the first intimation that anything was wrong. Hastily springing to arms, the engineers organized an improvised line on the slopes of Engineer Hill leading to Point Able. Within ten minutes of the first warning they were hard at grips with the advancing enemy. Service troops, cooks, and men of every kind of unit grabbed whatever weapons they could find, and fought together, firing on the frenzied Japanese at point-blank range, gradually building up and consolidating their forces.

It may fairly be said that the ultimate success of the whole Attu operation hinged on the ability of the Engineers to meet this emergency. Several small enemy detachments penetrated Clevesy Pass and attacked the Hogback in Massacre Valley just short of the emplacements of one battery of our 105mm. howitzers. This was the Japanese objective and it was nearly attained. Though fighting in this area continued long after daylight and throughout the day of May 29, the Japanese onslaught broke down before the tough-fibered resistance of the 50th Engineers, fighting as infantry in desperate hand-to-hand combat. On the eve of victory the American force had come close to losing all that it had gained.

May 29 was a day of confused fighting and the destruction of small groups of Japanese throughout the area of the counterattack, but final victory was never again in doubt. Few of the enemy surrendered; most of them preferred to die from their own grenades as soon as they realized that further resistance was useless.

In the late afternoon of May 30, when it had become evident that the situation was again in hand, the 2d and 3d Battalions of the 32d, the 3d Battalion of the 17th and Company A of the 4th occupied Chichagof Harbor virtually without resistance.

A communiqué of the Japanese High Command conceded the loss of Attu on May 30 in the following terms:

The Japanese garrison on the island of Attu has been conducting a bloody battle with a small number of troops against a numerically far superior enemy under many difficulties, and on the night of May 29 carried out an heroic assault against the main body of enemy invaders with the determination to inflict a final blow on them and display the true spirit of the Imperial Army.

Since then there has been no communication from the Japanese forces on the island and it is now estimated that the entire Japanese force has preferred death to dishonor.

The sick and wounded Japanese soldiers who were unable to participate in the last attack killed themselves beforehand. The actual number of Japanese defenders on the island was 2,000 and odd hundreds and their commander was Colonel Yasuyo Yamasaki.

The strength of the enemy, who was very well equipped, was about 20,000 and casualties on the enemy side reached no less than 6,000 up to May 28.

The island of Kiska is definitely maintained by Japanese forces.

The Japanese communiqué grossly exaggerated American effectives and casualties. In fact, American forces on Attu never exceeded 12,000. And our total casualties, including those from exposure who were temporarily evacuated, were considerably less than 3,000. Out of approximately 2,300 Japanese on the island, 29 prisoners were taken. For many weeks after the battle isolated snipers lurked in the mountains and the last surrendered in September 1943.

CONCLUSION

On May 30, 1943, the battle of Attu ended. For the next few days mopping-up operations continued and small groups of the enemy were located and destroyed throughout the battle area.

It has been said that Attu was primarily an infantry battle, and this is true. But in giving credit to the Queen of Battles it will not do to forget or to ignore the rôle played by the artillery and the Air Forces. Both played their positions on the big team and played them well. Again and again the infantry found itself powerless until well-directed and coördinated artillery fire opened the way for its advance. The weather handicapped the air arms of both the Army and the Navy, so that they had no real opportunity to give the effective aid they might otherwise have given. Nevertheless, when the final story of Attu can be written, it will be found that the air part of the battle was by no means inconsiderable. Aside from the technical difficulties of transport and supply which the engineers overcame, their epic stand against the Japanese counterattack in the early morning hours of May 29 will always be counted a legendary feat in the history of their Corps. To the Medical Corps it is hard to offer praise in measured terms. But for the selfless courage of its officers and men, the losses and suffering on Attu would have been multiplied many fold.

In short, every arm and branch of the service—every unit—carried its share of the burden and performed its allotted task. Mistakes were made, but they were not the kind of mistakes for which anyone need feel ashamed. They were simply the kind that are inevitable whenever troops inexperiencd in combat and unfamiliar with local conditions and terrain must fight a well-trained, thoroughly acclimated and strongly entrenched enemy.

There was never a faltering of courage, or a loss of faith in ultimate victory. The result speaks for itself: Attu—and Kiska as well—are again American.

PART TWO
PERSONAL NARRATIVES OF ATTU

FOREWORD

By

First Lieutenant Robert J. Mitchell, 32d Infantry

These are the incidents of battle: the stories of the men who move and kill and die, over mountains and mud—who mark the ground with their bodies, while the maps behind them are being marked with pins and pencil lines.

These are not the stories of heroes, though many heroes are mentioned here. They are simply the stories of guys who kill the enemy soldiers with rifles and bayonets.

They are the truth. They are the truth as it is remembered by the men who lived the stories—the truth, only so far as it can be represented by words on paper. Words, however colorfully arranged, can never flash like the muzzle of a machine gun firing through the fog, or rumble like artillery shells on a mountain, or grunt like a soldier when a bullet hits. Those are things kept secret inside of men who have lived intimately with battle; and they are shared, like prized possessions, only with other men who have lived with battle.

Often with such words as, "Sergeant, the Lieutenant is being sent around by the Chief of Staff to get some stories on the battle up on Attu," company commanders introduced me to their men. Then, invariably, with a look full of things the two had shared, and an uneasy glance at me, the soldier and I sat down to talk; sometimes in a mess hall or a CP tent, sometimes on a "cat" or a boat or the soldier's bunk; sometimes on the ground, the very ground where the fighting had been.

Most of the men were reticent; some were smugly reticent. They felt a personal ownership of their experiences, regarded the story of the bullets that killed their buddies as a cherished and private thing, not to be tossed about indiscriminately by outsiders. They always waited for me to start, even after I had told them the sort of thing I wanted; and it usually took a catalyst like "Remember that Jap machine gunner on Engineer Hill . . ." to start the conversation.

They remembered all right. They remembered vividly. As the battle reappeared in their minds, the effect was reflected in the face of every man I talked with. But men who have been in battle and felt the impact of combat on their bodies are like members who have been initiated into an esoteric brotherhood. And until I had a chance to tell that I was up there that day, that it was the day I had been wounded, and I knew what hell they were catching the stories were only lifeless statements. After that, however, the men talked freely. Most of the soldiers I talked to alone were shy, but when several got together their mutual memories dovetailed, and the stories built themselves. All the men preferred to tell stories about each other, the one in subject adding details and corrections, and saying, "Ah, hell, if it hadn't been for Joe. . . ."

They told the truth. For few men who have been in battle will exaggerate or

[24]

lie in the face of the men who fought beside them, and many of the stories cross-checked where the incidents overlapped. The men were embarrassed by the exaggerated misstatements published about them.

They remember just the incidents and are proud of their memories. They remember the men who fell and the way they fell, in the ten or twenty yards on either side of them. They remember the details of a parried bayonet, and the vicious snapping of close machine-gun bullets, and the dirt from a shell exploding beside them. They remember the little things like urinating into an empty shell carton and pouring it over the edge of a foxhole as the height of battlefield fastidiousness.

When the unit report states coldly ". . . the attack pushed off at 0600. The attacking companies advanced, under stiff enemy resistance, to within two hundeed yards of the objective and were repulsed," the man who heard his buddy drop and dived behind a rock as the bullets splattered against it, knows intimately and accurately how the attack was repulsed. And tomorrow night he will know intimately and accurately how the objectives were gained. He will have been there.

The big picture is plainly marked with black grease pencil over the flat contour lines of the map. The other picture is plainly marked, too, with scars, and laughs, and memories. It is the man's picture. I am proud to have seen it, and humble before it. It is the little picture. . . .

I: MASSACRE VALLEY

The main force of the 7th Infantry Division on Massacre Beach landed on May 11, 1943, pushed its two battalions of the 17th Infantry (one battalion of the 32d Infantry in reserve) up Massacre Valley to hold at Clevesy Pass (Massacre-Sarana Pass) and to force Jarmin Pass (Massacre-Holtz Pass). The eager Doughboys landed without meeting resistance at the beach and advanced toward the positions at the head of the valley that were the defenses of the Japanese 303d Independent Infantry Battalion.* Five days of bitter fighting were required to clear the area and permit the preparation for the assault of Chichagof Harbor.

The Landing of the Artillery

*Staff Sergeant Stanley E. West, Staff Sergeant Allen W. Robbins,
Corporal Howard B. Campbell*

Battery C, 48th Field Artillery Battalion

The advance party with Lieutenant James West were already moving up Massacre Valley into the fog, when the barges with the big 105mm. rifles and the heavy cats crunched against the sand of the beach. The motors roared and the cats backed the big guns out of the barges onto Attu.

In a few minutes they had turned around and were struggling over the steep bank up from the beach. Three of the guns had landed, and one was still coming in from the ship. The battery was busy getting up its own fire-direction center, as the big tractors lumbered onto the spongy, yielding tundra dragging the guns

---

*This battalion was landed on Attu 31 January 1943.

slowly behind. About seventy-five yards from the beach the treads of the first cat chewed through the tundra and began to slip. In just seconds it was wallowing helplessly in the black oozy mud. The other two cats soon shared the same fate. When the tundra broke, the big treads turned round and round and only dug the machine deeper into the mud. What the hell, seventy-five yards was far enough initially! The crews swung the big guns around and pointed them into the valley. They were setting up.

The radio to the advance party popped back into life. The tin voice said, ". . . encountered no enemy. . . ." The crews went ahead rapidly setting up the big guns. Lieutenant William Kimball was on the radio, the guns were getting ready. The first half hour passed. "No enemy. . . ." And Kimball said, "For Christ's sake, find something!" The guns were set, and the crews were moving ammunition in when the 610[1] spoke again, Lieutenant West's voice, "Enemy mortar position . . . map target 10." The battery knew where the target was, on the map, but they didn't know exactly where the guns were on the map's beach. The FDC[2] popped a pin into the map, took a deflection reading off the fan for target 10. The guns were already laid up the valley in the general direction of the enemy. Lieutenant Kimball was shouting, "No. 1, adjust . . . shell HE . . . charge five . . . fuze quick . . . base deflection . . . left two zero . . . elevation three two zero. . . ."

Eager fingers moved over the gun making adjustments. Then Private First Class Roy W. Watson said, "Set!" and Corporal Billie V. Vannoy, "Ready!" Lieutenant Kimball sang into the radio, "One on the way," then "Fire!" and the big gun slammed back into recoil. The trail log jumped eighteen inches into the boggy mud. The first round of artillery was whistling through the Attu sky toward the enemy.

For a long thirty seconds everybody waited, then the radio spoke, "eight hundred right . . . five hundred over." The computers, Staff Sergeant Stanley West and Corporal Howard Campbell, flipped the figures a moment converting the yards into millimeters. The muzzle of the big rifle moved slightly to the left and down. Lieutenant Kimball called, "Fire!" The trail log hunched deep into the mud as the gun roared another round at the unseen Japs ahead in the fog. The radio spoke again, "one hundred right . . . two hundred over," and again these figures were changed to millimeters and the big gun adjusted. The third round ripped into the enemy mortar position, and far up the valley Lieutenant West watched the burst as he reported, "Fire for effect!" When Lieutenant Kimball called out, "Battery, three rounds . . .," and the three guns roared in unison, Section Chief No. 1, Staff Sergeant Allen W. Robbins, looked over at Vannoy, his gunner, and grinned, "This is it, boy; we're gunnin'."

That was it. The beginning of twenty-one long, back-breaking, cold days and nights of fighting they would never forget.

---

[1]Field Artillery portable radio set.
[2]Fire-Direction Center.

Advance Into Massacre Valley — The Right Flank

Lieutenant Charles K. Paulson, Corporal Mike M. Brusuelas,
Corporal Paul H. Doty

Company F, 17th Infantry

"Land in Massacre Bay; move to the right. Protect the right flank of the battalion, block the pass through the mountains from Sarana Bay; move up Sarana Valley, and join the battalion in the vicinity of Clevesy Pass. . . ." The mission was clear. Lieutenant Paulson had the 1st Platoon of Company F, 17th Infantry, reinforced with a section of light machine guns and a 60mm. mortar.

When they say that an army travels on its stomach they usually mean that the men are traveling on the food in their stomachs. Well, brother, when that food is gone, and they still travel, they're traveling on guts. *That's the way Lieutenant Charles K. Paulson started his story.* You remember how it was when we landed, foggy and cold and mixed up. A little after 1600 on the afternoon of the 11th, it was, when we took off to the right and headed up into the mountains. The ground was new to us; the tundra and the holes and the snow gave us a bad time all the way. Some of the slopes were so straight up that we used ropes to haul our guns over them. We traveled all night the first night and got over onto the Sarana side early the next morning. God, we were tired!

We set the guns up in the pass we were to block, and then we came under scattered fire from across the valley on the other side of Lake Nicholas. The Japs were using heavy machine guns and big mortars, but the fire wasn't hot. We tried to return it, but they were out of range for our 60mm. mortars. We left one machine gun and a squad of men with Sergeant Rupert Schmitz to guard the pass and moved out with the 1st and 3d Squads. The Japs were in the valley, so we tried to follow the ridge along, but it was too tough going, and besides it led us off in the wrong direction. We had a -284[3] and a -195[4] along and tried several times during the day to contact the battalion, but neither radio would work.

It was getting late on the afternoon of the 12th when we decided to drop down into the valley and move up that way. It was dark when we got down off the mountain, and during the night we headed up the valley toward Clevesy Pass. We went along the left side of Lake Nicholas, between it and the mountain, and it was a helluva trip. We stumbled and fell and were soaking wet. It took us almost all night to get past the lake, and when it began to get light we were at the upper end. The two squads went up the hill to get in position around a nose, and the mortar and machine gun stayed in the valley and dug in.

Two patrols had been sent out—one with Sergeant Alex Lopez and Corporal Walter Johnson to investigate Sarana Nose across the valley; the other with Sergeant Leland A. Larson and Private Frank P. Campbell to move up the valley and investigate Clevesy Pass and try to contact the battalion. The patrols returned and reported Japs in both areas, but we didn't realize the situation until broad daylight arrived.

---

[3]Portable radio set.
[4]Walkie-talkie.

We saw the Japs. They were in a big horseshoe all around us. They were moving in the pass to our front, they held Sarana Nose, and they were almost behind us down in the valley, the way we had come. We sent the two Alaskan Scouts who had come with us back with the coördinates of the enemy positions, as the Japs began to fire on us. In each of the positions they had machine guns, mortars, and rifles. We were returning their fire with our machine gun, but the Japs were moving across the valley toward us. Corporal Mike Brusuelas was firing the gun, the rest of the squad had moved back to dig in higher on the hill, and Mike was blasting away trying to cover them. Sergeant Alonzo F. Atkinson, the section sergeant, jumped up to help Mike with the gun, and a Jap sniper cut him down. Joseph J. Cunha helped him back to a defile, then he went on up the hill to get some help. Sergeant Lopez and Private Campbell came down the hill firing tracers at the Japs. There were about twenty of them moving in on us from about 150 yards out in the valley. Mike picked up the gun and headed up the hill, and Campbell grabbed the tripod; the Japs were kicking up the tundra at their heels.

As the men worked their way up the hill lugging the gun and tripod, Sergeant Larson met them. The Japs were starting up the hill after them and had put a light machine gun in position near the foot of the slope. Larson hollered, "Keep going, I'll cover you." And he flopped down behind a rock and began firing. One after another, he knocked three gunners off the Jap gun, and the men made it up the hill to where the 1st Squad was. Sergeant Atkinson was hit hard and was in bad shape.

During the afternoon we watched about three hundred Japs working on Sarana Nose; they were digging positions and moving supplies. Sergeant Lopez saw them getting artillery pieces into position across the valley. Again we tried to contact the battalion with our radios, but failed. It was getting dark again, as we withdrew farther up into the protection of the hill and the fog. Sergeant Atkinson was suffering, and the men were so exhausted from two sleepless nights of aching cold and stumbling mountain climbing that they could hardly drag themselves along. The aid man was getting sick from hunger and exhaustion. He wanted to stay behind, so we arranged a little camouflaged dugout for Atkinson and the medic and left them all the scraps of rations that remained among us. Slowly and laboriously the remainder of the platoon struggled up the steep mountain to a defensive position.

The squads separated. One was to defend one side of the nose, and one the other side, but Sergeant Louis G. Techeira and his squad—the 3d—got lost and failed to make contact with the other squad. They moved along the ridge in the dense fog, following the ridge line. They were lost, and the ridge was leading them away from where they thought they should be going.

The men were getting sick, and some had vomited green bile several times during the morning. They had failed to contact the 1st Squad, and the fog had settled in, thick and confusing. They sat down to rest and to figure out the next move. Doty spotted a figure moving in the fog and called the password. The man ducked, and Doty called again. This time his answer was a bullet that cracked overhead. Doty raised up and fired, and the Jap fell behind a rock.

Someone threw a grenade and the blast sent the Jap tumbling over and over down a long snowbank. They decided to go directly back to Massacre Valley. They were lost and getting weak from hunger and lack of sleep. Doty had a watch compass and shot a back azimuth from the way we had moved, leaving Massacre. They started out single file, kicking footholds into the deep snow.

Meanwhile, the 1st Squad and the rest of the party had moved up the mountain far to the right of the lost 3d Squad. They were on top of the ridge, and it was bitter cold. The wind was whipping the wet fog and ice particles over the crest in a torrent of stinging little knives. They came upon the Japs suddenly and ducked as the bullets snapped out of the fog at them. It was a combat OP dug into the mountain at the foot of a rocky ledge facing Massacre Valley. There were eight Japs in it, armed with rifles and grenades and a light machine gun. Luckily, they were dug into the mountain in such a way, facing Massacre Valley, that they had to get out of their holes to really fight. For a few minutes the battle was terrific. Grenades were being thrown at fifteen yards, and men were firing from the hip. The Japs were beaten back into the shelter of the ledge, and they bunched up under a large rock. Our fourth grenade landed right in the middle of them, and they were finished. Several of our men had small wounds from grenade fragments, and Brusuelas had been hit in the knee pretty hard. We set up the Jap gun and our own light gun and prepared to defend the position. From down in the valley we could faintly hear a cat motor and some firing. It was getting late in the afternoon; some of the men were vomiting again.

The 3d Squad, which had been lost, moved straight over the mountain toward the sound of the cat motors in the valley. The fog was thick, but they could still hear the sound. It was a slippery treacherous descent. They were walking single file across a snowfield—the leader kicking steps in the snow, and the rest of the squad trailing behind in a line. The fog, which had hung around their ears like a veil all morning, suddenly broke and lifted. They could see the valley below, the first tents, the start of a road, the boats, and the tractors. Then they saw the guns on the beach flash, and a 37mm. shell landed below them with a crash. In seconds machine guns, rifles, and carbines were hurtling bullets at the squad strung out across the snow. The squad broke and ran, taking cover in rocks at the edge of the snow. The barrage continued for several long minutes, and the men in the squad were confused. They had no orange panel to identify themselves, and the carbines sounded like the Jap's caliber .25. They wondered if the Japs had counterattacked, or landed a new force and held the beach. One man was hit in the hand. They kept asking each other if they were wounded as the barrage continued. They lay in the cover of the rocks for a couple of hours after the firing subsided. Then the fog settled down again, and Doty got up. He could see six men in the fog, besides himself. Two of them thought Doty was a patrol from the beach, and they hollered from their cover that they were Americans, 17th Infantry, "same outfit as the guys on the beach." Doty finally got them together, and the seven men worked their way back up the mountain.

They discussed their situation the rest of the cold afternoon. They were irrational and weak and freezing. Doty thought someone should go down at night and tell the beach party who they were. The BAR[5] man thought the Japs held the beach. Two others insisted they wouldn't go down. It was getting late, so Doty decided he would go down after dark.

In the meantime, the 1st Squad and the weapons had dug in around the Jap OP and were ready to defend it. With a couple of men, we started out to see if we could find any trace of the lost 3d Squad. We wandered down the slope of the mountain and started edging off toward Massacre. We found Jap tracks, identified by the little hobnails, and then farther on we found Leo M. Chinuge's pack and first-aid kit. It had been dropped on a trail above a big snowbank. The faint trail, marked with American footprints, indicated that the 3d Squad had made it down OK. (Chinuge and a couple of others went on down after they had been separated from the squad during the barrage and made it all right. Chinuge had his sleeve torn off by a 37mm. shell and was badly shocked. He told a delirious story about the Japs attacking the squad and wiping it out. He even went into details where he had seen Japs bending over Doty and rolling him over, and when Doty spoke they killed him. The man was in bad shape.)

After we had found Chinuge's pack we moved back to the rest of the party. It was almost dark when we found our defense area near the Jap combat OP.

Doty and six men, who had been shelled, were moving along the ridge top. Doty had decided to try getting down the mountain himself. He told the rest that if he didn't return by morning they were to move back to where they had spent the afternoon and wait for him. They were to use the only password they knew, the one they had used the first night. Doty moved out alone, and soon was swallowed by the fog. He climbed straight down the mountain, crossed by the snowbank, where the squad had been fired on, and moved down. He had no idea of the current password and had no orange panel, but he carried a white rucksack cover and hoped to God that might stay the finger of a trigger-happy sentry until he could explain who he was. It was late, almost 0300 when he reached the valley floor. He moved across the flat a short distance, when he stumbled into a good deep hole. He decided he would wait there until daylight, then go in and identify himself. The hole was wet but it was deep and the wind didn't reach him there. It was warm, after the biting cold of the mountaintop, and Doty was exhausted. He fell asleep.

Some time later he woke up with a start. A great mechanical voice was shouting, "Let's go. Coffee ready for the men. Everybody out," and then some instructions about unloading boats. Doty was so stiff he could hardly move. The hole was luxurious; he lit a cigarette. The voice was shouting something about coffee again, and Doty climbed out of his hole. He moved warily a few steps, not knowing whether he'd be shot or not. No one paid any attention to him. He walked over to some engineers and asked who was in charge. Captain Paulard was found farther down the beach. Doty was grimy and muddy and almost dead on his feet. The captain asked him if he was one of the men who had been fired at on the mountain the day before. Doty told him enough of the story, while he was eating his third ration, so that the captain made arrangements for a party of MPs to go up and find the rest. Doty heard of the others who had come down

---

[5]Browning Automatic Rifle.

or been picked up. Sergeant Louis G. Techeira had been hit in the leg with a caliber .50; James M. Reaume had been hit in the finger; John Marchel and Victor Bonella had come down with them; and they had found Chinuge and brought him down.

After Doty had changed into some dry clothes, he wanted to go back up the mountain with the MPs to be sure that they found the other six men. The climb up the mountain was slow and tough, and even the three rations and soup and fresh clothes were hardly enough inspiration to keep Doty on his feet, but he managed, on sheer guts, to make it. He led the MPs to the place where they had rested the afternoon before and they began to holler for the men. They looked and shouted for about half an hour before Doty finally found the men. They had crawled back between two big boulders, out of the wind, wrapped up in all the shelter halves that they had, and were sleeping all in a pile.

It was late in the morning of the 15th that our party, the 1st Squad and the weapons and the radio men, stumbled down the mountain into the beach party. God, the chow was wonderful! And the valley felt like the breath of spring. We got dry and warm and our bellies full of soup, for the first time in four days.

I interrupted Lieutenant Paulson's story to ask what happened to Sergeant Atkinson and the medic who had been left behind. He said that he guessed nobody knew for sure. A few hundred yards from the dugout where they left them, they found the medic. His body was shot up pretty badly. And later, Sergeant Atkinson was found down near the head of Sarana Valley. He was dead, too. They didn't know if the Japs had moved them after capturing them, or if they had tried to move themselves.

I'll never forget that platoon, *he continued.* Those men can take it. And you can't tell me an army travels on its stomach; because long after it gets through traveling on its stomach it continues to travel, on its guts.

Advance Into Massacre Valley — The Left Flank
Private Raymond V. Braun, Company I, 17th Infantry

Were you there when this mushy-mushy hyee stuff got started? I asked Braun. Sure, *he said,* It'll work I guess, too. It started just after we landed on May 11. Our landing on that rock was screwy. We had been in boats all day long waiting to come into the island. Then we landed in fog as thick as mashed potatoes, expecting a wild dash across the beach with bullets flying, and there weren't any. We were supposed to be the left-flank protection so we headed for the flank, and it seemed like half of the Army was heading the same way. It turned out to be Company F, 32d Infantry, going to Temnac Bay. As they marched by, practically stepping on us, just as if they had gotten the wrong drill area, we attacked the first Jap tent. A firing line was set up and we covered the tent with fire while some other men worked in close and threw grenades. The tent was deserted, and we discovered that Company F's point had already grenaded it.

We pulled back and started up the left side of the valley. There was smoke coming from a draw to our front and it was a camp which the Japs had burned out before leaving. We stopped to rest; it was getting well into the evening, when three figures approached across the valley from the direction of the beach. We challenged them, and they stopped. Two of them were oriental, and one was an American colonel. They didn't know the password, and we almost opened fire. But while the platoon covered him, Lieutenant Odus E. Long went out and talked to the colonel. It turned out that they were a colonel from the Alaskan Scouts and two Japanese interpreters. Lieutenant Long checked their papers and then signaled us "OK."

We were planning to move on into the pass that night, but it was getting dark, and the colonel warned us about quite a number of Japs supposedly in that area, and Lieutenant Long decided it would be better to wait until daylight before going any farther into the pass. We set up an all-around defense, and made camp about five hundred yards from the smouldering Jap camp. The colonel and the two interpreters spent the night with us.

The next morning we moved up to the Jap camp. There were equipment and trash all around. We began snooping through the Jap stuff—the colonel picking up scraps of maps and documents, the GI's picking up pieces of sake bottles and cigarettes.

Finally we got ready to move on, and the colonel told us, in parting, about a Jap trick that might come in handy. In effect it was this: if we were ever confronted by a Jap who was not immediately trying to blow our heads off or stick a bayonet into us, because he was not yet sure we were not his cousin from San Francisco, he might say "Mushy-mushy." This apparently meant something like "Hiya Joe. What's cooking?" Now if the Jap was in defilade when he called "Mushy-mushy" so that we could not blow his head off or stick a bayonet into him, we should reply "Hyee!" accent on the "ee." This seemed to mean "Nothing much, Mac. How's the wife?" The Jap, then thinking we were his cousin from San Francisco, would stick his head up so we could blow it off.

The words had no more than gotten out of the colonel's mouth and into our freezing ears, before the men in Sergeant Anthony S. Bumbico's squad, farther up in the pass, attracted our attention to four Japs approaching about six hundred yards away. The platoon was immediately deployed in firing positions. The Japs had stopped and were looking at us and pointing. We held our fire and they continued to walk toward Bumbico's squad. It was obvious they had seen us, but apparently they were not sure we were not their cousins from San Francisco, because they got to within two hundred yards of us before they stopped. They seemed so close we could see the slant of their eyes, but they were the first Japs we had seen. One of them carried a light machine gun. They stood there in whispered conference for a moment, then one of them hollered "Hyee." For a minute there I expected him to say "Hyee fellers." I thought quickly with my freezing brain that something was backwards here. "Hyee" was supposed to be the answer. Well, maybe it would work both ways. Lieutenant Long suddenly shouted back "Mushy-mushy." The Japs jabbered away in their own tongue for a moment. Then Lieutenant Long hollered "Open fire."

The four Japs immediately hit the ground. Two of them jumped into convenient holes. The Jap machine gunner opened up but only got off a couple of shots before we got him, and another lying close by him. Then one of them who had jumped into a hole jumped out again and ran toward the gun. We shot him. Bumbico's squad grenaded the other one out of his hole, and he was still moaning when Sergeant Bumbico got up to him so he bayoneted him, got his bayonet stuck, and had to fire to get it loose. One of the Japs was an officer, and Sergeant Bumbico took his saber, undoubtedly the first Jap saber taken on Attu.

Well, "Mushy-mushy," buddy. I'll see you in the mess hall. It'll be the vogue before the season's over.

Attack on Jarmin Pass

Sergeant Louis Adami, Company G, 32d Infantry

Even coming up on the ship, the name Massacre Valley spooked the boys. They weren't quite sure just who was going to massacre who in that valley, but they were sure as hell willing to find out. And on May 14 they thought they had found out. The 2d Battalion had been ordered to advance on Jarmin Pass, capture it, and destroy the enemy there. Company G was advancing up the right side, and Company F was advancing up the left side. The attack pushed off early in the morning at about 0630 and immediately the Japs opened up. The first casualties were being hit in the back from guns high on the mountain to our left. It was demoralizing because we couldn't spot them. And the fire from the front was increasing in intensity all the time. They had machine guns all over the place, and knee mortars were systematically blasting holes in our advancing lines. Lieutenant John J. Young had caught a piece of mortar shell in his neck but was still able to navigate. He had taken cover behind a little wrinkle in the ground, when he saw Lawrence K. Isaacs get hit. He was running right into the fire with his head high, just as always, when a bullet got him right in the stomach. He rolled over once holding his stomach; then he got up and walked over to a little creek which ambled over the valley and got down behind its bank. Louis Adami came dashing up from the rear and flopped down about fifteen feet from Lieutenant Young. "Are you hit bad, Flash?" he asked. And before Lieutenant Young could answer, a burst of machine-gun fire ripped the tundra between the two men. "No, just got the back of my neck scratched," Lieutenant Young hollered. And tuktuktuktuktuktuk! the Jap gunner fired again. He was traversing toward Adami. A mortar shell burst near them and they buried their heads. When Lieutenant Young looked again Adami had his face screwed up into agonized lines and machine-gun bullets were striking all over him. "Are you hit, Adami?" Lieutenant Young shouted. He felt foolish asking it, he had seen the whole burst hit the man. Adami shouted back, "Yes, just in the leg." "Can you run?" Adami shouted, "You're goddamn right," and they both jumped up and ran into the creek. Isaacs was there but he was very pale and seemed almost out. He didn't recognize the men, or at least gave no sign that he did. He raised up, and leaned on the bank facing the ocean. For a long time he just gazed down the valley then he slid down into the creek, dead.

The first dead one you see makes you grit your teeth, but unless you go crazy you get over it at once. A little fellow had just tumbled into the creek with them, all out of breath and white as a sheet. It was Joaquin R. Del Castillo. He had been everything from latrine orderly and dining-room orderly to the captain's orderly, the kind of a little guy that putters around with odds and ends and hardly knows which end of a rifle gets hot. Lieutenant Young and Adami were just ready to move ahead, and Castillo said, "Flash, do you want me to go forward or wait for a medic? I've been hit twice, I've lost my rear sight, and my rifle is jammed." They laughed, and the chill of watching Isaacs die passed. Thomas R. Stapp, the runner, hollered over from behind a little clump of tundra and said, "Castillo, I'm going back; you can come with me." Castillo in a weak voice asked, "Have you got a covered route?"

Adami was looking at the wound in his leg and began to check up. When the machine-gun burst landed on him, in addition to getting hit in the leg, there were two other holes in his rain pants, one in his sleeve, a rip down his back; his canteen and his pack had been hit; his rifle sling had been cut; there was a hole on the edge of his helmet and a piece of shell fragment in his gunstock. Lieutenant Young said, "Let's go, Adami," and out they went.

They did not capture the pass that day, and they didn't destroy the enemy. And Company F on their left didn't capture the pass nor destroy the enemy. But they learned many things, and they lost many men; they got colder and hungrier, more exhausted and more determined.

The Signal Corps in Foxholes

Captain Fred E. Kyer, 7th Signal Company

Walter Kalinowski and Isadore Eisenberg, a couple of inseparable wire men in the 7th Signal Company, were constantly throwing shady deals into one another, but remained good buddies in spite of it all.

It was a rough afternoon on May 14, at that early stage in the battle when the lines were just becoming fixed, and the two forces were really getting down to business on each other. Kalinowski and Eisenberg had been given the mission of laying a wire to a battalion on the line from the regimental CP, and they had gotten about three-fourths of the way out to the battalion with their reel of wire when a Jap machine gunner spotted them and opened up. The two Irishmen dropped their wire and dove headlong into a shallow little hole, in which there was barely room to lie side by side.

Kalinowski was lying on the uphill side of the hole, and the persistent Jap gunner poured a stream of zinging bullets past his shirt tail. Kalinowski quivered. The Jap fired another long burst, and Kalinowski quivered. After a few minutes and several more bursts, he nudged Eisenberg. "Say, buddy, I'm cold over here. How about swapping sides?" "Sure, pal," Eisenberg answered. So while Eisenberg rolled up, Kalinowski rolled over him and into the deeper security of the downhill side of the hole.

The Jap continued to fire at the two men until the fog settled down and curtained them. Then they crawled gingerly out of the hole, picked up the reel of wire, and accomplished their mission. Nothing was said of the swapping of sides in the hole until they were almost back. Then Eisenberg looked out of the corner of his eye at Kalinowski. "Say, buddy," he asked, "were you really cold on your side of that hole?" Kalinowski grinned, "Man, I was freezing to death." Eisenberg raised an eyebrow. "Yeah," he said, "those bullets stirred up a very chilly breeze, didn't they, pal?"

Early in the battle, when the Japs sprayed the top of the hill every time anything moved up there, Bernard L. Hillers, a wire man in the 7th Signal Company, was sent up to Major Smith to lay a wire from the 17th CP to an OP located on the top and forward end of the Hogback.

The gang had moved out from the CP and had gotten up onto the top of the Hogback with their wire when the Japs across the valley picked up the activity and began blasting away. The gang broke and took cover in some very shallow, hastily prepared, slit trenches as the bullets ripped over them. The cover was just barely deep enough with maybe a couple of inches to spare. It was a nasty, tense situation, lying out there helpless and quiet—the only sound being the vicious crack of the bullets inches overhead.

Then, easily and resignedly, the faint sound of a harmonica drifted out over the shallow foxholes. Hillers, our boy, had rummaged around in his pockets and found his damn mouth organ. There he lay, flat on his back, while the bullets cracked over him, playing the plaintive *Too late, too late.* . . .

Artillery Sniping

Lieutenant John W. Edrington, Company F, 17th Infantry

The gunners on Attu got pretty fancy before that thing was over, and some of them were plenty good at the start; but I watched one gunner work who was good and took the pride of an artist in his work. After several days the 37s had been moved well up onto the Hogback in Massacre Valley and were pounding hell out of the Nips in their rocky nests all over the mountainsides up there, sometimes even shooting a few rounds at extra-troublesome snipers.

It was on the afternoon of May 16, I think, and one gunner had been firing off and on at machine guns on the nose of Black Mountain and at positions over on Cold Mountain and around, and then he had a long slack period where nothing happened. The war for the 2d Battalion consisted of blocking Clevesy Pass, and life for us just amounted to sniping back and forth and trying not to get blasted out by mortar fire and slowly freezing. This gunner sat talking idly with a couple of riflemen for quite a while not apparently paying any attention to his business at all; then, all at once he began to twist wheels and peer through his sight and urgently juggled around to beat hell. I looked out across the pass and there, running up the hillside, was a Jap sniper. The muzzle of the 37 moved smoothly under the gunner's manipulation, and suddenly he pressed the trigger. The shell streaked across the pass and hit the Jap squarely between the hips. He just disappeared in the explosion. The gunner was serious. He looked at his friends and with a gesture of absolute perfection he said, "I led him just a hair."

Caring for the Wounded in Massacre Valley

Staff Sergeant Ernest Briggs, Company B, 7th Medical Battalion

We had tried to reach the stranded aid station the afternoon before but we had been driven back by heavy sniper fire. It was imperative that we get to the men because they had only meager equipment, and the wounded had been lying in the wet for two nights already. They were pocketed in a deep ravine cut sharply into a steep slope of the mountain near the foot of Point Able. All of the approaches to this draw involved wide open stretches of ground against which moving men stood out clearly in the Jap gunsights high on the ridge above.

The morning of the 14th was drenched in fog, which swept up the valley and over the Hogback in great rolling curtains hiding the mountains almost to the bottom, and at times, when it dropped down, it reduced everything to hazy gray shadows. This was our chance. We heaved our rucksacks, loaded wih medical supplies, onto our shoulders; and with Captain Lyle Koontz and Major Robert J. Kamish leading, and fifteen men carrying litters and supplies following, we started out again toward the aid station.

It was a long haul up the valley, but we got to our destination with nothing but the treacherous holes in the tundra to worry us. The fog persisted, flowing around us like a wet blanket and hiding us completely from the Jap snipers above.

The little aid station was a pitiful mess. In the narrow gorge just at the lower edge of a great bank of dirty snow, the tiny area was kneaded by the crisscrossing footsteps into a gooey bog of mud. A brook flowed from under the melting snowbank and the spongy tundra on both sides had spread it several yards wide.

On one side of the draw near a vertical wall of rock lay the ten litter cases, some were wrapped in shelter halves, some in blankets. Several seemed sleeping; others, with pale lips puckered, watched us intently out of gray-circled eyes.

Everyone was delighted to see us. The doctors and aid men began immediately unpacking our gear, eager to get at the supplies. The litters we had brought up were almost jerked out of our hands, so happy were they to have them. While the wounded men were being taken care of, we dug foxholes into the steep walls, guarding against the probability of the fog lifting later in the day. Much-needed morphine had been given to the more painfully wounded, and each of the hurt boys was resting on a litter with a fresh blanket when the fog began to thin. The doctors had been discussing the plan of evacuation, and the lifting of the fog simplified their problem only in eliminating the easiest route of withdrawal. The enemy began to fire onto the valley floor blocking the lower mouth of our draw. That left the one remaining possibility of climbing straight up the walls of the draw onto the main hill slope and crossing straight over to the Hogback. With luck, after we got out into the open near the Hogback, we could make the 17th Infantry CP, and our job would be done.

Getting the men out of the draw up the nearly vertical sides presented a big problem. The sides were soggy where the tundra grew, and slick as grease where they were barren. We tied the patients onto their litters, and several men scaled the wall taking a long rope with them. We fastened the end of the rope to a litter, and six men moved up the wall with the litter. They would pick it up off the ground and the men would pull the rope, moving the litter and the patient as high as the crew could reach. They would set the litter down against the hill and repeat the process. It was hard, exasperating work, jumping the litters up these walls, three feet at a time. Often the crew would slip, and someone would roll clear to the bottom. The patients were a nervy bunch, and they would never admit they were hurt, but cheered us on, telling us we were doing wonderful work. By the time they had reached the top, several of them had slipped so far that half of their legs were dragging off the litter.

Five men, the walking wounded, had started on ahead. The route was simple to follow, the only danger being enemy fire when the fog lifted. One of the men should have been a litter case, but he was sure he could walk in, and if a man was able to get back under his own power it was a tremendous help to us. None of our boys could go with them because we needed every man to work the litter cases out of the draw.

A machine gun continued to fire into the valley, and eventually a sniper began working on us, through intervals of clearing in the fog. When he fired we hid our patients behind clumps of tundra and in small ditches, and the rest of us slid down the wall into the draw. It was during one of these sniper attacks after we had all the wounded out and were moving our own personnel out, that Morris J. Creppel, an extremely short little man who had the reputation of not being able to wear a .45 without dragging the sight off it, put on his show for us. He was the last to leave. He had put on his rucksack, which seemed a tremendous thing on his tiny back, and we were pulling him up the wall. First one shoulder strap came loose, but he hung on and was about halfway up when he slipped and the rucksack slid off his other shoulder and rolled down to the bottom. He was having a terrible time, his short legs were churning away in the slick mud of the wall, and he had definitely decided to abandon his rucksack and devote his energy to getting up the hill himself. He was almost to the top when the sniper opened up on us, two shots which cracked close over our heads. In desperation we turned loose of the rope and dove for cover. With a shriek, Creppel slid all the way back down into the draw.

It was 1830 when we finished getting everyone out of the draw, and our bedraggled column started down the slope onto the open flat toward the Hogback. The fog, our best friend in this situation, was getting very fickle. We were hurrying over the rough ground, four men carrying each litter, and ten of us carrying rucksacks and other supplies that we had been able to bring with us.

We had moved away from the hill onto the flat about one hundred yards when our fears were materialized; the fog thinned out to a few fast moving wisps. In just a matter of seconds crack-crack-tuk-tuk . . . the Jap machine gunner had picked us up. We scurried for the protection of a tiny draw, in which we parked the patients, some of them were rolled off the litters so they would lie lower, and we, with rucksacks, jumped into whatever small holes were around. There we awaited the next move, for nearly forty-five minutes, in water or soggy tundra with our rucksacks sticking up like turtle backs. The fog, which had so treacherously lifted, once more faithfully descended. The Jap fired a few more rounds then stopped completely. We found that two litter bearers and their patients had been hit. None of the wounds, luckily, was too serious, but it made the going tougher.

We moved away from that spot in a hurry, after a hasty reorganization. We heard someone coughing on our left and then we saw the boy who had started out with the walking wounded earlier in the afternoon, all alone, half sitting, half lying on his side in a spasm of painful-sounding coughing. Two of us without litters went over and picked him up. He was a concussion case. A mortar had landed practically on top of him two days before and, while no wounds showed, he was spitting blood when we came upon him. We got him on his feet and with one of his arms over each of our backs, we ambled slowly along, stopping every few feet to let him cough. He had been willing to try to get back alone but he told us he had stopped so often to rest to relieve a pain that hung like a weight in his chest that he had fallen behind the others. He said he realized now that he could never have made it back alone and alternately apologized for going so slow and praised his good luck that we had found him.

It was getting dusky when we passed through the OP line around the CP and we were happy indeed to see the end of our trip. Some of the patients were dropped off at the aid station near the CP, but a stream of casualties was beginning to drift back from the front, and outside each echelon of treatment, like water at a dam, a growing pool of wounded men waited their turn with the doctor or transportation to the next echelon rearward.

We were exhausted from our eighteen-hour day's work, but each litter squad picked up a patient at the aid station and moved him down to Company D, the clearing company, and there each picked up a hospital patient and carried him to the beach. It was nearly 0500 when we stumbled into the 7th Medic Headquarters kitchen and gladly burned our lips on some good hot java. . . .

The Contact Between Southern and Northern Forces

Lieutenant Winfield Harvey Mapes, Headquarters, 3d Battalion, 17th Infantry

On May 17, Colonel Zimmerman, the regimental commander, had been observing Jarmin Pass all day, and he had decided that there were no enemy there.

This appeared strange, for the past three days concerted attacks against Jarmin Pass had been beaten back by the enemy firmly entrenched in the pass itself and high up on the steep slopes on each side. But the colonel had studied the pass all morning. His conclusion was that the enemy had withdrawn. It was getting well into the afternoon when a patrol from Company K, 17th Infantry, was sent out under Lieutenant Morris C. Wiberg to determine if the enemy machine gunners had gone from the mountains in front of the pass. Lieutenant Mapes waited at the Company K CP for a report from the patrol. They had not returned, but they could be seen up near the mouth of the pass. Mapes and Colonel Zimmerman started out to meet them. The patrol, on its way back, reported that they were not sure about the interior of the pass, but they hadn't been fired on and had walked up close to the machine-gun positions and had drawn no fire from there either.

The Colonel turned the patrol around, and we started back toward the pass. There was one way to find out for sure that the enemy was gone. That one way was to walk through the pass and see. The patrol, with the colonel at the head, and scouts out, started up the right side of Massacre Valley. Ahead, the tableland lay pockmarked with shell holes and cut by trenches. It was very quiet, ominously quiet. The scouts moved across the gully on the right and walked slowly and carefully up onto the table. Not a shot was fired. The patrol followed the scouts up onto the table. It looked as though they were going to make it. Colonel Zimmerman sent Lieutenant Mapes back to bring up a platoon of Company K under Captain Charles T. Frazee. They waited until they saw the platoon moving across the valley toward the table; then they started up into the pass. It was getting late, and the fog that hung across the peaks had begun to settle into the ravines.

Colonel Zimmerman motioned the four scouts spaced across the pass to move out.

It was very quiet. The only sound was the sloshing of the heavy boots in wet tundra, as the patrol walked slowly up into the pass. Steep rock walls jutted sharply up on both sides of the patrol, and high overhead huge rock forms seemed to move in the wisps of heavy fog slinking around them toward the valley. The patrol sloshed slowly deeper and deeper into the deathly silence of the pass, working slowly toward the high point.

The enemy, the treacherous Jap, had held the pass in force just the day before. The pass had been alive with their biting, barking fire; now it was quiet and deserted. Three bodies were huddled in a pile. The patrol stopped momentarily while the scout checked for death in the lonely three Japs and then moved on.

A runner was dispatched to bring Company I up. Captain Frazee's platoon had set up their weapons on the table behind the patrol, and the voices giving orders echoed hollowly through the empty pass under the descending fog.

Colonel Zimmerman waved the wary scouts forward. Cautiously, they moved up the last steep incline toward the high point. Beyond lay Holtz Bay, and somewhere out there was the Northern Force. It was getting dark, and the fog had crept down among the rocks until the scouts were vague shadows moving up ahead. They were almost in the center of the pass now. A grenade filled the pass with rumbling echoes as a scout blasted a suspected cave in the rocky wall. The rest of the patrol moved quickly up the last incline to the high point. They could see down the other side. Over a long bank of snow was a little valley, with a lake on the right. And then, about five hundred yards beyond was the long steep hill that dropped abruptly into Holtz Bay.

The Colonel ordered Company I, when it arrived, to occupy the pass. Captain Frazee's platoon was to outpost the high point until Company I got there and then was to move forward and block the Holtz Bay end.

Lieutenant Wiberg, Lieutenant Mapes, and two volunteers started down the back side of the pass toward Holtz Bay. About three hundred yards down the hill they came across the first Jap hut. It was deserted, but around it were strewn ammunition of various kinds and the usual litter of a hastily evacuated camp. Farther down, by the lake, were two more huts, empty. From behind them, Captain Frazee began moving his men through the pass. Mapes and Wiberg moved down to the edge of the hill overlooking Holtz Bay. At the right of the waterfall, which plunged two hundred feet down to the valley floor, they stared into the gathering darkness and fog. Out across the east arm, on the high ground, were troops moving . . . the Northern Force. Captain Frazee arrived and began setting up his defenses. Lieutenant Wiberg took three men and dropped down the crooked zigzag trail onto the valley floor. It was 2200. At 0230 the next morning he had met a platoon of the 7th Reconnaissance Troop. The Southern Force had contacted the Northern Force.

During the night a small patrol returned from somewhere to the pass. They stumbled into the guns of Company I, unaware that the Japs had evacuated, and the Americans had moved in.

Lieutenant Mapes, leader of an intelligence and reconnaissance platoon, returned to his battalion headquarters after dark that night. He stumbled and fell over the several treacherous wet miles to the battalion CP. He was unnerved from the weird advance into the silent pass, and the long walk back with a high explosive shell pressed to his chest. He had found a large Jap 90mm. shell and was bringing it back to G-2 for identification. He stumbled, almost exhausted, into the Battalion CP, and proudly laid the big explosive shell in front of Captain Harry L. Beatty on the table.

Captain Beatty raised his haggard eyes from the map and said, "Get the hell out of here with that damned thing."

The Attack on Clevesy Pass — 1

Sergeant Alastair Finlayson, Sergeant Emil H. Roethemeyer,
Corporal Raymond C. Gantner,
Company E, 17th Infantry

For a week the 2d Battalion of the 17th Infantry had occupied wet, soggy, cold positions in the mouth of Clevesy Pass, blocking it from the enemy, who perched on every piece of high ground around them and peppered their holes constantly. The 3d Battalion of the 17th Infantry and the 2d Battalion of the 32d Infantry had tried for four brutal days to bulldoze their way into Jarmin Pass through flanking machine-gun fire and murderous mortar barrages from positions concealed in the fantastic rock formations of the mountains and screened by the eternal fog. Finally, on the night of May 18, Jarmin Pass was opened up and occupied, and preparations were under way for a push through Clevesy Pass. The Japs held both flanks of the pass and had strong entrenchments across the saddle itself. Company C of the 32d Infantry had been sent up the impossible slopes of Gilbert Ridge to envelop their left flank. But the morning of May 19 came with the Japs still holding both flanks of the pass. It was another damned hard nut. Company E of the 17th Infantry was ordered into the right side of the pass and Company F into the left side, with G in support behind F. The 2d Battalion of the 32d was to move in and pass through the 17th when the flanks had been cleared.

Company E moved out at 1000. We came under long-range machine-gun fire, and mortar shells began to drop around, but it didn't bother us too much. We headed straight into the pass, initially, and our artillery fired smoke on the Jap positions, lessening the pressure on us. Under cover of the smoke we made good progress. We knew the Japs were up there, but we didn't realize they were as close as they were. The first thing we knew we were right among them. It was a mad scramble for a few minutes. Sergeant Roethemeyer and some of the boys in the 1st Platoon contacted them first and moved right in. Elias J. Montoya, the

BAR man, and Corporal Joseph B. Moreman were working as a team flushing out the Jap trench. Montoya would jump up and spray a stream of bullets down the trench while Moreman dumped grenades in; then when they went off Moreman would move in with the bayonet with Montoya right behind him.

The 2d Platoon had bad luck that morning and had lost all their leaders. Lieutenant William H. Becker had sprained his ankle when a snowbank caved in, and Staff Sergeant Paul L. Neavill had been knocked out by a mortar, and the platoon guide, Sergeant William J. Boland could hardly walk on his badly frozen feet. They had been split up, and about half of them had come with the 1st Platoon; the other half was over on the right with the 3d Platoon.

The 3d Platoon had worked their way up a little draw until they were close under a Jap trench. For several wild minutes the boys dodged Jap grenades. Then they moved in. The first Jap they contacted was huddled down in a hole. Sergeant Finlayson hollered for him to come out but the Jap cowered lower and repeated, "No, no, no, no." So Finlayson tossed a grenade in on him. Some of the Japs withdrew out of the first position before we got there, and the twenty-two who hadn't pulled out were shot or grenaded. We moved into their holes and reorganized. We were almost ready to move out again when we spotted a group of Japs coming up a draw in the gap between the 3d Platoon and the 1st Platoon. They had a machine gun with them, but between the 1st Platoon's grenades and our BAR fire they never got a chance to use it. Sergeant Finlayson had jumped out of his hole and was crawling forward when this group of Japs was spotted, and Corporal Raymond E. Martin, from the machine-gun section of the weapons platoon, had jumped into the hole that Finlayson had just left. The Japs opened up and hit Martin before we got all of them.

A few minutes later a Jap officer and a soldier tried to come to the top of the hill and set up a light machine gun. Our 3d Squad was spread out crawling forward when our machine gunner spotted the Japs. It took a couple of minutes of yelling and waving and signaling to get some of the 3d Squad out of the line of fire, but our gunner got the job done and cut down the Japs. His bullets flew over the heads of the 3d Squad by only a foot, but he killed the Jap officer and drove the gun off the hill.

The 3d Squad, with Sergeant Finlayson, was about halfway across an open piece of ground between the first Jap trenches and our new objective when a Jap gunner began firing from our right front. Corporal Gantner spotted the gun and took off for it. In the first dash he ran about seventy-five yards, then we saw him fall, and we all thought he had been hit. But he got up and dashed again; a bullet had gone through the sole of his shoe and never touched his foot. We saw Sergeant Finlayson working his way toward the gun, too. Then Gantner appeared right over the hole. He jumped up and emptied his M1 into it. The position was really two holes, and one was cut back so that from his position he could not shoot into it. He emptied his rifle into the Jap and then he ducked down the hill from the position. Finlayson raised up and hollered, "I'll cover you while you load up." Gantner loaded his rifle, then ducked while one of the Japs left in the position threw a grenade. Gantner and Finlayson each tossed a grenade into the hole and that finished the job.

We finally worked the whole platoon across the open and up under a little hill. There were six Japs in holes not over twenty yards from us, yet in all the time we stayed there they made no move to get us. We were pinned down by fire coming from both flanks for nearly three hours before we could move. First Finlayson would peek over the crest at the Japs, then his buddy would peek over. Maybe the Japs figured that they would let us by-pass them, and then they'd shoot us in the back. But they stayed in those holes, all huddled up and quiet, and died like rats the next time we attacked.

Company E of the 32d Infantry moved up on the hill in the early evening. At first we thought they were Japs. They had on rain suits, the first ones we had seen. Staff Sergeant William D. Liles crawled over to get a good look and found out they were E of the 32d. An attack had been set for 2030. When the time came, we all got up together and took off, knocking off the six who had sat right in our laps all evening.

We drove the Japs off the hill, moved over to the Sarana side, set up defensively, and had some food.

The Attack on Clevesy Pass — 2

Private First Class Ira Clawson, Company F, 32d Infantry

On May 19, when we started into Clevesy Pass, anything could have happened. We had good plans and good organization, but somehow things got a little confused. In the first place we thought both flanks of the pass would be secured before we started into it, but they weren't. The Japs had the high ground on each side of us. And then, as we started out into the pass itself, Company F of the 17th was having a hard time on our left, so we lent them two of our platoons. That left the 3d Platoon out in the pass alone.

To make the situation worse, the Japs wouldn't show themselves. Some of them would crouch down in their holes and never look out. They didn't know where we were or where the rest of their outfit was; and we were in the same boat. Things were really mixed up.

Clawson and Wilbert J. Schroeder and Sergeant Eugene M. Rider were moving up to some Jap holes that had been vacated and were about twenty-five yards from them when a machine gunner on Point Able spotted them and opened up. They hit the ground and then made a dash for the Jap holes. Rider and Schroeder jumped into one, and Clawson made a dive for another. The one Clawson was making for was a nice deep hole with a partial roof over it, and as he flopped down just outside he noticed a figure in it. "Hey, how about sharing your hole, buddy?" said Clawson; and since you don't stand much on formalities when you're under fire, he started crawling in. The little figure hunched down in the corner looked back over his shoulder at the two hundred pounds of Clawson about to crawl in with him. To Clawson's great surprise the little fellow, who incidentally had slightly slanting eyes and buck teeth, did not wish to share his hole with anybody who weighed two hundred pounds and called him "buddy." So he made a grab for Clawson's rifle. Clawson, like most soldiers in battle, did not wish to part with his rifle, so he grabbed it back. The Jap grabbed it again and Clawson grabbed it back. As the Jap grabbed it again Clawson felt that something should be done to break the stalemate. The Jap apparently felt the same way, and he made a grab for his knife. Clawson, being a quick-thinking American boy and having a heavy pair of very wet boots on, kicked the jap in the mouth. Rider and Schroeder had watched the fun from the adjacent hole; and at this quick turn of events, the Jap machine gunner having ceased fire, they came over and Schroeder shot the Jap. Schroeder fired again and an explosion filled the hole, ripping the little roof off and knocking the three down. Schroeder said, "Gee, I must have hit a grenade. Those Japs sure are tricky, even dead ones." "Yeah," said Clawson, "I thought that one was a Mexican out of the 17th."

The Attack on Cold Mountain from Jarmin Pass

Staff Sergeant Charles H. Roberts, Company I, 17th Infantry

The idea of the thing was to envelop both flanks first, then push through the center of Clevesy Pass. Captain Charles W. Murphy, Jr., and Company C of the 32d Infantry were freezing and stumbling along fighting practically in single file along the crest of Gilbert Ridge, trying to knock out Point Able, a natural rock fortress on the right flank of the pass; and Lieutenant William E. Brown had received the mission of taking his platoon of Company I of the 17th Infantry, up the mountain from Jarmin Pass and attacking Cold Mountain, the left flank of Clevesy Pass.

It was dark, the night of May 18, and bitter cold when the platoon started out. We knew there were Japs up there, and we knew they had three heavy machine guns at least, that would be blasting hell out of the men going into the pass when the attack started, unless we knocked them out. The hill was a steep, slippery, rocky, sonuvabitch; and there was ice forming on the tundra as we slowly stumbled up toward the Japs at the top.

We saw the first one at 0430 in the morning. He was a sentry, and we were within fifty yards of him. He stood up against the skyline and was shaking out a grass mat. Lieutenant Brown motioned us to get up under a little ledge to our front, then he shot the Jap. The shot must have awakened others and as we worked up over the ledge a Jap machine gunner began firing at us. We stayed down until the first excited bursts had gone over, then we raised up and returned the fire. Several Japs had holes near the edge of the ledge we were under, and they began to throw grenades over, but the hill below was so steep that most of the grenades rolled down and exploded out of range below us. Sergeant Anthony Bumbico was hit on the side of the head, but only slightly. Sergeant David I. Santos hollered to his second in command, Corporal Lyle C. Blow, to bring half of the squad around to the right, and the Japs heard him. Then they began to holler, "Brow, over here!" The machine gun was firing again, but several of the men were close enough to the ledge to lob grenades over. The machine gun itself was out of grenade range, but some of the Japs near the edge caught hell from the grenades.

Lieutenant Brown had the radio man try to contact the battalion, but the radio wouldn't work. Over our heads the Japs began to shout and raise hell, and then four of them with bayonets and an officer waving his saber rushed over the crest at us. Private Paul C. "Goat" Smith, the BAR man, saw them coming. He was lying on the ground slightly to the side of where the Japs came over. He raised up on his knees and fired three quick bursts, and the Jap bayonet assault was over. From somewhere back to our left another machine gun opened up, and we withdrew down the hill to reorganize.

Lieutenant Brown tried again and again to contact the battalion or the artillery with the radio, but the set refused to function. The radio man worked with it and tried again, but failed. The platoon was reorganized, and we started up. We got as high as the ledge once more and had started over the top onto the table above, when the Japs opened up with machine guns again. We needed artillery and needed it bad. Every time we stuck our nose up, a hailstorm of bullets cracked across at us. The radio man was trying frantically to contact anybody in the valley below us, but the set remained silent. Several men had crawled around to the left and thrown grenades at the Japs near the edge of the table, but the machine guns remained out of grenade range, and they drove the men back to the cover of the ledge. Corporal Jess D. Baltierra, Jr. had been hit in both hands, and George Rose had a slug in his shoulder. . . . Artillery, if we only had artillery, we could observe the fire! We knew where the guns were. We'd walk over the damned mountains. The radio man was desperate. He tried the set again, but it was silent. In a rage he threw it down the hill.

We tried once more to move around the flank and get to the Jap guns. It had been broad daylight for some time, and the big attack was to push off before long. But as we appeared over the hill where the Japs were, an impossible stream of bullets drove the men back. We withdrew down the hill. Lieutenant Brown sent messengers down the mountain. Then, a few minutes later, we heard the guns in the valley begin firing. The attack was on. We had failed, and we felt bad about it, but you just can't go into that stuff sometimes.

The Taking of Cold Mountain
Sergeant Walter G. Moesch, Company H, 17th Infantry

On May 19 our section of heavy machine guns was attached to Company F, for the attack up Cold Mountain on the left of Clevesy Pass. It was called Massacre-Sarana Pass then, but I was with Lieutenant Samuel W. Clevesy, Jr. when he was killed there in the pass, and it was named for him. The attack had moved across the flat in front of Cold Mountain without much fire but long-range mortar and some 37. And we had gotten to the first Jap position almost without opposition. But when the attack moved up the hill, hell began to break loose. Company F was driven back with lots of casualties, and Company G had moved through them and around to the left, and they were getting all shot up. Then Company F of the 32d Infantry came through on our right flank, heading right out into the pass itself, and they combined two of their platoons with the remainder of Company F, 17th, and we started up again.

The Japs were holding the pass on the high ground on both sides and to the front, too. The ones on the right could fire into the backs of the attackers on the left and vice versa; it was rough going. Our first section was in position right below where we had first entered the lowest Jap position, and the second section was around to the right, into the pass about 150 yards. Lieutenant Clevesy was down near the first section when I saw him. He was mad. He had been hit once in the arm and was skinned up, and he wanted to go right back into the fight. He got me and we went around to the 2d Section to get them started up the hill. The attack was going OK, but it was awfully tough; bullets were flying all over the hillside. Just uphill from the second section was a Jap 37. We had watched the fire from that position several days before, and we knew there were Japs in that trench. The main attack was moving around to the left as we started up the hill. Finally the fire got so heavy that the machine-gun squads took cover in a little draw until we could grenade the trench above us and clean it out. Then they were to come on up. Sergeant Thomas P. Kovacik, Private First Class William H. Marshall, and I started up with Lieutenant Clevesy. We had crawled on our bellies to within about twenty-five yards of the trench, when a sniper raised up and shot Marshall in the ear. We shot at the sniper and threw grenades into the trench. We crawled up rapidly then, ready to move in behind our grenades, and another sniper popped his head up out of a hole above us. Lieutenant Clevesy fired his carbine just as the Jap fired. The lieutenant toppled over a little bank and lay still. He was dead. I was just bringing my rifle up as the Jap ducked.

Then, from across the valley the Japs spotted us, and they gave us hell. Machine guns, rifles, and a 37 began pounding the area. A man from Company G, who had gotten too far to the right and had joined us, began to swear. We thought the 37s were our own guns, back on the Hogback. The Company G man pulled an orange panel and he raised it and began to wave it frantically, all the time cussing the dizzy bastards firing the 37 at his own goddamn men, like they didn't have it tough enough without that kinda crap! A shell from the 37 screamed over and crashed into the hill above his head so close it almost ripped the panel from his hand. Then we realized that it was a Jap.

Finally the intense shelling slowed down, and we dashed for the open end of the Jap trench we had grenaded. The trench led around the point of the hill and was wide enough to drag a 37 along. We crawled down the trench and found where the Japs were located. Then we stuck our heads up right in the face of a burst of machine-gun fire.

Some men from Company F had come over to help us, but we were stymied. We couldn't raise up long enough to fire, and we couldn't get close enough to throw grenades. Finally we decided to see if we could get mortar fire on the position some way. Corporal Alfred P. Hehman started back to check up on the mortar possibilities, while we waited and rested. The Japs in the position were slightly below us and about a hundred yards farther into the pass. They were firing almost constantly at troops we could see moving out in the valley and on the opposite side of the pass. We were quite high up on Cold Mountain, and we could see Japs moving way across the valley on Sarana Nose—moving supplies and digging.

After nearly two hours of lying in the trench and waiting, one of the men behind hollered, "Here, Hehman, up here." Hehman and another man from Company H of the 32d Infantry were crawling along up a little ravine laying wire. They had found a mortar of Company E of the 32d, and had a line right to it. The big fight up on the mountain had gotten almost to the top, but the forces across the pass were getting hell from the guns below us. We got the phone all set and carefully poked a little hole in the dirt side of the trench so that one man could see the whole Jap position below. Then we called the mortar, and the fun started. We were only about a hundred yards from where the shells were striking, and the ground shook. They fired several rounds close, and then they began to drop right in the position. Perhaps they could have wiped out the position completely with mortars if they had continued firing, but they stopped. The leader of the Company F men who had come over told us to call and tell them we were moving in and not to fire.

The position was a big wheel-like affair with holes all around it, and the spokes were connecting trenches with a big, center installation at the hub. Two Jap machine guns and the 37 that had fired at us during the previous week were captured and destroyed there. We tossed six dead Japs out and then brought our guns up and set them in the Jap holes. There we sat that night, just daring the little bastards to come up. Man, what positions they had!

The Taking of Engineer Hill
Corporal Tony L. Pinnelli, Company E, 32d Infantry

It was shortly after 1000 on May 19 when Lieutenant Anthony J. Bellas waved "Follow Me" and started around the front end of the Hogback and turned toward Clevesy Pass. The Japs began firing at us from two long trenches on the right side of the pass. That was our objective. Mortar shells were bursting through the company as we worked down into the deep draw that cut across the pass from left to right. Then one by one we crawled over the big snowbank and wormed our way closer to the Japs on the high rise in front.

It was afternoon before we got to the lowest Jap position on the right of the pass. It was vacated by the Japs, so we moved in. Above us, from time to time, we could see the round helmets of the Jap soldiers as they changed positions in the trench, and we exchanged shots back and forth. Somewhere to our left was a strong Jap emplacement. We couldn't see it, but we knew it was there; it would be impossible to get the Japs on the high ground above us, without getting the ones on our left first. Sergeant William D. Truffelli and I argued about the exact Jap location. From time to time I had seen a large puff of white smoke rise from behind a small knoll as the Japs fired their trench mortars at us, and I was sure that the position could be grenaded. Finally we asked for volunteers to go over and try it, but there were none; it would be a rugged job. It was my idea, so I asked Truffelli to look after my squad and give me some covering fire, while I went up and tried the thing myself.

It was tough all right. I moved as far down in the defilade as I could get from the Japs up above. Then I started crawling straight up the hill at the little knoll behind which I had seen the smoke. I made it to the knoll without being seen. The Japs were behind it, like I figured, and they were watching down the hill toward our left flank. I crawled up on the rise of ground and threw a grenade. The first one was short. I tried another, and it fell into the Jap hole, but they threw it out.

They still hadn't seen me. I threw several more grenades into the position. One of the Japs spotted me and tried to throw one of my grenades back. He grabbed the thing and was ready to throw it when it exploded by his ear and blew his head completely off. The platoon heard the commotion and began to advance up the hill. The company's light machine guns opened fire on the trench as the platoon advanced. Several of the Japs jumped out and tried to run back, but the machine guns cut them down. Then the whole company moved forward into the new Jap position, and the fighting was pretty hot for awhile. We accounted for about fifty Japs there in a few minutes. When I jumped up over the little knoll to move up with the company a Jap sniper on Point Able shot me in the leg. The bullet went into a muscle near my crotch like a hot needle. It bled and stung for a while, but it wasn't bad enough for me to have to go back.

In the evening the Japs began to retreat over the whole right flank of the pass, everywhere but at the top of Point Able. It was sometime after 2000 and the Japs were firing furiously and falling back.

One heavy machine-gun squad of Company H had made it up the hill with us and was firing into the Japs. Robert H. Greene, the gunner, started the belts through full on one side of the gun and his crew pulled them out empty on the other side, then Greene shoved a new one in. The gun got so hot that we poured canteens of ice water on the mechanism to cool it off. Lieutenant Thomas D. Hindman let out a terrific Rebel yell, and we took off to assault the last Jap position on the pass. As we started Corporal Francis J. Flynn saw a Jap setting up a light machine gun. He opened up on it and drove three crew members away from the gun. As the company charged up the hill at the last position of the Japs they gave up and pulled back, leaving their gun.

We made it all right. Company E of the 17th Infantry moved into the center of the pass as we took Engineer Hill. My leg was getting stiff, and the medic wanted to send me back, but there is something about being with the boys up there where they're fighting their guts out, that makes laying in a hospital a hell of a thing. I stayed with them, too, until a grenade shook me up on Buffalo Ridge. Then they sent me back.

The Taking of Point Able — 1

Lieutenant Donald E. Dwinell, Company C, 32d Infantry

The day I was wounded I cursed long and bitterly, cursed Company C as lazy gutless fools because Company C was supposed to have cleared Point Able of the enemy and secured the right flank of Clevesy Pass, and the machine gun that got me was fired from the right flank of Clevesy Pass. . . . But that was all while I was tired and hurt and mad and long, long before Lieutenant Donald E. Dwinell and I sat on chairs, in a warm tent, smoking and talking about Point Able.

Point Able marks the inland end of Gilbert Ridge, a ridge rising two thousand abrupt feet up from the sea, with Massacre Valley on one side and Sarana Valley on the other; Point Able, joined to the rest of the ridge by a low narrow saddle, is a conical mountain crowned with a huge bare rock, a fortress.

Lieutenant Dwinell related the story of Point Able very matter-of-factly, for two months of comparative quiet had done much to replace the veneer of casual-ness that combat so brutally rips off. But as the story went on, however matter-of-factly, Dwinell began to light one cigarette from the butt of the preceding one. . . . You could tell that he was remembering, remembering how a man thinks in terms of how many he has left, not how many he has lost; remembering the cold that stiffened the joints like a fist closing over them; remembering the obsession of moving ahead with the fear of death hanging like a weight on your neck.

The first time we attacked Point Able was the 16th of May, *Dwinell said.* It was our first real fight, and we had orders to attack straight up the hillside toward the point. We got up to within 600 yards of the top when the fog lifted off the point and there we were, like ducks on a pond. We were driven back, with losses, and we were wiser.

We were ordered to move up the next time on the night of the 18th. This time we were to climb up Gilbert Ridge from a point near the beach in Massacre Valley, then to move along Gilbert Ridge and attack Point Able from the high ground. We were loaded with all we could carry, and it was gruelling work of about five hours to get to the top. We had our whole company and a section of HMGs from Company D. We carried two days' rations and the outside of our sleeping bags. We reached the top and stumbled through the dark on very difficult ground. This ridge is only about four feet wide at the top and drops off very sheer on both sides. Finally we found a little level pocket where we stopped and rested. After about an hour and a half it began to get light. We dropped our packs and went to work. Our attack had already been planned, the two 6-man patrols started out, one on the right and one on the left. They carried rifle grenades. They were to work as close as possible to the point and then the company was to attack along the ridge top. The patrols dropped down on each side of the knife-edge and worked their way forward, and then, after about a half-hour, the company started forward. My platoon was leading.

It was getting fairly light now, but the fog was heavy. We moved slowly along the ridge, the company strung out behind me in almost single file on the only level ground up there, the very top of the ridge. Suddenly the fog cleared and we were about 600 yards from the point. We could see one patrol, Sergeant Roger A. Carpentier's. They were under a ledge in a deep bank of snow, about forty yards under the point. The Japs had spotted the patrol and were working on them. They still apparently didn't know the company was there. Most of the men took what cover was available and those of us who could see watched, fascinated. The patrol was in a tight spot. The men had laid ammunition out in front of them in the snow ready to fight it out right there. The Japs were firing rifles and machine guns, but the patrol was just barely in defilade from the flat trajectory weapons. Then we saw three Japs move out of their trench where their MGs were and start crawling out toward our patrol.

They were going to grenade them. Sergeant James G. Bruce and Sergeant Horace A. Lopez took a BAR man, Joseph C. Frydrych, and moved forward to good firing positions and opened up. The three Japs dashed for cover, and the patrol tried to break out of their tight spot. The Japs opened fire as the patrol ran for some rocks, and one man was hit. He stumbled and fell, and as he raised up again fog drifted over and blocked our vision. When the fog raised again we saw the main body of the patrol behind a ledge of rock that was at the top of the hill along which they could pass with cover to Gilbert Ridge itself. But Joe E. Fislar, who was hit, was forward of them and a bit below. About sixty yards of open ground lay between him and the covered route where the patrol was. Fislar shouted, "They can't get away with it, damn them!" and he fixed a grenade on his rifle. As he raised up above his rock to fire, the Japs cut loose with a burst of machine-gun fire, and it caught him dead center. He was knocked backward, and he rolled for a long way down the hill.

We moved forward then, slowly. The Japs had spotted us by our firing, and they added to the difficulties of mountain climbing by almost constant machine-gun firing. It took us until well into the afternoon to get to within 250 yards of the point. That was as far as we got that day. One man from the platoon had been killed, and several were wounded, and we still had made no noticeable impression on our objective. Finally, orders to withdraw were received, so we moved back. It was late, and the cold was intense. It made you ache dully all over; it was a wet cold. We tried to sleep, but it was fitful. We would wake up with spasmodic shivers every little while. At 1630 we got the men up. We were going to try it again.

We had received word that Company E was attacking the point from the Clevesy Pass side, and as it got light we could hear machine guns firing from that direction. We moved out, my platoon leading again, and as we moved along the now familiar ridge top we passed four Jap bodies, men who had been killed by artillery fire four days before. One of the men remarked, "If we don't get your buddies this time, Tojo, we'll have to take a dry run on you just to keep in practice." The fog was thick as it swept over the ridge and it eddied around a man like water. As we neared the positions we had held yesterday, we could hear the fire from Company E down below and on the opposite side, and we could hear the Japs returning the fire from the point. It took some time to get our heavy machine guns into firing positions, and while they were setting up, my platoon moved out under cover of the fog, two squads to the left and one to the right. I took William W. Rehfeld with me. He was a wire man and had a set of sound-powered phones with him. If we got close enough we could direct fire, even through the fog, with the phones.

We worked along the steep slopes, clinging to the rocks, tooth and toenail. We decided against moving along the top of the ridge because even the sound of our voices or footsteps would draw fire which had been fixed to cover this one easy path at the top. We got to the saddle between the ridge and the point without too much fire and had worked almost to the point when, without warning, the fog along the whole ridge lifted. There were the Japs right before us. We fired several shots almost simultaneously with diving for cover, and I'm sure we hit three or four of them. There was a pause, while Sergeant Bruce and I jumped into a 105 hole and Rehfeld made a dash to join us with the phone before they opened up with machine guns. Rehfeld was too late by a split second. The burst caught him as he jumped into the hole. He was hit several times, bullets passing through his body from left to right. It was terrible in this small hole with the wounded boy lying on top of us and asking where he was hit and what hit him. We dug. We dug with a trench knife and our hands while the bullets cracked over, clipping the snow and tundra on both edges of the hole and tearing Rehfeld's jacket. He died in just a few minutes.

We lay in that little hole all afternoon. The Japs apparently didn't know where we were exactly, because after about an hour they pulled the old trick of putting coats and helmets on rifles and moving them along their trench trying to draw our fire and thus expose our exact position. Some of the boys from farther away fired at these "targets," and then the Japs would dump mortar over the hillside for a while. The sound of digging in our hole always brought down machine-gun fire, but we kept at it off and on. Somewhere, during the advance, I had lost one leg of my rain pants and the exposed leg was getting numb from cold and dampness. And there was poor Rehfeld's body still lying across our backs. We were afraid to move him out because the Japs would spot our hole then, so he lay across us all afternoon. I finally managed to get the phone into the hole with us and made contact with Captain Charles W. Murphy and Major James H. Keller back on the ridge. At first we talked in normal tones, but the voices brought down a barrage of rifle and mortar fire, so from then on we whispered. The sound of the voice from the ridge warmed me it seemed, whispered though it was. It was a strange series of conversations, all whispered. We tried to control the heavy machine-gun fire by the phone but we failed. We could not see enough through the fog to do much good. A sniper finally began to peck at us, coming so close that the bullet would ring with that peculiar shocking high tone that very close bullets emit. Sergeant Bruce and I would each flinch and then invariably ask the other if he were hit. Each time I would move, trying to ease some aching muscle, I'd groan or grunt into the phone, and Major Keller would ask in a violent whisper, "Dwinell, Dwinell! Are you there?" The bursting of mortar shells around the hole developed into a kind of a game. The major would hear the explosion over the phone, and I'd describe where it hit—"that one was ten yards to left front," and so on. We thought they were hand grenades because none ever lit behind us like a mortar does, but they told us that no one was throwing grenades that they could see, and through breaks in the fog they could see the white puff of a mortar being fired.

We were beginning to suffer from the cold again. I could only move far enough around to hold the phone in one hand without shoving Sergeant Bruce out of the hole, and three fingers on that hand were frozen. We were numb all over, wishing to God that Company E or the other squad on the Sarana side or somebody would get close enough to unpin us; or that the fog would lift so that a little accurate machine-gun fire might be directed on the point for a while. Finally reports from all the attackers were in, and the Japs were going to hold Able another night by the look of things, so we were ordered to pull out. We hollered around and got the word passed out to the men who began to move out very carefully one or two at a time. It was quite a trick to jump up suddenly and run like hell along a very steep slippery slope to the next cover, then dash across a wide band of soft snow to the next cover, and then rush or creep or crawl to the ridge itself, but somehow most of the boys made it through. Finally it came our turn to try it. Sergeant Bruce jumped up and sprawled into a hole about fifteen feet behind me with a burst of fire right on his tail. I tossed him Rehfeld's rifle; the thought of leaving a fine M1 for the Japs to get and use on us later made me furious. Then I jumped up and made a dash for it. A machine gun fired over me just as I flopped into the hole. I lay there a few minutes and dashed again. I don't remember the whole return trip, but by the grace of God I finally was crawling along Gilbert Ridge with the sound of the firing behind me.

We counted noses. . . . Most of the boys had come through. . . . Some were missing, but we found that several of them, Lupe S. Vera, Johnny Hall, Ernest C. Brown—were wounded and evacuated. Some we didn't find. We moved back to our little bivouac area, our "pocket," and slept.

The point was taken the next day. We advanced and held our side while Company E assaulted the position from the other side, after a big mortar barrage. One of our mortars had the sight shot off it and the gunner was killed during this fight. And there were many others. . . . It was rugged. The whole damned deal was rugged, like attacking a pillbox by way of a tight rope . . . in winter. . . .

The Taking of Point Able — 2

Private Anthony G. Simonic, Company G, 32d Infantry

Point Able was rough. It is a big pinnacle of rock that crowns a barren hill at the inland end of Gilbert Ridge. Lieutenant Harry Gilbert of Company G lost his life in a valiant effort to move up the coverless slope of Point Able. At its foot lies Clevesy Pass, and the day before troops had fought through Clevesy Pass. The Japs holding the point were isolated, but they fought like cornered weasels against Company C on the ridge, against Company G moving up from the Sarana side, and against Company E on the Massacre side; they had been pounded by artillery and heavy mortars, and still they hung on.

Lieutenant Gilbert's platoon, whittled down to a single squad, was working up on the right. Lieutenant Stanley J. Wolczyk went to the left. Machine-gun fire grazed the tundra from the big rock 800 yards ahead and up above us. We moved farther to the left where a shoulder of the hill jutted out and shielded us from the machine gun. Then we started to climb. We got to within 150 yards of the Jap trench before they stopped us. Jap rifles were snapping from the trench, and a machine gun rattled off a burst. "Christ, they've got a machine gun in there, too," someone said. Corporal George Barker said, "There's gotta be one. The Japs have always got a machine gun." We were lying under some small rocks at the edge of a big bank of snow. Out in the snow were several jagged boulders, and George Barker began to work his way out across the snow to a big one in the center. We covered him as he crawled. He seemed to take an hour to get out there about 75 yards, but he said he didn't think he had been gone ten minutes when he came back. He had tried to get close enough to see how many were in the trench. He said he figured there were about a dozen. Lieutenant Wolczyk sent back for a mortar.

It took a long time to get it up to where we were hanging onto the slippery mountainside, but eventually it arrived. The mortar crew overshot the first couple of rounds; then they cut the range down to 125 yards, and the shells began to drop right in. They dumped six shells right into the Jap trench. Then Lieutenant Wolczyk hollered, "Drop one more in, and we'll assault." He began to place us. There were eight of us in all—me to the left, Barker to the right. Victor Rakusan wanted to go to the right and get one that had been shooting at him as he covered Barker. The mortar crew hollered, "We'll drop two, just for luck."

Lieutenant Wolczyk said, "Check your bayonets." When the second round burst in the trench we jumped up and started across the snow. As soon as we got to our feet the Japs opened up. The BAR man was doing his best to cover us, but they were throwing everything—mortars, rifles, grenades, machine gun. I will never understand how we got as far as we did. Rakusan got his sniper and another; Barker was yelling his head off and had killed two; I got one I'm sure of and maybe another; and little Jose P. Benavidez, who had come up with the mortar "just for the ride," had gotten two. I glanced to the right and saw Barker holding his rifle like a pistol and shooting, while he pulled the pin on a grenade with his teeth, just like in the movies. A grenade went off right behind me and a piece of it cut the handle off my shovel. I remember thinking for just a second, "May God curse them, my mess kit's been ruined." Somebody hollered, "Barker, you're taking too much time with them." He replied, "I am like hell. I want to be sure they're dead."

We got to within thirty yards of the trench, to a row of big jagged boulders, and ran into a nest of snipers. It was fast desperate work, and it was more trouble than we could handle. We fell back.

In the dark the following morning at 0300 the point was finally taken. The machine guns were silenced. It had cost lives and energy, but the big thorn in our side was out.

II: HOLTZ BAY

The Holtz Bay sector was attacked initially by one battalion of the 17th Infantry which landed on Red Beach. This force was reinforced a few days later by a battalion of the 32d Infantry. The bitter fighting in this sector forced approximately 1,700 Japs of Yonegowa Battalion, Aota (AA) Battalion, and administrative troops from their main supply base into the secondary sector of the Chichagof Harbor area. This retreat was hastened by the assault in the rear, made by a Provisional Battalion composed of the 7th Reconnaissance Troop and 7th Scout Company. This last force suffered severely from exposure and lack of rations because of the difficulty of supply over the snow-covered ridges leading back to Austin Cove, where it had landed from two submarines.

The Attack on Holtz Bay

Sergeant Frank J. Gonzales, Company B, 17th Infantry

The company moved up onto the hill the evening of May 12. It was a foggy night and visibility on the jagged hill was very poor. That and our unfamiliarity with the Japs are probably why we got so close to them without seeing them. We got in some cases to within 25 yards of their camouflaged dugouts, and we didn't see them. The company was spread out on the ridge with three platoons abreast, the 1st on the left, the 2d in the middle, and the 3d on the right. The 1st and 3d

Platoons saw some Jap positions in the evening and fired at them, but the 2d did not fire. As a result, the Japs probably figured that the area where the 2d Platoon was, was unoccupied, because during the night they tried to infiltrate men through our area. The first one I saw was one I almost stumbled over in the darkness. He was half-sitting, half-lying in a small natural hole in the tundra. I hadn't seen him there before, but he was playing dead, and as I pushed him he rolled over. My rifle was a few feet away in a foxhole, so I called another man who was near to stick a bayonet into him just to make sure. Apparently the man didn't do it, because the next morning, just prior to the first Jap assault, I'm sure this same Jap that I had rolled over in the night was shot and killed as he tried to get a light machine gun in action about 20 yards behind our lines.

It was still dark. I don't know why Frank J. DeMeo did it, maybe he just had a hunch. Anyway he came around and alerted the platoon. The sky was just beginning to get gray, and we had been awake about ten minutes I guess, when we saw bayonets moving behind the crest of the hill. We threw grenades at them, and they threw the grenades back. It was then that we learned to sizzle our grenades, and sometimes we'd hold them and count as high as four before we threw them. The Japs charged with bayonets after their first grenade barrage. They charged in small groups of ten or so, rushing out of the gorges and over the crests of the rough hills. We beat the first bunch off, and lost some men. Harry Sutton, Jr., had both his shoes blown off by a Jap grenade but was unhurt.

The second time they came at us, they tried to get around our left flank and ran into the 1st Platoon. The platoon sergeant, Sergeant Malcolm Word, moved over to the left flank, so I went to the right to check that flank. Firing was getting very heavy, and it was hard to move around. The right flank was in bad shape. I found that two men had been knifed during the night—Frank G. Galante and Robert E. Ney. They were both in their holes and had been stabbed before they could cry out or do anything. The squad leader of the 3d Squad had been hit in the hand, and the corporal of that squad had a bullet in his lung. I started back toward the left to report that our right flank was very weak. I had just got started when the Japs rushed us on that flank. I heard rifles being hit together, and then I saw Henry G. McDoniel and a Jap in a fight with bayonets. McDoniel got him in the throat. He moved toward the right to give some help and dashed into a burst of machine-gun fire. I started that way to take over for him when a few more Japs came in on us. I got their squad leader myself. I remember his bayonet going past my head on the left, and he seemed to run right onto my bayonet. I got him in the stomach. When I tried to withdraw, my bayonet stuck. I tried to work it free and even loaded my gun and tried to shoot it free but it stuck. I unsnapped it and left it in the Jap.

It was strange to me how the Japs would charge us, and the machine gunners behind them would continue to fire. I'm not sure that they killed their own men, but I don't see how they could have missed.

Ack-ack opened on us finally. It was bursting about ten feet over our heads. I took cover, so I couldn't get over to report that our right flank was about gone. I saw where Lieutenant Alfred J. Palmer had taken cover too, and while I watched I saw a shell burst right over him. I thought he was dead, but he crawled out of the hole and told Sergeant Word to take over. He was shell-shocked, and Sergeant Word was out of his head, too. He ordered the platoon to withdraw. The ack-ack was still bursting as the men began to fall back. We suffered quite a few casualties in trying to get off the hill. Four of us stayed up on the hill and watched the platoon move back. Charles H. Walsh, DeMeo, and Corporal Nello R. Giaccani and I stayed up. I decided that something had to be done. The four of us couldn't do much good toward holding a whole platoon front by ourselves, and we couldn't permit the two flanks of the 1st and 3d to remain exposed. We decided that all four of us had better take off and get some help. On the way down the hill we came across Lucien L. Brodeur and Garland M. Curry. Curry had been hit when we had crawled up to the crest of the hill and tossed grenades into two groups of Japs who were getting ready to charge us. Brodeur had been dragging him down the hill on a shelter half when he got hit himself. I saw them again later in the day. They were walking back toward the aid station, holding each other up. That was the last time I saw them.

I finally found Captain James R. Tisdale, our company commander. I told him what our situation was, and he sent me back up into position with my three men. Our orders were to hold the hill at all costs. Captain William R. Davis showed us a spot on the right side of a saddle where we could cover the front with fire anyway. We attached ourselves to the left flank of the 3d Platoon. Luckily, during the rest of the afternoon, no large group of Japs tried to break through our sector. One Jap machine-gun crew tried to move in, but we knocked it out with grenades.

During the evening we reorganized and pushed on over the ridge top. We counted between forty and fifty dead Japs, two of them officers, and captured seven machine guns. One Jap gunner was slumped over his gun and his blood was running down and dripping off the end of the barrel. It made me feel good to see him. I thought that might have been the gun that shot two canteens off my belt during the day and got McDoniel right in front of us.

Five days after our fight on Hill X (Ack-Ack Hill), what was left of the company was moving across the west arm of Holtz Bay in an attack on the high ground between the east and west arms. It was May 17. Japs who held the high ground were placing a lot of fire on the units to the right, so their progress was much slower than ours. We crossed the river first and started up the hill almost 1,000 yards ahead of the other troops.

We were under long-range machine-gun and sniper fire, but it didn't bother us much as we started up the hill. Captain Davis led us up a narrow path, very steep and rough, where a misstep would send you tumbling down the hill into the ocean. We didn't know what was up ahead, but for a good part of the climb up the mountain we were defiladed from all firing, so we did not think there was much opposition up there.

We had one casualty on the way up. Our runner, Ignatius R. Koszara was hit in both hips. And near the top of the hill we had to cross about twenty yards of exposed ground over a very tricky little trail. The trail was only as solid as the tundra, and eighteen of us got across before the trail wore out and got so slick it was impossible to cross. The Japs began firing at us as we crossed, and another man was hit in the neck; James Lowery was his name. We were just below the high point of the hill, so while the rest of the company looked for another route for advance to the top of the hill, Captain Davis took me and Sergeant Charles D. McNeill and six others on up to the high point to our front, about thirty-five feet higher than the shelf we were on. So far we had had no opposition, but a gun was beginning to fire over on our left, so we had a vague feeling that there was trouble brewing. They hit us just as we reached the top of the hill, not over fifteen yards away. First they threw grenades, then they came up over the crest of the hill. We were firing from the hip, like a bunch of wild men. The Jap officer was out in front waving his saber, and he was coming up right in front of us. Then he must have seen Captain William R. Davis, because he turned to the right and made directly for him. Several of the boys saw him and fired. The Jap officer flopped down almost at Captain Davis' feet, riddled. The ten men we had left behind on the shelf were firing through us and trying to get up to us, and we were firing madly ourselves. The fight only lasted a few minutes. Some of the boys who had just come up grenaded a Jap machine gunner on our right flank, who had just set his gun up. They got him before he fired a shot. Corporal Ellis C. Berg and Francis McKastle had both been hit, and even old "Wild Bill" Davis, the captain, caught a grenade fragment in his shoulder and received a bad cut over his ear.

As soon as the Japs at the bottom of the hill saw that the bayonet assault had failed, they began dumping mortar shells on us. The machine gun on the left continued to fire, and in addition to everything else, an ack-ack gun spotted us and opened up. I tried to give the captain first aid; there were no medics up there, yet. He sent me down to find the rest of the company and any other help we could get. I found some of our men almost straight down the hill and told them to get into position to guard the left flank from a short distance in the rear. Even while I was getting them into position a few Japs tried to get in on the left flank but our boys made short work of beating them off the rugged, rough ground they had to cross. They tried several times to go around our left but failed each time. I found the rest of the company trying to climb the hill from the right rear, but machine-gun fire was harassing them. I told them the captain had been hit and needed them up there, and it was a thrill to hear them say, "To hell with the machine gun!" and take off for the hilltop. Finally we got our two mortars and a heavy machine gun from Company D up there too, which we put in position in rear of the center of the company line on the ridge.

Fire on the ridge was terrific. Our heavy was getting in some good licks. It would fire at one flank, then at the other, and it discouraged hell out of a lot of Japanese who tried to flank us. The fog which had settled in broke just long enough, however, for the Jap gunner on our left to get a crack at our heavy. He killed our gunner and drove the assistant away from the gun. Our own light machine gun was still down the hill a ways having a duel with a faraway Jap gun on the right flank. I could hear him down there pounding away, and eventually they brought the gun up. They said they had just got tired of the sonuvabitch biting at them, when it was tough enough climbing that hill without being shot at. They had silenced him.

From somewhere a couple of wiremen had shown up and they had a line into Battalion. The ack-ack was firing again when I got the first call through. I told them our situation and took the phone to Captain Davis. We were digging in under the pounding fire and consolidating our position. From down on the right flank other troops were gaining the high ground, too. We gathered up our wounded—there were about a dozen now—and put them in a little sheltered pocket. Before long Lieutenant Colonel Albert V. ("Little Caesar") Hartl appeared on the scene. He told Captain Davis to go down and get some aid. The captain was so reluctant to leave that the colonel had to give him a direct order. Sergeant Diego Rubiales took over as the next senior and continued the fight. Sergeant Charles D. McNeill was shot through the neck, and before long Rubiales caught a mortar fragment. "Why, to hell with them!" he bellowed and stayed on the line. We lost eight men killed that day and about a dozen wounded. It was costly, for they had surprised us; but of the forty-five wise Japs who tried that bayonet assault, forty-five Jap bodies were counted in that area, and Captain Davis has the Jap officer's saber, too.

The next day was a knockout affair, too. Our troops were pushing hell out of the Japs, and they wanted some fire on the reverse slope of a hill. The rifle companies had requested the fire with -536[6] radios, and what they wanted was a barrage just on the reverse slope of the hill. So we got them to adjust our fire for us with -536 radios too, and it worked beautifully. We gave the Japs a helluva time and got a lot of them. And once or twice we got the message: "Push them out a ways farther; the last round landed in our laps." We were firing fast and really getting results. It was the first time we had fired hard and fast at a live target, and Andrew Taraba, No. 2 in the squad, got so excited and enthusiastic that he'd pull the pin, plant a big luscious kiss of genuine affection on the old HE shell, and slide her down the tube. He loved it.

Jeeps at Red Beach

Private First Class Morris R. Madison, Company D, 17th Infantry

It was about 1200 on May 12 when they hoisted my jeep out of the hold of the transport *Bell* and into the landing barge. We had the barge about half-loaded maybe, when we got an alert for a Jap air raid and were ordered to disperse the landing barges. We left the side of the ship and cruised around for a while. Then the transports got a submarine alert, and they put out to sea. We had to spend the night on the ocean in the landing barge because we couldn't risk going in with subs and aircraft around, and during the night the sea got very rough, and the jeep was rolling back and forth in the half-loaded barge until I thought it was going to burst out a side.

The next morning the barges were taking on quite a bit of water, so we hurried over to the *Bell* to try to reload the jeep and the other stuff back on her, but the winch broke down so they ordered us to take the jeep and load it on a destroyer and leave it there until the evening. I got on the *Bell*, and the jeep was loaded onto a destroyer. Along toward evening a barge that had picked up my

[6]Portable radio.

jeep pulled alongside the *Bell*, and I got into it and we landed. The jeep had to be winched up the steep incline from Red Beach, and we were harassed by artillery fire a bit in getting it done, but it was a good system. I had no sooner got to the top of the rise when I was ordered to pick up a load of mortar and machine-gun ammunition and head for the front. The tundra was terrible to drive over. It was treacherously soft and full of holes. I wasn't used to it at all, so of course I got stuck—and right on a skyline, too.

Another jeep came along and we started to pull mine out, when a Jap sniper began pecking at us from clear across the west arm. We spotted him and returned the fire until he left us alone.

It was only a matter of minutes to get me out of the hole and on my way again. I delivered the first load without any more trouble and started back toward the beach. Carl Mancuso, another jeep driver, and I arrived on the hill overlooking the beach about the same time, and we pulled up about fifteen feet apart and were talking when suddenly the ground furrowed up between us. A Jap dud had landed with a thud, right between us. We dove for cover as another shell landed and exploded over on our right. Billy L. Gassaway had just driven up, and he dove out of his jeep and into a hole as a shell burst right in front of him. The shrapnel ripped up his radiator, blew out a front tire, and smashed his windshield.

We worked back and forth between the front and the beach for several days, hauling ammunition and chow up and casualties back; and finally we moved around to Holtz Bay, on the 25th, I think.

We had it pretty easy going over there, except for one spot. That was between the Jap airfield and the beach. It was another hill that we had to be winched over. A stretch of low ground just before we got to the hill was bad too, because the Japs would invariably dump a bunch of mortar shells at us every time they saw us start across. We'd dive like hell and get over to the cable at the hill; once we got over the hill, we were safe.

One night I was going to take the jeep around the point by boat, and I was waiting on the beach for a barge when the Japs opened up with their damned artillery. I tried to get the jeep off the beach and to do it I had to cross a creek. I went splashing out into the creek, which I had crossed many times before, and drove right off into a submerged bomb crater. The jeep sank right out of sight, and I jumped off and waded out. I didn't get it out of there until the next day at noon, when a boy came along with a captured Jap cat and pulled it out. All the gas and oil had to be changed, and everything had to be dried out. It was a helluva mess. The drivers worked hard, and so did the machines; they were wonderful. A guy gets so he loves his own machine, you know? They can take it.

Crossing the Ridge to Holtz Bay

Staff Sergeant William B. Pack, Company A, 17th Infantry

On May 14 we were ordered to advance over Hill X and attack the Japs in position in the valley below. Hill X had been pretty much of a nightmare, and our attack over it on the 14th was bound and determined not to change the reputation. It was to be all-out assault, preceded by naval gunfire, then bombing and strafing by the planes, and then the infantry was to move in. The Navy shelled all right, but the weather was so bad that the planes didn't show up, so the Doughboys were ordered to move in. The hill we had to cross was practically straight down for forty feet, except for one little draw that cut through this steep bank and made a fairly gradual slope to the valley below.

From our experience with Japs the day before, we had learned to throw two grenades over a crest before we went over, because the Japs had a nasty habit of waiting just under the crest of a hill, on the reverse side, for guys who popped over the top. The two grenades were expected to discourage that sort of stuff.

We moved into the little draw and started forward, when the Japs spotted us and began shelling us with ack-ack. The first shell burst, and the men dove for cover. When the firing stopped, I moved around and got the platoon going again, and the Japs started shelling again. Everybody stopped and dove for cover. This happened two or three times, and I was getting damned sick of it. During the times we were advancing between ack-ack barrages, I had moved close to the crest, where the draw sloped abruptly downward. I hollered to several of my platoon who could hear me and said, "Hell, this is too hot for me; I'm going over!" I tossed my two grenades and took off. The slope just below the crest was steep and bare—naked snow—for about fifty yards. The Japs were covering this opening with machine guns in addition to their ack-ack. Once I slipped against a rock in the middle of the snowbank, and I thought they had me. But about fifty yards farther down the hill was a field of big boulders, and I made a dash for them. Honest, it felt just like walking in the front door of home when I jumped into the rocks, it was so safe.

The platoon kept coming over one or two men at a time until about half of them were in the rocks with me. No one had been hit. The only casualty was a sprained ankle. We stayed in the rocks waiting for the fire to be neutralized to our front, and while we were waiting grenades began going off in back of us. I worried about that plenty. I thought at first Japs had slipped in our flank, but then I discovered that a support platoon of the adjacent company had gotten orders from somewhere to precede over the crest of the hill with grenades, too. That made our spot nice and warm, with Jap machine guns, ack-ack, and our own grenades bursting around.

Company D was supporting our attack from the ridge behind, and before long they had begun to really get the Jap guns. We found that every time our guns fired we could dash with comparative safety, but the minute our guns stopped firing we had to get underground and get there fast.

It was getting late in the afternoon, practically evening, and we had advanced down into a draw that led into the west arm of Holtz Bay. There were about half of the 3d Platoon of Company A and about half of the 3d Platoon of Company C there. We were out maybe 150 or 200 yards ahead of the main body of troops. We moved on down the draw a few yards farther, and then we discovered that the troops on our right had stopped advancing and were pulling back.

The platoon leader of Company C was in bad shape, shell-shocked and sick, so he turned the platoon over to the platoon sergeant, who decided he would pull his men back.

There wasn't much the seven or eight men of Company A could do up there alone, so we withdrew to where the rest of the platoon was in the vicinity of the rocks. We dug in there and prepared to spend the night, but at 0200 we got orders to withdraw back to the vicinity of the battalion CP, which was about 1,000 yards behind.

We got to the battalion without a mishap, unless falling down in the little water pockets a few hundred times can be called mishaps. We were tired out and cold, but the cooks had a big batch of hot chocolate to feed us, and we drew new K rations.

We were back on the lines before dawn, in positions along the ridge from which we supported the attack of the battalion the next morning.

It was a miraculous business, that advance the day before, through the draw, under ack-ack and machine-gun fire. The boy who sprained his ankle was our only casualty that day.

The Gunner's Revenge

Private First Class Melvin J. Nelson, Company D, 17th Infantry

On the 17th we had made a big push across the west arm of Holtz Bay and up into the first hills in the high ground between the arms, and the going was getting very tough. The Japs were pounding away at us with everything they had, and we were pounding back, trying to shut them up long enough to get our footing anyway.

Our gun was in position over near the left flank, and the gunner was raking the Japs on the hills to the left front without a letup. He was getting in some good licks too, from what we could see through the fog, and the men were getting positions they could fight from, and then the damned fog broke over on our left flank. A sniper over there somewhere fired and got our gunner right through the head. Mel Nelson jumped behind the gun and continued to fire, while the section sergeant tried to spot the sniper. He saw him when the Jap raised up and fired at the gun again. Nelson was hit in the stomach, and it hurt and he was furious. The sergeant hollered where the sniper was and pointed. Nelson kicked the gun onto free traverse and swung it over, just as the Jap raised up again. He fired a long stream of tracers right into the sniper's head and chest; then he laid back, and a couple of the boys carried him away from the gun.

"The little sonuvabitch," he said, "I guess that'll teach him."

Night Patrol

Sergeant John C. Salvino, Company L, 32d Infantry

All day long on the 16th they had tried with mortar and machine gun to silence the damned Jap, but after they thought they had destroyed every living thing in the vicinity of that litle shelf across the valley and had turned to something else—or Company K in the valley tried to move—the Jap would be there popping away in the ripping little bursts that had kept their faces in the grass.

It was 2300 when Lieutenant Paul M. Coty and I and four men crawled up to a ridge, while the Company K boys told us where this gun was located. We were to be a combat patrol to move out after dark, across the valley and up on the bench to knock out the Jap gun, and if possible to bring it back.

It was quite dark as we passed Company K's OP and moved out into the valley. Lieutenant Coty was leading and I was in the rear. We had gone very slowly and quietly, keeping low, for perhaps two hundred yards; then we stopped for a moment and listened. Everything was quiet. Lieutenant Coty whispered for us to move out and keep going straight ahead. Somehow we got separated from him, and we had gone another hundred yards or so before I discovered that he wasn't with us. It was shortly after that I saw a figure following along behind the patrol. I assumed that Lieutenant Coty had rejoined us and was trying to catch us. The figure was about fifty yards behind us at first.

The scout, up in front, had stopped again. Then he crept forward very slowly and carefully. We were at the foot of the shelf where the gun was supposed to be located. The figure behind us was coming up very slowly. The rest of the patrol moved up behind the scout, who was lying on his belly looking over a tiny ledge onto the shelf.

We crawled up beside him. We could see two Japs, one standing at the flank and one walking slowly along in front of the trench that was supposed to have the Jap gun in it. We were still too far away to throw grenades, but we could see the Japs and the trench clearly. There was no machine gun in it.

We moved around the little rise and looked carefully along the Jap emplacement. The two Japs were moving again, but there was no machine gun in the hole. We didn't know how many more might be sleeping in the hole, so we decided to return. As we backed down from the hill and started across the valley, the man who had followed us across and who I assumed was Lieutenant Coty, took up our trail again. He was about thirty yards behind our column and kept pace with us. Finally I stopped the patrol and called, in a whisper, to the man behind us. No answer. I called louder to him and still no answer. We began crawling toward him until we knew there was no chance of his not hearing us. Then I called "Lieutenant Coty," and the man jumped and ran low into a shell hole. We crawled to within five yards of the hole, and I called "Lieutenant Coty" again, and still we got no answer. One of the men raised his M1 and shot him.

When we got back to Company K's OP we found Lieutenant Coty. He was waiting for us. He asked us about the shot a few minutes before, and we told him about the Jap and how we thought it was him for so long. He had a similar run-in after he got separated from us, only the Jap had done the shooting and missed.

Captured Mortars

Corporal Jerome G. Job, Company L, 32d Infantry

From the fighting a few days before we had captured a few Jap knee mortars and some ammunition, and by experimenting around with them Lieutenant

Robert A. Green, of the Cannon Company, found out that after you screwed the fuze, which had a left-hand thread, on tight, you had to take a half turn to the right before the projectile would go off. At first it sounded like a sabotage plot, but after we got onto it, we could lob shells out pretty good. The mortars had all the leveling bubbles torn off when we got them, but to guys who had shot slingshots and paper wads all their lives, a little Kentucky windage on a mortar was a cinch.

It was the 21st or 22d, on the hills above the east arm, that we first got a chance to use the mortar like it was supposed to be used. The troops had a firing line built up along the ridge in front of us and the firing was going like mad up there. There was a lot of Jap machine-gun cross fire on our line, so Lieutenant Colonel John M. "Mickey" Finn called up and sent me and Sergeant Richard H. Mason and Lieutenant Charles W. Nees up with our little old Jap mortar and a sound-powered phone. We got up on the line and got in position by some rocks. The colonel was on the other end of the phone when we started to fire, and he could see our bursts. He kept calling the shots for us, and we kept dumping the rounds over on the Japs. We were after an emplacement up near the top of the next ridge, that was dug into a bank up there and had a roof on it. Some Jap machine gunner was giving us a rough go, but we were down on the ground blasting away and coming close. Colonel Finn had just called back the last burst, when the Jap gunner fired, blowing the mouthpiece clear off the telephone. Lieutenant Nees turned over the stub that was left in his hand and shouted into the earphone. Then he put it up to his ear, and by hell, the colonel's voice came over! He suggested that Nees talk a little louder and mentioned something about a 105 going off in his eardrum—goddammit! But we kept firing, and he kept calling the shots. The machine gunner cut in again, just as we caved in the roof on the Jap emplacement. I was up against a rock, and one bullet went over my head maybe an inch, another went under my leg, and another splattered against the rock under my armpit, and we decided to withdraw and cool off.

Duplex Foxhole

Sergeant Richard H. Mason, Company L, 32d Infantry

The Attu fog that draped over the gaunt mountains like a wet shroud was alone confusing enough, but add to its blurring wetness a couple of quarts of warm sake, and, brother, you've got "the department of utter confusion."

Company L had moved up on Hill 3 above the east arm of Holtz Bay during the day, and we held a line across the hill a little over halfway up; some points of the line were almost to the top. The Japs had holes all around the place and were still holding the high ground. It had been foggy during the attack, and toward the end the exact disposition of the forces was somewhat confused, not to mention the soldiers.

About half of my squad, on a flank, had crawled up during the fighting to within seventy-five yards of the Jap lines, and we had taken over some Jap holes there, while we waited for orders. It was getting well along into the evening, and we could hear the Japs up above us talking and clinking their gear around. We were in a nice joint as foxholes go—a duplex job, one without running water, which was something especially nice. But the neighbors weren't so hot—a bunch of drunks—although they were hospitable enough in a confused sort of way.

We had waited about an hour, I guess, when who should come trotting down the hill, his rifle slung jauntily over his shoulder, but our first caller of the evening. He ran up to within twenty feet of our hole just like he was going to move right in with us, and then he stopped. His slant eyes bulged even farther out of his head as he spotted the grimly smiling faces, and the business end of an M1 came hulking up out of the hole at him. He turned to run back, as the M1 barked, and he fell.

We sat back and waited some more. The party upstairs was getting good. The clinking of gear and the talking were boisterously rising almost to the pitch of normal conversation. It sounded funny on the battlefield where you're either whispering so you won't be heard or screaming your lungs out so you can be.

We had waited about another hour, I guess, and it was getting pretty dark, when we saw another one hop up out of the hole and start down the hill. He had his rifle slung over his shoulder, and he almost skipped down the hill toward us. As he came closer we saw that he was all gassed up, practically drunk, and he was carrying a bag of dried fish and rice balls right up to our front door. This little character kept coming until he was ten feet from us. Then he stopped. He stared at us, sort of dazed, like he had suddenly remembered he forgot to turn the water heater off, and he began backing up. We raised up out of the hole without rifles, and in good English he said, "Don't shoot, don't shoot!" But his rifle had a fixed bayonet on it, and he had gotten it off his shoulder. It looked, somehow, as though he might be going to stick us with it, so we cut down on him.

We weren't bothered with callers any more; we stayed awake all night, just so we could be sure we wouldn't snub anybody who might drop in and find us asleep. I guess our neighbors had a hang-over the next morning, because they were in a lousy mood, and even tried to kill us as we went up the hill.

Memories

Staff Sergeant Arthur Benevich, Company A, 17th Infantry

It certainly is strange the things that stick in a man's mind about the battle. Sergeant Benevich and I were talking about the fighting in Attu, and I agreed with him that it is very strange what men remember and what they forget.

Now me, for instance, *he said*, I didn't realize what a terrific problem it is to identify troops at a distance. And on May 12 when we were advancing on Hill X we were getting casualties. But they weren't being hit from the front, like they should have been. They were getting it in the back and in the right rear of their legs. We hadn't received any fire from the front yet at all. Finally we spotted a group of men a long way off on the right flank. We were supposed to contact the Scout Company out in that area somewhere, and we thought they might be scouts even though we could see them firing in our direction. We studied them for about half an hour and still couldn't positively identify them. The men were getting mad as hell at them, whoever they were, and began to return the fire. Then one of the group pulled out. He got up and began ambling back. He carried his entrenching shovel with him, and we saw that it was larger than ours, and didn't have a cross-handle. They were Japs, so we let them have it. One after another they got up and moved out slowly. We got four of the seven. I remember how funny I felt when I saw that shovel and knew for sure that they were Japs.

Another strange thing happened that day. We got to within thirty-five yards of a Jap machine gun before it opened up; that is, our lead scout, Walter J. Imbirowicz did. Some Jap rifleman fired, and we all hit the ground, and Imbirowicz was out in the middle of a snowbank. Just above him this Jap machine gun opened fire. Imbirowicz was lying crumpled up on the snow. We were pinned down, and for the fifteen hours that we lay there, Imbirowicz was absolutely motionless. In the evening the Japs pulled out, and the medics went up to look at him. I saw them bending over him, and I thought they must be taking off his dog tags.

Then suddenly he jumped up and ran down the hill toward us. I thought for a second I was going crazy. He had two slight wounds, one on the hand and one in the arm, from grenade fragments.

I went through some pretty tough fighting up there, but I don't believe I was more scared at any time than I was one morning on the tableland up from the east arm when we were moving toward Chichagof. We were flushing out Jap foxholes, and they had taken a terrific beating from our mortars and artillery. It was about the 28th, I think. Anyway, my buddy, Private Louis J. Adamski, and I were working close together. I walked past a gruesome little picture of a Jap in a hole who had his head blown completely off, and his body was lying in a very grotesque position. I passed it in a kind of a hurry. It was a very unpleasant sight.

I'll never drink a cup of coffee again as long as I live, I guess, without thinking about the platoon runner. He was just a kid, a volunteer about eighteen years old, and up there with a bunch of men who were supposed to be fighting a war. This kid—his name was Roy L. Kitts—was a damned fine runner. Whether he was too young to realize the danger, or whether he just simply wasn't afraid, I don't know. But he ran messages over some of the places I didn't think that a mosquito could get through without being hit by something. And it was always "the shortest way is the quickest way" for him, regardless. But that's not why I'll remember him. The reason I'll remember him is that he was never without coffee. I don't know where he got it, but he always had some. He'd pass it around for the guys—good hot coffee. When you'd sell your soul for a kind word, here would be Kitts with his canteen cup full of steaming coffee. I remember one day in particular we were catching a lot of hell from all over. It was cold and miserable and raining, and we had taken a Jap position on the center arm, and they were giving us a fit. There were dead Japs sprawled all around, and here was Kitts down in a hole rolling this Jap out so he could have room to work. He pulled a shelter half over his head, lit a can of Jap canned heat, and made a full cup of coffee. With bullets flying around every which way, here he came with his cup. "Have some coffee, Sarge," he said. I told him he ought to drink it himself. "Aw, hell no. I never touch it myself," he said, as he handed the cup over. I got to thinking back, and I don't believe he ever did.

It sure is peculiar the strange little things that stick in a man's mind.

Lost Opportunity

Lieutenant Joseph A. Gray, Battery C, 49th Field Artillery Battalion

You almost have to know Lieutenant Joseph Gray to appreciate his experience with what the men called the "Red Ball Express." Gray is a big man. He must weigh a good two hundred or more—the kind of a guy you'd gladly walk down a dark alley with, but would hate like hell to crawl into a ring with.

He loved to throw shells at the enemy with his 105 and only felt bad because he was so far behind the front he couldn't throw them by hand. He was genuinely worried that he would go all through the battle and never get a chance to get close enough to a Jap to shoot his tommy gun. But he had it ready, at all times, hoping against hope that sometime he would get his chance.

It had been a drizzly night, but everything was sparkling in the bright morning sun. The men were all puttering around the gear, drying it and stacking loose things up out of puddles that had formed, when someone spotted an airplane. It was flying low, quite a ways out to sea, and as it circled about we could hear the rumble of explosions. We believed it was an American plane probably searching out a submarine. And then it swung in close over our position. As it banked around and the light hit her side, there, big and glaring, was the huge red ball—a Jap! Beach guns began chattering their frantic challenge, men were shouting and diving for cover, a few rifles cracked insolently, then the big plane swung on out over the water and disappeared.

Men crawled out of their holes, talking excitedly, looking into the plane's wake, their weapons still hot in their hands . . . all except Gray's. He continued to sit in his foxhole, utterly downcast. Ruefully, he fingered the immaculately clean and oily pieces of his completely disassembled tommy gun. His only big chance had come and gone in a matter of seconds and caught him with his piece down.

The Landing at Austin Cove

First Sergeant Fenton Hamlin, 7th Scout Company

The company got aboard the submarines, the *Nautilus* and the *Narwhal*, at Dutch Harbor on April 28 and started rehearsing our debarkation. The crews of the two submarines had worked with Marine Corps raider battalions and they completely revised our methods, cutting the time required right in two. Their system consisted of inflating the rubber boats and shoving them onto the afterdeck. Then, with the men sitting in them, the submarine was partially submerged, leaving the rubber boats floating free.

It was bitter cold at 0100 on May 11. We were about four thousand yards off Attu as the black water gurgled around the submarines, and the rubber boats floated free. The men began to paddle and the little boats moved silently through the foggy night toward Scarlet Beach (Austin Cove).

It was a long way in, and the men were tired when they hit the beach. There was no resistance. The two sections made contact and moved inland, as a signal light blinked out to the submarines that the landing was complete.

The column of men moved slowly along a tiny creek, heading up and north. The mountain was huge and precipitous. All day the company moved on and up the great steep slope, expecting the Jap. As the company was near the top of the mountain, the supply plane flew over and dropped rations and ammunition. Patrols fanned out and reconnoitered the mountain top, while the company rested. It was decided that we would bivouac for the night on the mountain top. We were about four miles due west of the west arm of Holtz Bay. At 2100 a runner reported that the 7th Reconnaissance Troop had bivouacked about a mile and a half north of our position. The ever-present cold and fog of Attu closed in on the men, and they shivered and tried to sleep.

At 0400 the next morning, the company began the descent into the valley. It was daylight before we reached the head of the valley and moved into attack formation. The descent into the valley was thrilling. The 1st Platoon had gone down first and worn grooves in the deep crusty snow. They were moving like specks at the bottom of the incline as the rest of the men jumped fourteen feet onto the snow and then slid at breakneck speed, like human toboggans, down the grooves made by the ones before them. There was a grimness about the men, laughing as they slid into the valley, and the Japs were there.

They began to fire at us. Long-range machine guns and dual-purpose anti-aircraft batteries concentrated on us as we moved ahead. At 1200 the artillery began bursting at the mountain top; the Japs had picked up the 7th Reconnaissance Troop as it moved down.

As we advanced toward the Japs in the canyon, one platoon was in the bottom, one platoon on the high ground on the left, and two platoons on the right of the stream on high ground over there. We had surprised the enemy, but they were fighting back as the distance between us became less and less. Machine guns in the valley slipped streams of bullets up at us, and on the high ground on the right Japs scurried about lining other guns against our advance.

Late in the afternoon we were close to the Japs. They had felt only the caliber .30 rifles and light machine guns. Moving farther down the canyon, like little specks against the snow, other Japs were walking insolently out into the open, coming up to support their front lines. At 1800 the 81mm. mortar arrived with the Reconnaissance Troop, and as the big shell burst down the canyon the little specks of approaching Japs scurried like ants, back into the protecting wall.

From their emplacements in the valley and on the hill to the right the Jap machine-gun fire held up the advance down the canyon the rest of the night and the following morning. The wet fog and persistent cold were taking their toll, and the faces of the men were drawn. Fatigue showed clearly around their eyes. The rations were almost gone. Overhead, somewhere in the fog, the motors of the supply plane roared back and forth, as the pilot tried to locate us; then they faded out over the mountain.

Late in the afternoon we hit the Japs on the high ground to the right. Two platoons of the Scout Company supported by a platoon of the 7th Reconnaissance Troop with two caliber .50 machine guns made the attack. The Japs were driven back, but from the valley machine guns chattered frantically, and reinforcements were moving up from the west arm. It was dark when our advance stopped.

The bitter cold numbed their joints as the men huddled in the rocks. At the CP a cave had been dug into the snow and the wounded were lying in it side by side on shelter halves. Even when they were unconscious their bodies trembled violently from the cold. Empty shell cases, ration boxes, anything that would burn, had been torn up and consumed in tiny fires to heat the last packages of coffee and warm stiff fingers for a moment.

"Damn American dogs, we massacre you!" the Japs had taunted during the night. "Damn American dogs, we kill you!" they continued in the morning, between bursts of their machine gun that almost continually sent bullets splattering through the rocks. Hasrata was cold and hungry and mad. He called back to Lieutenant Robert Engley several times for a machine gun. Engley assured him it was on its way. "Damn American dogs!" the Japs taunted and sent a burst crashing into the rock behind which the excited Hasrata crouched. He jumped up and waved his fist. "Go to hell, you little bastards!" he shouted and then ducked as another burst splattered against the rock.

Bolger, the machine gunner, arrived. The bullets were streaking through the smoky air of the canyon. Bolger was a wild man. Instead of lying down behind the gun, he just crouched on one knee sideways to the gun, and riding it like a bronc he'd fire a burst, laugh, and fire again. Hasrata moved forward and threw a grenade. The Jap machine gunners threw grenades back at him, and Bolger sprayed them with his machine gun. Hasrata threw another grenade, and with a whoop, rushed into the nest with his bowie knife flashing.

The situation was stabilized. We had repulsed an enemy counterattack the morning of the 14th, and the fight had settled down to bitter, deadly machine-gun duels and grenade and sniper fights. We were bottled up in the canyon and only very slowly making progress to get out. We needed supporting weapons. The ammunition for the 81mm. mortars had been exhausted, and other ammunition was getting low. Overhead the motor of the supply plane with food, ammunition, and sleeping bags, roared blindly through the fog making futile efforts to locate us. The fog pressed in like wet cotton around the signal flares we had fired as the plane went over us. Finally the motors droned away again over the mountain. The men looked at each other, silently, then rolled back to face the Japs.

It was the third day in the canyon. The cold was intense and some of the men were vomiting green bile from their empty stomachs. We could catch glimpses of the Japs ahead through the fog, as their bullets twanged off the rocks around us. The situation was tense, and nerves were drawn as tight as fiddle strings. No one was talking. A vicious burst of machine-gun bullets crackled over the heads of Sergeant Thomas and his gunner, Morochek. Thomas looked at Morochek and very matter-of-factly broke the silence. "You know," he said, "I think those guys are trying to kill us." He stated, so calmly what was so terrifyingly obvious to everyone, that they laughed. It broke the tension. Some of the cold, hungry men even moved forward to better positions.

Two men limped and staggered on their frozen feet back to the CP carrying a man between them. He had been shot in the chest. They laid him down carefully on the snow in front of the cave. He wanted a drink of water and later a cigarette. Sergeant Hamlin lit it for him, and he took a deep drag. Hamlin was sure he had been hit in the lung. He pulled back the man's parka expecting to see smoke issuing from the neat hole in his chest.

Two sleeping bags were borrowed from the shore-fire control party of the 7th Reconnaissance Troop for the wounded men. They slipped the new fellow into one, and he immediately passed out. The next morning he was white and motionless. Hamlin was sure he had died. It seemed impossible that he could have lived through the night, but Hamlin just touched him and the man opened his eyes. "How you feel?" the sergeant asked him. "Fine, fine. Gotta smoke?" The doctor came over and probed for the bullet. It wasn't to be found. The only explanation seemed to be that the bullet had bounded off his breast bone.

The supply plane was droning overhead again. It was exasperating. The men in the canyon were freezing and most of them were vomiting bile now with every drink of water they took. There, overhead, like a promise from heaven, was a load of food and ammunition and sleeping bags. But it was foggy. It was always foggy. The fog was cold and wet and thick and blinding. The frustrated men even thought of firing tracers up at the plane, but realized that the pilot would think they were Japs if they did.

We needed supporting fire badly but the only time that the shore-fire party had been able to contact a ship, a submarine scare had driven the ship out to sea.

Scott, a runner, and several other men had gotten lost in the fog. It was easy to get completely turned around in the thick moving mist that made everything vague. On their way back they stumbled face to face with a Jap machine gun that loomed up out of the fog suddenly in front of them. The men behind Scott ran, but Scott had no time to run. His tommy gun and the Jap machine gun roared almost muzzle to muzzle. The men with him got back, but Scott did not return.

It was the fourth day without food. Lieutenant Stott and Sergeant Petruska were in a foxhole together when Lieutenant Stott found two old dirty pieces of candy that had been in his pocket for weeks. Petruska's eyes got as big as saucers and he began to drool over the beaten-up, lint-covered candy sprinkled with tobacco grains. Lieutenant Stott claimed that Petruska would have murdered him if he hadn't offered him a piece of candy. Petruska said, "Gee, that was one of the best things that ever happened to me." Later that day the plane was heard again, feeling its way through the fog above. It dropped some rations just with the chance hope that they might come close, and one small bundle fell where we could get it.

During that night, the 15th, the enemy pulled back, and about 2300 we got a message from the 3d Battalion of the 32d Infantry, informing us of their attacks from the north. We pushed off down the canyon. The Japs had left in a hurry, leaving guns, ammunition, and dead bodies strewn everywhere. We found Scott. He was draped over a stone parapet around the Jap machine-gun emplacement. There were four riddled Jap bodies in the emplacement. Scott died firing his tommy gun. It had jammed, and three slugs were smashed together and a fourth had split the barrel and had started out the side when the gun stopped firing. The Japs had hit Scott in the face with a burst of fire.

We limped out of the canyon on frozen feet, and our flank patrol killed three snipers, the last vestige of resistance in the canyon. We contacted the 32d Infantry at 1600 near the beach in the west arm.

It had been a long, hard ordeal. The evacuation of the wounded was begun that night, and continued into the next day. We had lost an officer and ten men killed in the bitter six days since we paddled the rubber boats to the beach. The freezing cold and fog had been a harder enemy to fight than the Japs. Ninety per cent of the Scout Company and three-fourths of the 7th Reconnaissance Troop suffered from severe exposure.

It seemed an eternity ago that the black water had gurgled around the submarines, and little boats had moved silently into the fog.

III: THE BATTLE FOR CHICHAGOF

After the Jap evacuated Holtz Bay and was forced out of Clevesy Pass, his position represented a perimeter defense of Chichagof Harbor from Sarana Bay across Sarana Nose on up to the Pass leading from Chichagof to Holtz Bay. The Massacre and Holtz Bay forces then began coördinated attacks up the steep snow-covered slopes, along ridges above the fog line, and also along the soggy floor of Jim Fish Valley.

The Attack on Sarana Nose — 1

Captain John J. Womack, Company H, 17th Infantry

Late on the night of May 21 Lieutenant Colonel James Fish called the heavy-weapons company commanders together. The following morning the 3d Battalion of the 17th Infantry was going to attack the enemy entrenched in Sarana Nose. The nose stuck out, insolent and huge, into the valley where Jim Fish Valley meets Sarana and the only approach to it was across the open valley, flat and coverless, 800 yards wide. We were going to give supporting fire to this attack from Engineer Hill and the slopes of the mountain below Point Able. Colonel Fish said simply, "We want all the fire power on that thing possible."

We split the target three ways vertically. Company D, 32d Infantry, was on the right; Company H, 32d Infantry, was in the middle; and Company H, 17th Infantry was on the left. We were going to give them fire power. During the night hours everything was set. The guns were put in carefully and ammunition brought up for the mortars and 37s. It was getting light and the big hulking shape of Sarana Nose gradually reared into distinctness as the zero hour approached. The attack was set to jump off at 0650 on the 22d. We were to prepare for ten minutes prior.

Finally 0640 clicked by on the watches across the front and the thunder started. Thirty-two heavy machine guns began pounding hot streaks of bullets at the lowest Jap positions. Eight light machine guns on the flanks began to chatter. From along the ridge top to our left rear fourteen 37s barked out, sending their shells screaming across the valley; and behind them twenty-three 81mm. mortars heaved their heavy power onto the nose. Down in Clevesy Pass a section of mountain 75s began pounding targets higher up the hill; and behind them, in Massacre Valley, a battalion of 105s, their muzzles pointed skyward began roaring again and again, hurling tons of fury at the top of the nose.

At 0700 the troops began moving across the deadly open. The Japs in some few positions fired random mortar shells into the valley, and once, as Company K neared the foot of the hill, a Jap artillery piece fired from behind the hill at them. But they were getting across. They weren't falling. They weren't being cut down by machine guns and rifles, by a hundred hidden muzzles in the nose. The muzzles were blinded by the hail of bullets. Over Company K's head was a roof of screaming, snapping tracer bullets.

From the hill the streams of tracers looked like a bridge across which you could walk to Sarana Nose. The noise was a terrible symphony, deafening, and maddening, and exhilarating. The guns were getting hot, and still we fed the belts into the gulping receivers. The rate of fire was terrific (so terrific that we got our tails chewed about it later), but the attackers were moving up the hill.

We raised our fire to clear them and the fog raised with us. They had passed the first Jap positions and were moving through the second ones before the machine guns ceased to fire. Then, a little later, the mortars and the 37s ceased and waited for targets of opportunity.

The gunners were grinning and burning their fingers on their guns. The gun barrels were smoking hot, and practically smooth bore. Some of the boys claimed that the last couple of hundred rounds came out sideways. Some gunners had pushed four thousand rounds through their guns in twenty minutes. The mortars had fired ninety to one hundred rounds in about a half an hour, and the No. 2 men at the 105s back in Massacre Valley were wiping the sweat off their chins.

The guns took a beating, because we were short on spare barrels. They had been lost and left from time to time in the heat of battle, and when we needed them we didn't have them. But the 3d Battalion was well up on Sarana Nose, and faintly the popping drifted back across the valley as they mopped up the dazed remnants of the Jap defenders. It had been a beautiful show.

The Attack on Sarana Nose — 2

*Sergeant Francis W. McLean and Staff Sergeant John Bacoch, Jr.,
Company K, 17th Infantry*

At 0200 on May 22 the shivering men of Company K moved from their bivouac up on the mountain below Point Able and slid and stumbled and fell down a tortuous trail to the valley floor below. An attack was prepared to shove off at 0700 against the Japs entrenched on Sarana Nose. The attack was to move out with Company I on the left and K on the right, with L in support, and included an elaborate setup for supporting fire by three heavy-weapons companies, fourteen 37mm. guns, and a battalion of artillery.

The Company I commander, Lieutenant Ward J. Redmond, had become exhausted trying to find a route to the valley from the bivouac area; and after twenty continuous hours of climbing over the rocks in the fog, he fell and injured his already bad leg. He failed to get back to his company in time for the attack, and so when 0700 appeared on the watches across the front, Company K started out alone across the valley.

From the ridge behind them forty streams of tracer bullets cracked overhead, and higher up on the slopes of Sarana Nose the big mortar and artillery shells began to rip at the Jap trenches.

The first Jap resistance was mortar shells that landed in the company as they were crawling up the first, almost vertical bank out of the valley floor; and one big Jap artillery or heavy mortar shell burst at the foot of the incline. Sergeant Robert W. McAmis and Sergeant William E. Chislett fell, wounded with mortar fragments. Then, as another shell burst, Technician Fourth Grade Jesse H. Pomroy and Corporal Ernest F. Dwight rolled away from the exposion with shell fragments in their bodies. As the big shell exploded, a fragment broke several cartridges in Private First Class Per Thompson's belt and his clothing caught fire. Corporal Ray E. White was almost under the shell, and it knocked him several feet. He was shocked badly and began to shake and weep as he tried vainly to follow the attack up the hill.

The company crossed over the first Jap emplacements and found them completely deserted. Then, as they moved up, the leading scouts fired at a Jap in the next trench line up the hill. The scouts, Joseph J. Petres and Carl F. Burroughs, passed through a series of foxholes without resistance, and most of the platoon with Lieutenant George W. Thayer had passed through. They were pushing up on the hill, when Lieutenant Thayer and Staff Sergeant Chester H. Brown noticed some Japs still alive in one of the holes. They went back down and got to work on the Japs. The Japs were beaten by the great wave of supporting fire that had plunged into the hill from across the valley, and offered almost no resistance as Thayer and Brown moved from hole to hole killing them. Thayer had accounted for fifteen live Japs that the company had passed over, when he was hit in the leg, and Howard H. Roberts killed ten.

Over on the right flank a similar fight was in progress. Sergeant Bacoch had stopped to rest by some holes that the platoon on the right had passed over, when he saw a Jap head pop up. He fired and killed the Jap, and then two more popped up. He hollered for some of the 2d and some of the 1st Platoon men just moving up the hill, and they flushed everything clean of live Japs on the right flank.

Meanwhile the attack had moved rapidly on up the hill. Two of the machine guns that had delivered such a beautiful support fire dropped down into the attacking troops; the fire had almost stopped, the guns were nearly at the limit of their range, and Massey and Ralph Mesa caught bullets in the back. A shell fragment had hit Sergeant Brown in the hand as he and Lieutenant Thayer moved slowly up the hill. Thayer's leg was almost useless.

The leading scouts, Petres and Burroughs, had moved up on a little knoll and saw several Japs working on ammunition chests over to the left and behind the knoll. The Japs spotted them at once and opened fire. Petres fell and Burroughs ran back through some Japs to warn Lieutenant Thayer and the men. The light machine guns were brought up and moved over to the left flank, one set to fire to the left and the other set to fire uphill ahead. The BARs, Kenneth Stell, James M. Secrest, and Lawrence W. "Pappy" Ryker, moved up onto the hilltop and began returning the fire of a machine gun that had opened up below us. Corporal Okel Lockamy had just set his light machine gun up on the flank when he saw not fifty yards away a Jap light machine gun firing like mad down into the valley at Companies I and L moving across. Behind it about fifty yards and about twenty-five yards to the flank was a heavy, also pounding away at the troops in the valley. Neither crew had seen the Americans move up onto the hill, so intent were they on their firing. Lockamy directed his gunner to fire on the heavy, and he cut loose at the light crew with his carbine. He fired three shots and the three crew members slumped over behind their gun. Our light gun was in a good position, hard to spot immediately; and for the next few minutes he played the old machine-gun drill of "fall out one" with the Japs, and they were good at it, too. He got all set and fired a burst, and the first gunner slumped over. The Japs grabbed him and pulled him out of the way, and another gunner got behind the gun. Our gunner squeezed the trigger, and the officer fell out, too; they were very persistent but they had no idea where the fire was coming from.

Lieutenant Thayer warned us about the Japs at the bottom of the hill below us. We heard the wild yells as fifteen of them, led by an officer, came storming up the hill at us. The scene at the little hilltop was pure hell—grenades bursting, both machine guns blasting into the charging Japs; bayonets flashed, the .45s jumped in the hands of the machine gunners as the Japs got close. One of the Japs stood over Petres, who was wounded and lying about twenty yards in front of us, ready to bayonet him. Someone shot the Jap, but as he fell the weight of his body pushed the bayonet into Petres. The Jap officer screamed at his men, and waved his saber, then a BAR hurled a burst of slugs into his chest. The bitter little fight was over in minutes.

Over on the right flank James M. Gillock, Sergeant Edwin Dittenbir, Joseph Dias, and Private First Class Ferguson walked into a nest of Jap holes and were surrounded before they realized their position. They shot the first Jap that appeared; then the others opened up and the four men dove headlong into the nearest hole. Gillock got safely in the hole, and Dittenbir went right in behind him. Dias was hit and slid into the hole, and Ferguson was hit and groaning just outside. Dittenbir raised up from the bottom of the hole and was hit in the head, the bullet crashing between the rocks that made a small parapet around the hole. As other men in the platoons on the right moved over the hill and contacted the Japs, they began firing, and soon had the situation under control. Gillock had a crease under his eye from another bullet that had come through the parapet.

Lieutenant Thayer was getting sick from the wound in his leg, and the attackers held up in the little flat below the hill. They reorganized the platoons and ate their K chow. They had almost finished when the Jap artillery on the shelf above began pounding them. Sergeant Bacoch dashed over to the machine guns and directed fire against a 37 the Japs were trying to get into position near the edge of the shelf above. They could see the muzzle being pushed out over the edge and they opened fire, keeping that vicious snout back and out of sight. The mortars were set up and Corporal Dick Kastrup dumped round after round behind the shelf and finally silenced the big Jap gun firing in defilade behind the shelf.

As Companies I and L began to move over the hills to the left, the Japs withdrew completely off Sarana Nose, and by night the attackers were digging in on the top of the Jap stronghold. Jim Fish Valley was vulnerable. The Japs were being squeezed a little tighter.

Over the Hill

Corporal Dan H. Manges, Company L, 17th Infantry

"What were you busted for?" I asked Corporal Dan Manges, who only yesterday was Sergeant Manges.

"Well, I goofed off and went over the hill for three days, sir," he said.

"You are referring to the 'garrison hill,'" I said. "But you went over some hills on Attu, too, didn't you?"

"A couple," Manges said.

The first hill Manges went over, was in Massacre Valley, on May 14. We had started a big attack up the floor of Massacre Valley, against the Japs in Jarmin Pass, and on the hillsides around the pass, and they began to dump everything they had on us; mortars, machine guns, rifles, some mountain guns—the works.

Under this first impact of heavy fire the attacking troops bogged down. Company L was on the right of the attack, and Captain John E. Jarmin came running up to the front, trying to get the attack moving again. He shouted, "Who in hell are the leaders around here? Let's go!"

Corporal Manges was a leader. He jumped up and took off for the table in the mouth of the pass. He shouted for the men to follow as he ran, thinking that if they saw him heading out they would follow him. He ran through the fire, and among the mortar bursts without hitting the ground, until he stopped, out of breath, up on the table itself. He saw the Jap trench, and when a Jap raised up and looked at him he shot the Jap.

He shouted and waved for the men to come on up to the table. But he was alone and unheard. Artillery began to register on the table, began to blast along the Jap trench that ran across the lip of the table. Manges jumped from hole to hole dodging the bursts of the 105 shells. Most of the emphasis of the barrage was on the left of the table, and Manges was on the right, but enough was falling all over the thing to make anyone exposed extremely uncomfortable. For nearly an hour the 105s blasted and ripped at the tableland.

Eventually the barrage lifted. Again Manges waved and screamed down at the valley for the men to come on up. They were nearly two hundred yards behind him, and the machine guns were clipping the twigs off the little willow bushes over their heads.

Some of the Japs who had moved during the artillery barrage were coming back into position. From a trench over on the right of the pass, Japs began to fire. Manges looked back into the valley. He watched the Japs moving in on both edges, right and left. Suddenly he jumped up and turned around; then whoosh! he came off the hill and down into the valley.

On May 22 Manges went over the hill again. The 3d Battalion had made their big attack on Sarana Nose. Company L had moved up over the left side of the nose and had gotten well up on the hill before they encountered any stiff resistance. From positions down in Jim Fish Valley Jap machine gunners were firing along the left of the nose, supporting the Japs on the top of the nose itself. Manges and his squad were the left flank of the company as it moved up the hill, and the fire from the Japs ahead and fire from the valley below were giving the squad a bad time. Finally they spotted it, a Jap heavy machine gun, with a two-man crew, firing from the foot at the left side of a small hill. Manges crawled up and round the right side of the hill. The squad behind him covered several Jap snipers over on the right as he moved over the hill. Then he saw the two heads behind the heavy gun. He fired twice and killed both Japs. Manges jumped into the Jap position and tried to turn the heavy gun around, but he couldn't move it alone. He saw Sergeant Lester B. Thistle and hollered for him to come over. Between them they turned the gun around and opened fire on the Japs down in Jim Fish Valley.

Another dogface came in as I finished the notes. I must have looked very official for the newcomer asked Manges what was cooking. Manges said that we were just talking about the Battle of Attu. "Are you going to get a medal?" the new guy asked. Manges said: "Hell, you don't get medals for just going over the hill, fella." Manges and I grinned, and the new guy said: "I don't get it."

Direct Fire
Lieutenant John C. Patrick, Battery B, 49th Field Artillery Battalion

This was an artilleryman's dream. The same kind of a dream a fisherman has when the big trout he has tried to catch for three seasons in a row swims right into his landing net.

The battery had been set up on Bagdad Hill, to fire a preparatory barrage for the Doughboys' attack on Sarana Nose on May 22. It had been a long and good barrage, and the infantry was moving over the hill in the attack. Our immediate job was done, so the colonel called up and turned the battery loose, to fire at targets of opportunity.

This was the first time in all the fighting that the battery had been set up where we could actually see Jap positions and live Japs running around on the hills, so naturally we were all excited and anxious to get our licks in, where we could watch the results first hand.

We had picked as a base point the southwest end of Lake Cories, where a little tip of water lies closest to the foot of the mountain, and had registered on it the night before. We were studying the valley and the surrounding hilltops for targets, and we had fired several rounds at machine-gun positions here and there during the late afternoon. S-2, Captain Oscar M. "Nick" Doerflinger, had come up to the battery OP and we were making small talk about steaks and salads and the virtues of scotch over bourbon, when suddenly Nick stopped talking and said "Look!" There up the valley came five Japs, walking close together along a path that led around Lake Cories next to the mountain, and crossed directly over our base point. We all got the idea at the same instant I think. "It's a fifty-second flight," I said, referring to the shells from our guns. Nick began gauging the Japs' speed with his watch. It wasn't a legitimate artillery target, but it was just too damned good to miss the opportunity. The necessary data were phoned to the battery. . . . "Battery, one round. . . ." Nick was watching the Japs and his watch. . . . "Now! . . . Fire!" We heard all four of our guns roar behind the hill. . . . The next fifty seconds were endless. . . . The Japs continued to move along the path, without a pause, completely ignorant of the 110 pounds of high explosive already streaking through the sky . . . the little stretch of path grew shorter and shorter between the five Japs and the tip of the lake. . . . Now they were on it . . . now . . . NOW! A great flash ripped out of the very center of the tiny group, followed almost instantly by three other flashes, totally engulfing the five figures in a heaving mass of flying hunks of muck and smoke and rocks. The smoke hung in a big puff over the ripped area of our base point, and we could see five little piles of fabric lighter than the black holes over which they were scattered before the boom! baroomboom! of the explosions reached our ears. Probably no one but me remembers even hearing the explosions, because we were all cheering like a bunch of high-school kids at a track meet.

Patrolling the Heights

Corporal John B. Welde, Company F, 17th Infantry

Fog poured over the ridge tops like cold pea soup, and snow was driving into the tired faces of the soldiers and melting into icy rivulets that ran down inside the collars of their ragged rain jackets. It was Sunday, May 23, and the 2d Battalion of the 17th Infantry had moved up from Clevesy Pass and onto the high shelf near the ridge top along the left side of Jim Fish Valley. Somewhere over on the left, the Northern Force had moved onto the high ground too, and in the mountains to the front Japs huddled behind machine guns.

Captain Delbert L. Bjorck gave the patrol their orders. Corporal John Welde, Private Robert L. McArdle, and seven men looked up into the fog and stinging snow at the dimly outlined ridge top as Captain Bjorck spoke: The patrol was to try to contact the 32d Infantry troops moving in from Holtz Bay, to locate their outposts, and find the disposition of their front lines. They were to move along the ridge to their front about 1000 yards, where they would find a pass, then turn to the right. The 32d Infantry should be in that area. The men stamped in the piling snow as Corporal Welde replied, "No questions, sir, we're all set."

The nine men started out at about 1600 in the afternoon. The blizzard had increased and the men could see only five or six feet in any direction. "Anyway, the goddamn Japs can only see as far as we can," someone said as Welde led his men up the precipitous slope to the top of the ridge.

The ridge top was a typical Attu mountain. It was a knife-edged affair about three feet wide, and sloped away on each side of this narrow edge in almost vertical, jagged slopes. The enemy was somewhere in the fog and snow on the right. The men stumbled and slipped along on the icy rocks for about 500 yards. The soft silt between two rocks suddenly crumpled and two men fell over the side. They rolled a hundred feet down the side of the mountain and stopped against the rocks at the top edge of a huge snowbank. Corporal Welde heard their voices shouting up through the fog that they were OK, and the patrol moved on.

Welde, the BAR man, and one other man managed to crawl up a vertical incline that blocked the ridge, but Private McArdle slipped and rolled off the rock and fell twenty feet into a snowbank below. Ice was clinging to the rocks and the ground was piling with snow. Corporal Welde told the rest of the patrol to hold it up, he and the two men who had gotten across would go ahead, the rest should wait.

For about an hour the three men stumbled and crawled along the crest of the jagged ridge. Ahead, through the snow, they could see the dim outline of the basin and the pass. The ridge dropped sharply down. There was firing to the front. They stopped to listen. They could hear other firing coming from the left. Echoes and the fog and snow made it difficult to figure accurately where the fire was coming from. Captain Bjorck had said ". . . arrive at the pass, turn right. The 32d Infantry should be in that area." The Japs were somewhere on the right. There was firing to the front and to the left.

Corporal Welde decided to turn left, creep down into the pass and try to spot someone who was firing. His two men and he began climbing down on the left of the ridge. They moved cautiously, slowly, feeling their way through the fog and snow, stopping now and then to listen to the firing. They had worked down the mountain and were on a plateau about 400 yards from where the ridge sloped down into the pass. Suddenly, outlined against a big rock, they saw the rifle. They stopped and stared into the driving snow. A sentry was standing huddled against the dubious shelter of the rock, his back to the wind. They looked hard, he was only fifteen feet away, but with the fog and snow they were taking no chances on stumbling into the Jap lines. Then Welde called out, and the sentry grabbed his rifle and spun around to face them. Welde told him quickly that they were Americans and the password was exchanged; Welde even waved the orange panel he had brought in case they were spotted on a mountain top somewhere. It was the 32d Infantry OP. The sentry explained where the CP was and Welde started back. The sentry told the patrol the Japs were about 400 yards away in the pass at the foot of the ridge. Welde started, then he said, "Yes, we heard them firing." "Christ!" he thought, "We were heading right into the Jap lines up there."

At the CP they got hot coffee first and then a sketch of the outpost lines and the front lines, which they studied and left. "Nice afternoon for a walk, buddy," someone said as the three men left the CP. "Yeah, we always take walks in the hills on Sunday afternoons," Edward P. Jozefiak said as he slung his BAR and started after Corporal Welde.

The Japs were firing a few scattered shots into the fog below them as the patrol moved onto the ridge again. The snow was bad and the men were shivering and stumbling and cursing. Jozefiak slipped over the edge once and caught himself by plunging the butt of the Springfield he was carrying deep into the snow and hanging on. Welde had spelled him on the BAR; and if Jozefiak had fallen when he had the BAR he might not have stopped.

Two hours later the welcome sound of a rifle being snapped up to alert and a hostile voice calling "Halt!" through the fog let the patrol know that they were safe at home again. Welde reported his information and found that the other five men had come back after waiting a couple of hours on the cold ridge top. Another cup of hot coffee and some vigorous rubbing and a little determined cussing finally brought a tinge of red into the blue lips and hands of the patrol.

An Attu Sunday

First Sergeant Charles W. Laird, Company H, 32d Infantry

A little thing like a war going on couldn't stop First Sergeant Charles W. Laird from spending a good old American Sunday, although he admits it took a few field expedients to get it done. The battle had pushed through Clevesy Pass and down into Jim Fish Valley by Sunday, May 23. It was a very cold miserable morning; an icy drizzle of half rain, half snow was falling while Lieutenant Dean Galles and Sergeant Laird slopped around in the mud, digging in Company H's CP. They could keep their bodies warm but their hands and feet were freezing off. Sergeant Laird worked as long as he could, with mud sticking to his shovel, then he told Lieutenant Galles he was about to give up. He said he was going to take a walk and keep walking until he got warm. Lieutenant Galles told him to go ahead so Laird started off. He planned to visit all of his machine-gun squads, and during his tour he got off farther to the right than he planned. It was very foggy and unless you were careful you would suddenly look around and discover yourself lost. Laird did just that. He looked up into a draw in front of him and saw four well-hidden Jap tents. From the distance he couldn't be sure, but he thought he saw two men near one of the tents. The company had been firing into that area the evening before and Laird wasn't sure how far the riflemen had advanced. "Those men might be Japanese," was the cautioning thought he gave himself; but Jap tents always meant stores of dry socks, canned heat, and maybe matches and dry insoles. He decided to take a chance and go on to the tents.

When he got close enough to see some detail through the fog he saw smoke coming from the top of the nearest tent. He hurried up to it and then he heard American voices. He pulled back the flap and looked in. In the center of the tent in a large tin box some soldiers had built a small, very smoky fire. Sergeant R. L. "Pinky" Holman and Lieutenant William B. Frost from Company F were there and several others too, were huddled around the little fire. Their faces were grimy and whiskered and haggard, but they were smiling and muttering over the meager warmth of the fire. Pinky even had his shoes off and was painfully wiggling his doughy looking toes over the can. Laird went in and stood by the fire a few minutes.

Before long another character came in. He was just an ordinary looking soldier, beat-up, muddy, the weight of fatigue pulling hard at the edges of his face. He spoke to the men inside and added comments to the trickle of conversation about the fight, like any GI. Men were snooping through the litter in the tent, picking up a dry sock or a glove and then returning to the fire. For a small moment all the sound in the tent stopped and the newcomer was the only man standing. He said, "Well, it isn't exactly an appropriate place to hold a service, I guess, but this is Sunday. . . ." The circle of ragged roughnecks looked at him. No one spoke, and Sergeant Laird quickly thought, "What is this? Some GI pulling a wise one." Pinky courteously lowered his bare feet and shoved them down into his boots. Chaplain Clarence J. Merriman, the muddy, tired soldier, pulled out his small book of Scriptures and read. The circle of lined, gaunt faces watched the Chaplain, and they listened. They didn't hear the words, the words weren't important then. But they heard what each of them needed to hear for himself. And then as the helmeted heads bowed over their rifles, the Chaplain said the Lord's Prayer.

Lieutenant Frost coughed, and Pinky hung his feet over the fire again. The Chaplain said, "If you find any written documents or things around here give them to me and I'll take them to G-2." The men turned over several manuals and postcards and things to the Chaplain as he left to look for some matches. Church was over. Sergeant Laird went in search of matches himself, and he and the Chaplain and another fat soldier were in the tent across from the "chapel" when a Jap machine gun opened up. The tent popped as the bullets ripped into it and the paper on the floor hopped around like leaves in a whirlwind. The three men dived for the floor as another burst sang over their heads, tearing gashes in the fat boy's parka. The doorway was blocked by the fire so the Chaplain ripped a hole in the back of the tent and rushed through it, with the fat boy on his heels. Laird stayed low while the third burst struck, then he made a dash for the hole. Everyone else had miraculously disappeared. Laird jumped over a bank at the back of the tent and dashed to a creek bed in the flat below. He considered the possibility that his own guns were firing at him and thought he might even show himself and perhaps the firing would stop. He got up out of the creek and waved, then dived back into the creek bed as a burst of bullets ripped the tundra close to where he had been standing. For several long minutes he lay still, then slowly and carefully he began working his way down the creek bed toward Engineer Hill.

It was about twenty minutes after the first burst had hit the tent and Laird was on his belly moving across an exposed part of the creek bed when he saw a flash in the creek. His eyes lit up and he whistled through his teeth. The biggest trout he had ever seen had ducked under the bank right below where he was lying. Laird pulled up the sleeves of his shirt and jacket as high as he could get them and carefully slipped his outspread fingers into the water. Slowly he worked his hands over the bank and back under the overhanging grass and tundra. Then he felt the big fish. He made a grab with his right hand and caught the trout around the gills. After a round of violent splashes and grabs and grunts he rolled back from the creek holding a fine, big, solid three-and-a-half-pounder tight in both hands. He wanted to holler "Yippee!" and jump up but he remembered his little slant-eyed buddy with the machine gun. So, holding his fish tightly, he worked his way cautiously back along the creek until he was sure he was out of sight in the fog. Then he got up and quickly cut across to where Lieutenant Galles and the CP were located.

Lieutenant Galles was tickled to see the fish and suggested they roll it in mud and bake it. They had a helluva time. The mud wasn't the right kind and it kept crumbling off, and the fire wouldn't burn, but finally they got the fish baked and even without salt it was the best fish dinner either one of them had ever had. "Just like Sunday back home," Sergeant Laird was saying, "go to church in the morning and then go fishing, come home and have a good supper, and then . . ." a Jap 70mm. from somewhere up on the mountain had spotted them. A piece of shrapnel from the first shell ripped through a box of ammunition that Sergeant Laird had been sitting on. Lieutenant Galles looked up from his hole a few minutes later. "Laird, this may be like a Sunday back at *your* home," he said, and Sergeant Laird replied from his hole, "Well, I was going to add 'with some slight variations,' sir, but I was interrupted."

One-Man Army

Lieutenant Winfield Harvey Mapes, Headquarters, 3d Battalion, 17th Infantry

"Hell, I dunno. Just got all fed-up and disgusted and decided I'd get the damned thing over with, I guess." That was all that Fred M. Barnett of Company A of the 4th Infantry had to say about it, but you should have seen it.

It was the 23d of May. The big bend of Fish Hook Ridge was high on the right. The 2d Battalion of the 17th Infantry was up on the ridge and Company A of the 4th Infantry had moved across onto their left flank. Below the ridge two companies were moving across the rocks and snow toward Suicide Basin and the pass into the Chichagof area. From over on the right flank a Japanese machine gun, protected by a ring of riflemen, opened fire. The range and field of fire were perfect, and the Jap gun stopped the two companies in their tracks, flat.

The 1st Platoon of Company A was ordered to move down the mountain and knock out the Jap position so that the attacking companies could move ahead. The platoon worked their way arduously down the mountainside, slipping over snow-covered rocks and skidding down rock slides that sent small boulders bounding down the snow ahead of them. The Japs spotted them and opened fire. As they worked closer, the enemy opened up with an automatic rifle and pinned them against the rocks of the mountainside. The heavy machine gun continued to pound away at the attacking companies out in the rocky flat. No one moved for a long time; then quite suddenly a lone figure jumped up and ran across the open snow toward the nearest Jap hole. He had an M1 and a bunch of hand grenades. He threw a grenade into the first hole and began firing. He moved right on into the circle of Jap holes around the machine gun. Deliberately, he walked up to the edge of the holes one by one, looked in, then stepped back and fired or tossed a grenade. Nine times he did this; the 2d Platoon began a covering fire until the Jap machine gunners swung their gun around and opened up. He jumped into a Jap hole and ducked. Then he raised up and fired his rifle. Three quick shots and the machine gun was silent. The platoon moved down then and finished the job, mopped up the position.

Barnett is just a guy in Company A, 4th Infantry, who said, "Hell, I just got all fed-up and disgusted; and decided I'd get the damned thing over with," and voiced the words of a nation.

Pin-Up Girl

Sergeant Benjamin W. Wolfington, Battery C, 49th Field Artillery Battalion

We were firing at Hill 4. That didn't mean much to us back at the gun, except we knew it was a hill, and the Japs were on it, and our boys were on three sides of it, making a kind of U and our battery was firing at the Japs into the open end of the U. We were using high-angle fire, and it was a damned tricky mission, and the exec and the chief—well, all of us—were nervous as a bunch of hens. We could only fire one gun at a time because we had to fire right in there and couldn't take a chance on controlling a battery dispersion; yet we had to drop enough stuff at one time to make it effective. So we fired one gun as fast as we could for as long as we could, then we'd switch to another gun. No. 1 had started firing at 0800, then it got hot, so No. 2, started to fire. It was getting on toward 0900 when the exec hollered, "No. 3 . . . shell HE, charge seven . . . fuze quick, base deflection left 220, SI 360, one round, elevation 900 . . . Fire!" and we were off! Swede, our No. 2 shoved the big shell in, and wham! away it went toward Hill 4. "Betsy" jumped, rocked back into position, and continued to smile. Betsy was our pin-up girl. I don't know who she was really, but she was a dish of cheesecake all right, and we had her pasted on the rear end of a counter-recoil. She was an inspiration to us all, her smooth white gams were crossed coyly and her pretty smiling eyes seemed to look at each of us personally. Corporal Ralph J. Yorio, the gunner, had strapped a life jacket around the trail on his side and he used it like a saddle never taking his eye off the sight, "Boy, Betsy is gonna get a rough ride t'day!" The exec shouted, "No. 3, six rounds . . . fire!" And we swung into action. Swede had his own personal way of getting the shell into the breach of the gun, and he was a damn good No. 2. He'd lay the round over the bend in his left arm and shove it into the breach with his right hand. And now he was swinging like a pendulum, receiving the new round over his arm, while the gun bammed back in recoil, and shoving the new round in before the gun had returned to battery. "No. 3, six rounds . . . fire!" The exec kept repeating it mechanically, and we were batting this order to completion every fifty seconds. The sandbags around our position echoed the muzzle blast until it beat on our ears like a hammer. Even the waste stuffed into our ears did not prevent us from going deaf. The crew were shouting to each other now and hearing orders like voices are heard under water. Fifteen times we had executed the order "No. 3, six rounds . . . fire!" and still it came. The gunner had never left his lifejacket saddle but he looked up at Betsy once and hollered, "Hang on, kid, this is only the beginning." His eye was getting black from the beating the sight had given it. Swede's face was dripping with perspiration and a big wet spot was showing through his shirt. "Want some relief, Swede?" I hollered. "Hell no," Swede shouted back, and he swung again to shove a round in. "I could do this all day, and all night too, if it's helping those guys up there."

I had drained the recoil oil three times already, and the little knob on the gauge was sticking out again too damned far. She was getting hot, and the exec was shouting, "No. 3, six rounds . . . fire!"

The paint was getting sticky on the tube and heat radiated from the gun like a stove. The gunner looked over at No. 1 and grinned. "Better raise her a couple of mils, Allen.[7] I think the muzzle is beginning to droop," he shouted. Swede shoved a round in the breach and swore. Betsy was no longer smiling. Her pretty pins were hidden from the knees up in a film of oil that had oozed from the counter-recoil, covering her from the head down. "No. 3, six rounds . . . fire!" We bent to it. Swede shoved the fifth round in. Oil was dribbling out of the counter-recoil in a little river now. I checked the knob on the end of the gauge. Swede shoved the sixth round in. The gun whammed into recoil, and oil spurted from everywhere around the counter-recoil, bathing Yorio and Allen. "No. 3, cease fire!" Yorio, the gunner, and Lawrence Allen, No. 1, grinned like a pair of pickaninnies and wiped the oil off their faces. We tallied out 118 rounds in a little over forty minutes. Swede tenderly swabbed the oil from Betsy's lovely legs and with a tiny corner of a big gob of waste, he wiped her face. She was pretty beat-up, but she was smiling, too—and damned if I won't believe to my dying day that she winked at that big ugly Swede.

The Attack on Fish Hook Ridge
Sergeant Donald W. Wonn, Company I, 32d Infantry

The day of May 24 was the toughest day I remember during the battle. It is strange but I can only remember pieces of the day, isolated happenings, almost without continuity. I guess that's natural though; there was so much going on and so fast that it was like a three-ring circus with no holds barred, death on every side so close and so often that a man just got sort of dazed by it. That was the first day that we tried to get across what the boys called Suicide Basin. It was a big flat, scattered with boulders and huge rocks, just at the foot of the Bahai.

We started out from around Hill 4 and moved along the ridge line through the damned wind and cold until we got squared off above the basin, and then we got orders to attack the Japs in the basin and on the hill behind it. We moved out on the right of Company K and got out maybe five or six hundred yards. Then suddenly all hell broke loose on us. I remember running through several large explosions and hearing lots of bullets crack around, and then I was on my

[7]Pfc. Lawrence A. Allen.

belly behind a rock with Staff Sergeant James R. Carney, Dick Schuester, and a couple of others. The next thing I knew Carney was taking off his helmet. There was a hole in the front and a hole in the back, so far down that I kept looking at his head. I didn't think the bullet could go that way and not hit him. Carney swore. "The damned little yellow sonuvabitch! Now I can't even wash my face." "Hell, you're damned lucky, fellow," I told him, and about that time there was a crash around my ears and my helmet gave a lurch. I pulled it off and a bullet had gone through my own helmet in a similar place, ripping my wool cap clear through and not even touching my head. We compared the holes quickly and lined up where the sniper should be. The sniper fired again, and we saw him, but Schuester fell dead beside us with a bullet hole down low on his helmet. The Jap was 300 yards away and had a telescope sight on his rifle. One of the men had a BAR and the next time the sniper stuck his head up the BAR almost cut it off.

I remember getting up and leaving Schuester and running forward again. Lieutenant Paul Evans and Private First Class Walter C. J. Carter had gotten out ahead of the rest of the platoon and Carter ran right into a burst of machine-gun fire. He turned and fell, and the Jap fired again and hit him again. Lieutenant Evans hit the ground. The Jap fired again and three bullets cut across Lieutenant Evans' neck, part of his ear was shot off, and chips of rocks destroyed one eye and almost closed the other one. He had fallen slightly to the side and about twenty feet in front of a great rock as big as a house. It was wonderful cover and about half the platoon was behind the rock.

Over on the left Company K was getting hell kicked out of it. They began to fall back under the mauling the Jap guns were giving them. We were almost out of ammunition and it was getting late. As Company K withdrew we picked up part of their ammunition. Lieutenant Evans knew we were behind him and he kept asking if we thought he could get back. It was a tough spot; the Japs had it pinned down so hard it was sure death to move out into the open. We told him to lay still and not move, and we'd get him when it got dark.

From somewhere behind the company lineman dashed into the shelter of the rock, dragging his wire reel. He had a line into the company CP, but the man who had the phones had been hit. It was nearly dark and the firing had almost subsided, so we hollered back toward men scattered behind us to get another phone and bring it up. Lieutenant Evans was carried in behind the rock. It was 2300. Finally the phone arrived and we got back to the CP. I called Captain Thomas B. "Tommy" O'Donnell. I told him we were out there alone, that Company K had pulled out, and that we were short of ammunition. I wanted to know if we should try to hold the rock that night. He said he'd send another platoon up with extra ammunition and we should hold right there until morning.

The other platoon came up with ammunition and we organized the defense of the position. One OP was established in a small rock out about twenty yards in front of the big one, and a man with a Springfield and a man with an M1 crawled out to the rock. It was cold and dark by the time we were set. The men huddled against the rock and some of them tried to sleep between spasms of shivering. I must have dozed myself because the next thing I remember I was jumping about five feet away from a rock as a huge explosion ripped the silence of the night to tatters. I thought a 105 had landed in our laps. It was the little OP we had set up. At 0300 they had heard a party of Japs moving across the basin. They were rattling among the rocks and jabbering like they were drunk. Our men had waited until they were sure where the Japs were and what they were doing; then the man with the Springfield had fired an antitank grenade at them. In the morning we saw them, three Japs and a light machine gun ripped and scattered all over a pile of rocks about thirty yards beyond the OP. The boy had scored a direct hit on them in the dark.

In the comparative quiet of the early morning we had picked up Carter. He had twenty bullets in him. Plans were being set for a push against the pass on the 26th, so we were ordered to withdraw and it was nearly 1100 before all the boys got back in, just a short while before Captain Tommy caught his second Jap slug, the one that killed him, while he was observing the pass and planning the next attack.

Air Support
Private Anthony G. Simonic, Company G, 32d Infantry

The big bombers thundered power as they roared over the heads of the battered Infantrymen below. May 24 a big attack on the area of the Fish Hook mountain was being launched, and the bombers were swooping in to blast the Japanese positions and soften them up for the attack. "Make soup out of 'em, baby," a guy hollered at a big plane.

The targets had been marked with artillery smoke as the big planes zoomed by. It was a wonderful sight, the limitless power of the big machines that could get higher than the Japs for a change and drop great explosives on them. Everyone cheered the planes and put out the orange panels to mark friendly front lines. The planes flew up Sarana Valley, filling the canyons with roaring power; then the crump! crump! of the big bombs blasting into the Japs set everybody wild with joy. The planes circled and flew over once more, directly over. The muddy soldiers, looking up from their foxholes, could see the doors of the bomb bays, and the gunners crouched behind their caliber .50s.

Again the heavy crump! crump! of the bombs bursting and tearing big thirty-foot craters in the ground made everyone happy.

Then the planes flew back in the opposite direction. They were swinging over, directly over, the 2d Battalion. "Don't do it! Not here!" These thoughts were running through men's minds as the planes came closer, their path leading right over the 2d Battalion. The doors on the bomb bays were open. The planes were close. "Holy good God, they did it!" The bombs hurtled from the belly of the first big plane, whistling as they arched toward the ground, and the soldiers scrambled for the mud in the bottom of their holes. The big bombs landed blooey! right in the middle of the battalion. Mud and gobs of tundra flew in all directions. The bombers flew over and bombed the Japs; then, on the way back, they bombed the 2d Battalion again. Runners were dispatched, desperately, to check panels, phones were ringing, and radios were being shouted into. The mission was called off. The reserve companies had displayed panels too, and over on the windward flank a little smudgy fire sent smoke across the front. No one was hurt and nothing was damaged but nerves and morale. One machine gunner in Company H was dug out, along with his gun, from under a couple of tons of mud and tundra; and a boy from Company E had a slight tendency to stagger for a few hours afterward.

"Off we go, into the wild blue yonder!" Yeah? Nuts!

Mission Accomplished

Sergeant Neils Jensen, Company A, 17th Infantry

For several days units of the 3d Battalion of the 32d Infantry and the 1st Battalion of the 17th Infantry had been receiving a lot of troublesome fire from a nest of Japs who had dug themselves in under a huge rock set near the base of a ridge. The rock was as big as a large mess hall, and along one side a hill of dirt and grass sloped up about halfway to the top. The rock was larger at the top than at the bottom, and the Japs had dug in like badgers right at the base, and even tunneled under the sloping hill of soil, so that they could cover the open ground around the rock from any direction. The overhanging rock above them sheltered them from mortar and artillery fire like a great stone roof. It was a good position; 60s, 81s, and even artillery could do nothing more than shake them up, and the trench and tunnel were protected from fire of machine guns and rifles.

Troops were moving in along the ridges to the right, and were preparing to join the forces on the left for a drive against the pass through the Fish Hook and the mountains overlooking Chichagof Harbor; but still the Japs held out under their big stone mushroom and continued to hold up and harass the companies trying to get to the high ground behind the rock.

Early on the bitter morning of May 25, Sergeant Neils Jensen and ten cold, haggard, determined men left the CP of Company A with instructions to knock out the Jap emplacement under the rock. Sergeant Joe V. Alvarez was second in command, and as they passed the OP and started down the little hill onto the open ground he stopped the patrol. Sergeant Jensen gave them their orders. They were short and plain. The patrol would advance straight toward the rock, keeping spread out. When they got to a little rise out on the flat, Alvarez and six men would cover the rock while Jensen, Bert E. Roe, and Joseph T. Venuti worked up close enough to grenade the trench. They moved out.

A few scattered shots were being fired along other parts of the line, but the Japs were ominously silent. The patrol got to the rise. The seven men crawled up to the firing positions and lined their sights on the rock. Jensen and his two men moved on. The three spread out; Jensen moved to the left toward a small draw. As he dropped down the near side of the draw he was covered, but as he started up the other side he could look up and see the trench under the rock. He thought for an instant that he would get it there. He was wide open, like a duck on a pond. But the Japs under the rock held their fire. Venuti and Roe had gone to the right and were moving in. Jensen crawled out of the draw and began to walk toward the rock. He walked slowly and carefully, ready to dive for the ground at the first sign of a machine gun. He walked closer and closer toward the trench and still the Japs didn't fire. He could almost look down into the trench. Venuti was on the other side of the little sloping hill, walking toward the rock. Jensen was within eight feet of the trench. There, inside, rolled in blankets, with a wool cap down over his ears, sat a Jap. His rifle was leaning against the bank of the trench, his head was slumped down, and he had his back toward Jensen. A few yards away squatted the Jap heavy machine gun.

Jensen had come up very quietly. He raised his rifle, but he didn't fire. Something made the Jap stir; he started, then turned his head around and stared at Jensen over his shoulder. Jensen fired into his back and the Jap turned his face toward the muddy wall of the trench again. Slowly he sagged forward. Jensen fired again and the Jap straightened out. Venuti was firing from the other end of the tunnel, several rounds in rapid succession. He had been firing to block his end of the tunnel when he heard Jensen fire.

Together, they checked the Jap trench all around the rock. There was no food and the effect of the pounding the rock had received was obvious. It was skirted with shell holes and jagged fragments. One Jap, dead for several days, was sprawled outside the trench and another body was huddled in a corner under two rifles.

It was very cold. The rest of the patrol came up to see the Jap trench. Nobody said much. Firing was increasing down the line so the patrol returned to make a report: Mission accomplished.

Mortar Accident

Sergeant Charles N. Taggart, Company M, 32d Infantry

The troops had tried to crack Fish Hook Ridge the day before, on the 24th, and had been beaten back by the Jap machine guns along the ridge and the pass; so we were spending the 25th pounding hell out of their positions, softening them up for an attack the next day. We had been firing hot and heavy all morning, and the tube of our 81 was getting sticky from the heat; but we had a few more targets to go, so we cracked another cloverleaf[8] and started after them.

We were all set, the gunner ordered fire, and they slid the shell in just like they had done so many times before; but this time nothing happened. We raised up and peeked down the tube; about eight inches down from the muzzle was the nose of the HE shell. She had hung up. Sergeant Fred Rivas came over to unload it; he began beating along the sides of the tube after he had gotten the squad back away from the gun, but the shell was stuck tight. He decided to kick the base of the tube a couple of times to see if he couldn't dislodge it that way. He moved the guys back again and began kicking the tube. The shell slid down the tube all right, but instead of the kind of Bongk! a mortar shell makes as it flies out, the whole works exploded with a big blam! Sergeant Rivas was hit badly, and he died while we carried him down the hill. Platoon Sergeant Frank J. Chiorso was hit, too. The explosion blew about two feet off the base of the tube.

It was peculiar how it made us feel. Jap shells had burst around but that was

---

[8]A container holding three rounds of mortar ammunition.

OK. This thing made us feel vaguely like we had been let down by a buddy or something.

Passing the Ammunition

Lieutenant Darwin M. Krystall, Battery B, 49th Field Artillery Battalion

I was a forward observer during part of the heavy fighting and all day I had lain in the OP calling my battery, time after time, for the old "Battery, eight rounds" and getting it, too, smack on the target. I even cussed them out a few times when I thought they were a little slow in pooping the rounds out. Often during the fighting the Japs held positions in places where it was almost impossible to get to them with anything but artillery because the ground was naked as Adam; and so the 105s were pounding away almost constantly at one target or another while the Doughboys got up from behind little knobs in the ground that wouldn't adequately hide a small jackrabbit, and moved in closer.

But in the heat of a good fight you forget that "Battery, eight rounds" means hauling thirty-two heavy shells of 54 pounds apiece (almost a ton) a couple of miles uphill, over gorges and holes and mud knee-deep to a tall giraffe. This fact was brought home to me very vividly one night. It was raining and miserable and cold. The guns were set up several hundred yards away from the engineers' quagmire, quaintly called a road, and were on a hillside that had been cut by cat traffic until, with all tundra gone, the mud made it a horror to cross. The cats hauled ammunition as close to us as they could get and then it was hand-carried from there to the guns' positions. And all day long the men had been slaving across the mud, up the hill and down again, carrying terrible food for the ravenous 105s. The men were exhausted, but still the command, "Battery, eight rounds," continued to come in.

One little man in Service Battery, a fine worker and an excellent, cheerful soldier normally, was sodden with sweat and rain and fatigue when I saw him struggling through the mud uphill with a single round of 105 on his shoulder. Its 54 pounds pushed his feet almost to the knees in the sticky mud and bent his back. He was nearing the gun position when he heard the exec shout, "Battery, eight rounds." He stopped and straightened up. The gun roared over his head. Wham! One round . . . Wham! Two rounds . . . Wham! Three rounds. The little man raised his clenched fist . . . Wham! five rounds. He was shouting "Go on! Go on! Burn it up, you bastards, burn it up!" Wham! seven rounds . . . Wham! He had bent over and was tramping on up through the mud, his one round of 105 hanging over his shoulder. Hell, like a cross, I thought.

Advancing on the Fish Hook — 1

Sergeant Donald W. Wonn, Company I, 32d Infantry

The attack was going good. I guess we were a little cocky about it. The Japs had taken a terrible pounding from our artillery and 37s and mortars the day before, on the 25th, and Company I had moved down off the ridge and crossed the basin and had started up onto the table to the left of the pass with practically no resistance. We had been scrambling up the 150-foot incline below the bench, and were nearly to the top before the Japs up there gave us any trouble. Then one of them jumped up and ran out to the edge and tossed three grenades down along our front. Two of them went bouncing down the hill past us, but one went off right beside a man over on the left, and it seemed like a miracle when he jumped up and started on up the hill. We threw several grenades ourselves, and the Japs tossed a couple of them back at us. So we sizzled them for a while after that.

Over on the right Sergeant George W. Mirich and his buddy, Private Charles G. Keyes, had a little trouble, but better footing, and they got to the bench ahead of the rest of the gang. There was a big rock right above where they went over the edge, and Keyes saw a Jap run around behind it. The men tried to stop him but Keyes ran around the rock after the Jap and he was shot through the neck. He fell and slid a long way back down the snow on the hill; Mirich watched him sliding down the snow. A Jap near Mirich jumped out of some rocks and started to run and Mirich shot him several times. Then he rushed, all alone, across the bench toward the nearest Jap hole. Several of us were just coming up to the edge of the bench as he fired into the trench. He was standing over the Jap trench firing almost straight down; he fired again and the empty clip hopped out of his rifle with a cling! Mirich didn't wait to load again. He jumped into the trench and went to work. He made a furious lunge with his bayonet and it snapped off near the handle, leaving the blade jammed into the Jap. He clubbed his rifle and for a few moments the heavy butt rose and fell above the top of the trench as the raging Mirich clubbed the Japs to death in the hole; until a bullet ripped into his arm and he went down.

About ten men reached the top of the bench as Mirich fell, and then all the Jap emplacements were easily visible. For a few minutes the turmoil was terrific. Japs raised up from everywhere, throwing grenades and firing at point-blank range. Over on the right a BAR was chattering frantically. Sergeant James R. Carney jumped from hole to hole, bayoneting and shooting every Jap he could find. John F. Wendt jumped into a hole, then suddenly jumped out again and fired into it, then jumped back in. The supporting machine guns began to crack bullets over our heads at positions up above us, and from somewhere across the basin a Jap machine gun opened up on the bench. The men took cover with the dead Japs in the foxholes, and we tried to reorganize.

The Jap held us for nearly an hour before he was spotted and knocked out. It was getting late in the evening and the cold was numbing. But each man knew that if we didn't get the Bahai this time we'd have to move back and have the whole thing to do again tomorrow.

We moved out into the open and started up the ridge. Company K was moving up into the pass as we swung up onto the high ground into defilade from the Jap machine guns behind the pass. The ridge was narrow and steep and rugged. It was another of the now familiar razor-edged mountains that slope up steeply on both sides to a sharp edge that provides only room for men to walk along in single file. Fifteen men had stumbled and cursed past a hidden dud, then a man from the 17th stepped on it. It was a 60, our own and one of a bad lot. It exploded, nearly disemboweling the man and cutting others' legs badly. The men, jittery on the mountain's narrow trail and conscious of their vulnerability, all thought we had come under fire by Jap artillery and hit the snow for cover. It took a lot of prodding by Colonel Finn and the noncoms to get the column moving again.

The head of the column had almost reached the high point on the ridge before a Jap machine gunner picked us up. He fired a couple of bursts when Reuben E. Andersen, our BAR man, saw the flash of the gun. He ran forward a few steps and crouched behind a rock. When the flashes came again he fired, and with a few quick bursts emptied his magazine into the Jap position.

It was getting dark, and from below we could hear the explosion of grenades and the staccatto pounding of a BAR firing long, rapid bursts.

Company K was fighting in the pass almost directly below us. We figured we had pulled a sneak, that the Japs had left the ridge unprotected and we were almost in a position to fire down onto the backs of the Japs holding up Company K, when a grenade went sizzling through the air from below the crest of the hill and rolled down the opposite side to explode somewhere below, just like "ante-over." It startled us. Several men fired down the mountain in the direction from which the grenade had come, and Corporal Gilbert D. Montenegro and Andersen hit the ground and tossed grenades. The grenades rolled past the Jap emplacement and the two Japs began shouting "Friend, don't throw grenades. Friends!" We thought for a moment they might be Americans, but Montenegro began to swear in violent Spanish and the Japs answered in violent Japanese; so Montenegro rushed to the edge of the precipice and threw two grenades directly into the little snow trench while Andersen sprayed it with the BAR. It turned out to be a small affair with two Jap snipers in it and nothing more. But by then it was so dark we couldn't be sure. We sent back along the column for more grenades, and for the next few minutes we pulled pins and rolled hand grenades down the mountain into the darkness. It was not until the next morning that we found out what had really happened. Most of the grenades missed the target, which was the small snow trench just below the crest of the ridge, but almost all of them that had missed had rolled on down the hill fifty feet and had fallen into a larger Jap emplacement that we hadn't seen at all. There were eight mutilated bodies in it the next morning.

We had brought extra ammunition along up the ridge and consequently we could not carry our sleeping bags. So as the night wore on we got colder and colder. The wind blowing across the nose of the ridge drove the cold right into the center of our bodies, and huddle and shrink as we would there was always an ear or the back of a neck or a wrist that was being stung by the wind until the whole body was quivering. Andersen was on the nose of the hill covering the only possible route to the ridge top from the Jap side, and from time to time he squeezed off a burst just to discourage any enterprising Nip. It was nearly 0300 before they got the machine guns up and in position, and at 1000 the next morning Company L came shivering up the hill to relieve us. We were too damned cold and hungry by that time to even shiver.

Advancing on the Fish Hook — 2

Sergeant Glenn E. Swearingen and Sergeant Earl L. Marks,
Company K, 32d Infantry

It was the second attempt to take the Bahai. We had tried once before on May 24 and we had been beaten back hard. Now, on the 26th, we were going to try it again.

Company I was on our right working down the ridge, in front of the pass and across to the left, and we were working right up into the pass itself. The Japs had suffered from the beating our artillery had given them, and the casualties scattered over the ground proved it. Company I was busy dodging bullets and flushing Japs out of foxholes on a shelf to our left now, as we moved up into the mouth of the pass. A machine gun opened up from the flank and pinned us down until Company I spotted him and knocked him out. We were just below the Jap positions ourselves now, and Pete Adams and Sergeant Swearingen spotted two Japs in a hole. Pete shot one and Swearingen shot the other; then one of their buddies began to fire at us from some place so we made a dash for some cover. Adams jumped into a hole with a Jap in it by mistake and the Jap had a light machine gun. Pete still doesn't know exactly what happened then, but he did grab the machine gun and throw it out of the hole. Then he jumped out himself and started hollering for Swearingen who shot the Jap and then jumped back in his own hole.

After a few minutes we started on into the pass. Our own heavy machine guns were supporting from the rear and suddenly on a rock over our heads came a helluva clatter. I don't know what the boys were shooting at but for a minute there was what you might call damned close support! He was hitting the rocks right over our heads. The BAR man, James H. Byers, and Swearingen and I moved to the left into a little draw and traveled up it a ways. Just as we were coming out of it we spotted a Jap machine gun. Byers cut down on it with the BAR and got off a couple of bursts, when the BAR jammed. The gunner was getting back on his gun just as Swearingen lined his M1 up, and got him with it.

There were a lot of Jap foxholes along the table in front of the pass, but most of the Japs in them were dead, either from our artillery or the machine guns. Sergeant William Marcotte moved his 3d Squad up on our left and he had quite a wild and quick skirmish with about eight Japs who suddenly jumped up from some place. Two of the Japs tried to run. One of them was shot and toppled over the edge of a big snowbank and rolled down it. The whole battle seemed to stop for a moment while everybody took pot shots at the Jap rolling down the hill. But we got down to business again, but fast. A Jap raised up right beside us with a grenade sizzling in his hand. Swearingen took a quick shot and the Jap fell back in the hole just an instant before the grenade went off, and when it did go off it blew up two others in the same hole.

The battle that day was a strange thing. The Japs were beat-up pretty badly and offered only token resistance for quite some time. Then when we got them cornered or there was a bunch of them together, suddenly the fight would flare up and be hot as hell for a few minutes. The farther we went into the pass the worse it got. Once Private First Class Joe P. Martinez got caught in one of those hot spots and it made him mad. He had a BAR and he got to running from hole to hole spraying hot lead into each one until his BAR was empty. Then he grabbed an M1 from somebody and went on like a wild man with that. He was a tornado that day, too much of a one I guess.

We finally got whittled down to the point where there were 6 BARs and 18 riflemen but we were well into the pass. It was getting cold as hell and the incline was almost 45 degrees up to the crest at the high point in the pass. We had some trouble with snipers dressed in white and they kept pecking at us as we advanced. Swearingen and I finally spotted them and we did a little countersniping. We zeroed in with the tracers and got all set and killed three of them in a few minutes.

Finally we got to the top of the pass. We discovered that just at the high point there was a cliff about 15 feet high that dropped down the other side and it was a slight overhang. The Japs had a trench at the bottom of this overhang and we had a pretty hot little fight right there for a few minutes. Then Joe Martinez, all of a sudden, ran up the crest and put one foot out on a rock that jutted out beyond the edge a ways and started blasting the trench with his BAR. He stood there it seemed like an hour, exposed wide open and loaded and fired until the magazine was empty. Then he slammed in a new magazine and fired again. He loaded two or three times and then we heard it, a kind of crack and thoomp! Martinez fell backwards toward us. Before we could help him the Japs began tossing grenades at us, and we began tossing grenades back at them. We almost lost another BAR man when a grenade went off right beside him, but he wound up with a tiny fragment in his hip and a big bruise. And I thought for a second we had lost the whole outfit when a grenade went off in a box of Jap TNT that Staff Sergeant Vola C. Mounce was lying behind. It just scattered yellow powder all over him. Corporal Lester L. Hildebrand was creased and Leroy C. Strand was hit in his trigger finger. It was all over in a couple of minutes: six or eight grenades each way.

We were sure Martinez was dead but James F. La Voy said he saw his hand move. We crawled up to where he was lying. He had been hit through the edge of his helmet, a big jagged wound, and some of the brain tissue was torn out. We pulled him off the crest and cut his pack and gear off. Adams and Swearingen came up and Sergeant Earl Marks to try to move him back to the weapons platoon.

Swearingen put his jacket under Martinez, and he was starting to moan. We left Adams to watch him and we went back to get some help. We finally managed to get him to the weapons platoon but there were no litters around. We tried to get one but there weren't any so we decided to leave him until morning and move him back then. It was getting dark and the hill was steep. We'd kill him sure if we tried to take him down that hill without a litter.

We went back up to the crest and up the side of the hill away from grenade range and rested. We checked up and found we were out of grenades. That was something that bothered us. We were always running low. We had no damned place to carry extra ones except maybe in an extra canteen cover.

Daniel H. Schauff went back down the steep hill through the pass with a Jap shelter half and after a while he came back carrying the shelter half full of grenades. It was dark but we decided to blast hell out of the Japs anyway, so we crept up to the crest of the pass and pulled out the pins. We let the grenades sizzle for about three counts and then tossed them over. The Japs retaliated with some of their own grenades and the flashes kept the whole pass lit up for a while. We gave each other a damned rough few minutes that night.

We had outposted the pass, and things had quieted down. In the night it began to snow and we damned near froze to death. The next morning we found that the Japs who weren't dead had pulled out. We went on through the pass with practically no trouble, and on the way we counted 14 dead Japs in one trench and 26 in another.

Platoon Action

Lieutenant Eugene M. Reagan, Company D, 32d Infantry

Lieutenant Eugene Reagan was telling me about his platoon. Well, I don't figure they're much better or much worse than most others, but I'll go to war with them again—tonight if need be. . . .

I didn't need to ask why. The reason was in Reagan's voice: My platoon was sent up the hill with Company C when they climbed Gilbert Ridge to attack Point Able on the night of May 18. It was a long steep climb and we started at midnight with all our machine-gun equipment and lots of ammunition. It was a nine-hour climb for us and the men were so tired that at each break they just collapsed on their faces in the snow to rest.

At 0830 the top of Gilbert Ridge was in sight. And, by hell, we were tuckered out after lugging guns and tripods and ammunition chests up that mountain since midnight. We fell on the top of the ridge and relaxed. No one said a word. We just lay there. I remember how strange it struck me that there had been no beefing all the way up.

We had been at the top about five minutes when a patrol which had gone on ahead returned and said we were needed up in front. I told the men I hated to move them but by God we had to go set up.

Edward Hurt, one of my gunners, said, "Well, let's go, boys. This is no dry run." They stumbled to their feet, picked up their loads, and moved off without a word. I noticed a sparkle starting to show in some very tired eyes.

The old adage of "an army travels on its stomach" must have deep roots in truth if the actions of Corporal Carol E. Meadows on May 26 is any indication.

We were supporting an attack from Cathedral Rock toward Buffalo Ridge that afternoon. I had an OP on a little rise with one section of the guns on the left of the men and the other section on the right. We had opened fire ten minutes prior to the jump-off and were smacking the Jap positions good and hard. Then the Doughboys started out and the Japs saw them coming and started returning our fire. Bullets were snapping all over my OP and into the ground on both sides. The whole hill was being covered with a terrific, determined barrage to stop the attack and silence our guns. Holy-damn-smoke! I was scared to death! I looked over and saw Corporal Meadows. He was edging out of his hole and looking my way. I couldn't figure what had happened. Maybe a gun had been knocked out, or a gunner killed. But I could still hear both guns hammering away in that section below me. Corporal Meadows was in the open now, worming his way toward the OP, his belly and head flat on the ground, sliding forward, bullets kicking up rock and mud all around him. I didn't want him up on the OP with me; there was too much stuff hitting up there as it was. So I inched out of my hole and pushed myself down off the little rise in the ground.

Meadows was within shouting distance now and I was excited anyway so I hollered, "Corporal, what in the goddamn hell do you want now?" He looked up from under his helmet and asked, "Sir, what time are we going to draw our rations today?"

The next day we had been ordered to displace forward following a successful attack. The only rub was that the forces on the left had been held up and had not moved as far down as they should have, so the left flank was still uncertain. We knocked our guns down and I went forward to make a reconnaissance. A sniper went to work on us but by that time we had learned not to let that hold us up. I had finished my reconnaissance and looked back toward the old position, and sure enough, here came my first section, right on the ball, boy! They moved out into the open and a Jap gun cut loose on them. They all went down; but none was hit and they crawled into a little draw where they had cover. They were safe enough there but every time they tried to get out of it they drew a burst from our friend the Jap on the left.

Well, I couldn't help them, or even signal to them if I had had anything to offer, but the 1st Squad, acting on their own, had found a tiny wrinkle in the ground that led out of the draw near to the place where I wanted the guns to go in. First I saw Corporal Frederick C. Boodleman, flat on his belly, inching along this wrinkle. Then came William I. Boatman, the gunner, and behind him came Charles J. Kaczanowicz, No. 2. They were dragging their gun, knocked down into low-mount position, between them. All flat on their bellies, I don't think they had 10 inches' clearance, and the Japs were firing frantically just over their backs, ripping hunks of sod and pebbles off the lip of the little wrinkle of ground.

It seemed hours that they inched along, three men and a gun. I expected any minute to see them stop, killed. They had quit crawling and for a long time they lay there without a move that I could see. The Jap was firing only short periodic bursts and he seemed to be hitting a little way behind them. Then suddenly all three of my boys sat up, propped their gun up and put her in action. They just simply commenced trading fire with that sonuvabitch and flat-back froze him out! He'd fire and they'd all duck. Then they'd raise up, make a quick traverse, and fire right back. Soon they weren't ducking anymore but were firing steadily.

The 2d Squad moved up fast under this cover and set up where I wanted them. Then they got in action and covered the 1st Squad. Then the 1st Section fired together and the second moved up, clear sailing.

The hair on the back of my neck didn't lie down for three days, I reckon; but we got into position.

I don't figure they're much better or much worse than most others but I'll go to war with them again—tonight if need be.

The Rule of Chance

Captain Charles W. Murphy, Jr., Company C, 32d Infantry

Many strange and unpredictable things happen in combat. It's the greatest gamble in the world because all the chips are always down. Get a hunch and run just before the shell rips the ground you were lying on. Lie still and watch the shell blast the cover you were going to run to. Who can say whether to play the hunch or check?

Sergeant Peter J. Haid decided to play his hunch. Up there under the snapping bullets, where foxholes had to be dug into rock, changing positions wasn't just a simple matter of moving to another place. There had to be cover when you got there. But Haid had a hunch and wanted to move. He called over to his buddy in the next hole 15 yards away and put the proposition of trading holes up to him. "Sure pal," Jesse G. Foley called back. "It's OK with me."

At a signal the two men jumped up and traded places. A few minutes later a Jap machine gunner opened up and Foley, lying in the spot where Haid had been, was hit. The bullet ripped into his arm, inflicting a deep, painful wound that knocked Foley out of the fight.

Haid had escaped. It was a lucky break.

While Foley lay in the quagmire of the hospital on the beach five days later, painfully tossing on the dubious security of a canvas cot, Haid was killed in an assault on Buffalo Ridge.

Hunches are strange things. It's hard to tell.

The Weight of Numbers

Private Theodore Miller, Company C, 32d Infantry

We had huddled in our soggy foxholes resting during the day, waiting for midnight when we were to attack the Japs on the hill that is now known as Rock Quarry. It was a "Buck Jones" war in that country, with a lot of sneaking around and firing, then ducking while the enemy fired, chipping the rocks above your head just like the movies. Our squad was to be base squad in the attack so at midnight we picked up our gear and moved out. Our flank man tried to get contact after we had moved a short way but couldn't find anyone over there. The going was tough and we figured that the other squad was slower and would catch up with us before we contacted the enemy. It was pitch dark and foggy and we moved ahead slowly. I estimate we had gone about 300 yards when we heard digging up ahead. We stopped and the squad leader, Corporal James B. Braudaway, sent a couple of men around to see what it was. They knocked loose a rock that went crashing down into a little ravine and a machine gun cut loose from the direction of the digging noise. We spread out and lay low for a long time.

Finally Corporal Braudaway got us together and we started forward very slowly and quietly. The sound of digging had come again and we heard muffled voices from up ahead. We crept up between two points of rock to a place where the voices seemed to come from the left. Braudaway decided to split the squad up, sending half of us to the left rock and half to the right rock, to see what we could find out. The only sounds were muffled voices and the digging. I began to have a sneaky suspicion that we were out there all alone, 300 yards in front of our own lines.

Corporal Braudaway came with our half of the squad and we climbed to the top of the rock. We looked and listened but could hear nothing. Then one of the men came from the other point and said they had spotted some Japs digging in. Corporal Braudaway told us to go to the bottom of our rock and spread out and wait, while he went up to the other point to see what was there. We had waited about fifteen minutes when we heard voices coming, and three Japs carrying boxes of ammunition walked by within 10 feet of where we were lying. I nudged Roy Marino and whispered, "Should I halt them?" "Christ no, let them go by, you'll give our position away." They were laughing and talking in low voices. One of them stumbled over a frozen body laying just outside a small trench on the snow and almost fell. We were getting plenty jittery when another Jap came along carrying a shovel. He came close to where we were lying and then he looked our way and spoke something in Japanese. No one stirred. I was holding my breath. He came a couple of steps closer, staring at us. He spoke again in Japanese very low. Marino whispered, "Don't fire, Miller, don't fire." I had my bayonet fixed so I stood up slowly and motioned to the Jap to come over. He moved a few more steps toward me, staring at me. I motioned again and said, "Come here," kind of low like he was talking. He moved a few more steps. He was about 10 feet from me and my nerves were about to burst. Suddenly the Jap made a grab for his pocket. I lunged at him and caught him in the right shoulder with my bayonet. He fell down and screamed, rolled over a couple of times, then he got up and, still hollering, ran up the hill.

We ran down the hill.

The Radio that Turned Jap

Lieutenant Bruce Wells, Battery B, 48th Field Artillery Battalion

We had been using the -609 for fire commands all morning and the reception was beautiful. We were popping conversation back and forth without a burble and laying fire wherever it was wanted with no trouble at all. Then we got an order to fire a mission a long way down in Jim Fish Valley. I had finished sending the data back to guns and switched over to receive the answer when I jerked my hand back from the radio like it was hot. The damn thing was talking a steady stream of Japanese right at me! When I recovered from the shock I went to a telephone and phoned the data back, telling FDC about the radio. The mission was fired eventually but all through the firing I worried about my traitorous -609 and the peculiar Japanese voice.

The mission had been completed and still the radio continued to chatter on in

Japanese. Quite a group had gathered about it, listening to the not-to-be-understood tongue and wondering whether our enemy's words held anything significant for us personally. After perhaps twenty minutes the phone buzzed again, this time with a report that fifteen unidentified bombers were approaching the island from the west. So that was it! Now we began to get really excited over the matter-of-fact voice droning out of our -609; a meaning had appeared in the meaningless syllables.

Avid interest rising to apprehension began to show on the faces around the little speaker and one or two looked skyward from time to time. Still the strange intonations issued from the radio. Then swiftly, as they move, without warning, six sleek P-38s thundered their great power directly over our position, the wind hissed over their smooth contours as they streaked over us in the west.

It was a game now. We had forces against the enemy. The strange voice continued to flow steadily from the radio speaker. We listened with a fascination now; we were watching a show. We knew—and the voice did not know.

The unintelligible words continued from the speaker, unexcited, steady—then they stopped. We bent closer, straining to hear. The little radio suddenly jumped to life with such force that it startled us! A line of jabber as excited as a machine gun fairly leaped from the speaker! It was frenzied chatter that even in Japanese could only mean "Look! Look! P-38." They had spotted our planes! We were a part of this fight now, artillerymen lashed to this distant air battle by the tiny thread of our radio.

The tense circle of our faces pressed in on the little radio. We were holding our breaths. A frantic barrage of stacatto syllables gushed from the radio, then snap! Like that, it was over! For a long moment no one moved.

Then the little speaker hummed faintly. We all relaxed back and sighed. Someone said, "Well, I'll be damned!" Then the phone rang and our own battle started again.

Creature Comfort
Lieutenant Patrick C. Murphy, Company H, 32d Infantry

Comforts of life on the battlefield are indeed few and definitely far between, even to such a little thing as a cigarette, as no one realized better than does Lieutenant Patrick C. Murphy. It was on May 27 and Lieutenant Murphy had worked his mortar platoon up the steep slopes of the mountain to get into position for a push against the Jap entrenchments on Buffalo Ridge. It was gruelling work over arduous ground and the men, lugging their heavy equipment up the hills, constantly harassed by the enemy fire, worked the entire long Aleutian day to get located.

Finally everything was set, the guns were in position, the ammunition was brought up, and the 81mm. mortars were ready to dump the high explosives, at the battalion commander's signal, down Tojo's collar.

It was getting dusky and "Paddy" sat down to rest. Captain Robert C. Foulston was sitting near by with his back against a wall of rock. In those days when a man sat down to rest he had to rest fast; if he relaxed, the tension ran out of his nerves like water and his arms and eyelids got heavy. When Paddy sat down he relaxed. "I've got a cigarette, sir." "Good boy, light 'er up," Captain Foulston said. Paddy reached down in his pocket and pulled out a beat-up little box of K-ration cigarettes and lit one. The enemy was still firing at the new positions but enemy fire was just another accepted discomfort of life on the battlefield. Paddy took a deep drag off the cigarette and started to pass it to the Captain when a Jap mortar shell burst in front of them. Captain Foulston raised up from the mud and snorted, "Whew!" Paddy was cussing a long and heartfelt curse upon all Japs. His finger was bleeding but he didn't mind that. A piece of shrapnel had cut the cigarette off flush, leaving only a tiny stub which Paddy still clenched between his fingers. "And that's the last goddamn one, too!" he said.

The Attack on Buffalo Ridge

Sergeant Clent O. Brown, Company F, 32d Infantry

Lieutenant Dale V. Stice, the Kid, "Muscles Malone," was a young, cocky, good-looking guy, with life in his eyes and a fog-horn voice, and more guts than he needed. He stood up on a pinnacle of rock and looked down and behind Company G, working across the rocky flat from the "Rock Ledge" to Buffalo Ridge. Company F was way out in front, the going was rough, they needed help. The whole valley was filled with his huge voice as Stice cupped his hands and hollered, "For Crisake, Company G, get off your ass! You're strung out so far behind you look like a supply line!"

The attack against the ridge, made the night before, had been repulsed by the Japs' machine guns that lashed out from behind rocks and crags all across the front at the attackers as they struggled up the slopes. The line had broken and in wild, rolling, tumbling confusion, the men withdrew.

On the 27th another attack had been launched with Company C on the left and F on the right. The companies crawled, heads down, across the boulder-strewn flat at the foot of the ridge into the machine-gun bullets that snapped and whined away in crazy ricochets through the rocks. They were within two hundred yards of the ridge. The 4th Infantry was working on Points 3 and 4 on the Fish Hook and had practically secured the left flank. It was late in the evening. The pressure on the attackers was high as they moved closer to the Jap positions. They started up the slope to the ridge. Lieutenant William B. Frost was hit in the chest. "The little bastards ruined my fountain pen," he said after he had stopped rolling into a draw. From over on the right a great explosion sent a tattered boot flying into the air. Albert Novak, Jr., was in bad shape. Either a bullet had hit the grenades he was carrying or he had stepped on a mine. His legs were almost torn off when Sergeant R. L. "Pinky" Holman got to him. He was shocked very badly and moaned about his legs. Pinky said, "Don't look at them, Al. I'm going to try to move you." The men were exposed, and Holman started dragging him down the hill to cover but Novak couldn't stand to be moved.

Staff Sergeant Harold C. Wunsch was hit in the stomach, and Corporal James D. O'Connor and Corporal James L. Ferguson had dragged him into the draw with Lieutenant William B. Frost.

The attack had stopped. It was getting dark; over on the left some of the men of Company C were digging. Holman found the battalion wireman and they got a line in to the CP. Company G had been pinned down 200 yards from the rock ledge where the battalion was located, so the two companies, F and C, each consisting of about seventy tired and grimy and frozen fighters, were out at the foot of Buffalo alone. When Lieutenant Stice got on the phone Major Charles G. Fredericks asked about the situation and told Stice that they should withdraw. Stice insisted that the company was OK, beat-up but OK. They were right in the Japs' lap, but if they pulled back they'd have the whole goddamn nightmare to do over again in the morning. They stuck. The two companies scratched holes in between rocks and tried to rest in the few hours left of the night.

Early in the morning, before daylight, Stice was looking for a route of advance up out of the ravine. He had Bill Baggett with him and Joe E. Ruiz. They were working across the snow that blocked the head of the draw when they saw a Jap asleep in a hole. Stice walked over to him and jammed the muzzle of his .45 against the Jap's head. The Jap woke up with a start. Stice whispered loudly in his ear, "Do you want to surrender?" The Jap grabbed for his rifle and the heavy .45 jumped as Stice pulled the trigger. Six other Japs in the immediate vicinity were awakened by the shot and raised up. Stice shot two; Ruiz shot one just as he was ready to kill Stice; and Baggett, standing over the holes spraddle-legged, fired three times in rapid succession with his rifle at his hip. The noise of the little fight opened everything up again. Guns began firing all across the front and the fight was on.

From back near the battalion, Company H was blasting the top of the ridge as the troops started up. Company F's weapons platoon moved along with the riflemen, the mortars firing beside the BAR men. Nunzio J. Savino ducked and shook his head as a bullet ripped through his helmet. He turned the light machine gun over to the assistant and grabbed a pocketful of grenades and started up the hill. The Japs were rolling volley after volley of grenades down on the heads of the attackers. Baggett was trying to grenade a machine gun in a crevice of rock and each time he raised up a man behind him fired. Baggett hollered, "Don't shoot, don't shoot. It's Baggett," and he waved. But the Jap who was firing at him didn't care if he was Methuselah and almost got him before a grenade landed by the Jap. Corporal Manuel Andrade had rushed a Jap in a pile of rocks on the right and was bayoneted in the neck just an instant before Joe Ruiz shot the Jap.

Lieutenant Stice and about ten of the men had gathered under a tall ledge seeking shelter from the hail of grenades that beat down on them, and he shouted to Sergeant Clent Brown to try to skirt to the left around the ledge and flank of the Japs above. Brown started up, while the men under the ledge edged to the right to go around. They ran into more grenades. Just before Brown ran around the rock he saw Lieutenant Stice hit the ground and grenades were rolling down on him. Ruiz was firing madly up the hill. Over on the flank Zygmond P. Borucki, Raymond Gloe and Roy Perry were running up the hill through jagged rocks throwing grenades ahead of them. Big Albert J. Rofski fired his M1 into the rear end of a Jap draped over a boulder and an explosion almost tore the Jap in two. Ernest L. Redington and Sergeant Ullman B. Osborn had just bayoneted and shot a pocket of Jap machine gunners.

Then it was over. The firing ceased. Lieutenant Charles W. Farnham was at the top of Buffalo Ridge. Sergeant Brown came over and Farnham sent him to look for Lieutenant Stice to find out what was to be done now. The men had given out. No one talked and there was no firing.

Brown went down the hill to the ledge where he had last seen Stice and Ruiz. There was no one there. He moved up on top of the ledge. There below, to the right of the ledge, he saw them, Joe Ruiz and the "Kid." Lying a few feet apart, both dead. Stice had a hand blown off when he tried to pick up a Jap grenade and throw it back. Ruiz had several wounds from fragments and bullets. Sergeant Brown walked back up to the top of the ridge where Lieutenant Farnham was. He said, "You're the company commander, sir."

It was evening. The wild assault had taken the entire day. Company E moved out to secure the right flank. Company G filled the gap between F and C, and the 4th Infantry was on the left.

The company began to dig in on Buffalo Ridge.

The Unit Report, BCT 32-2, May 28, 1943, said, simply, " . . . Cos C and F assaulted Buffalo Ridge and seized their objective."

An Indian Game

Private First Class George H. Flyingnice, Headquarters Company,
1st Battalion, 4th Infantry

For several days the troops had been fighting in and out of the rocks and ridges on the left side of Jim Fish Valley and the afternoon of May 28 was following the same rough pattern as the previous days. Each morning we would make a hard push against the Japs, dug in among the rocks and snowbanks like badgers, and we'd put a lot of pressure on them. Then the afternoons would be spent trying to get reorganized, consolidating our positions and sniping back and forth so we could push them again in the evening.

Our troops had shoved off in the morning against a ridge held by the Japs and had made choppy progress for maybe 500 yards across a rough snow-covered valley strewn with pinnacles of lava-like rock and great jagged boulders. The Japs, wedged into the crevices of their ridge, hung on tenaciously and our advance was stopped some 350 yards short of the actual Jap line. The fighting continued sporadically all afternoon—sniping by the riflemen, arduous creeping forward of mortar fire back and forth across the lines and a general consolidation of positions for the inevitable shove again during the evening hours.

Our own weapons company was moving forward into position to fire on the present Jap line and also be able to fire at the next probable line the Japs would hold when and if we drove them out of their present holes. The terrain was such that they had to swing far over to our right flank to be effective and they were moving up to the edge of a great bank of unbroken snow, getting the mortars into position, when the first shell from a Jap 77 burst behind them. We had heard from his gun the two days before, but this was the first time they had fired today.

Flyingnice began to swear softly. He had cussed this big Jap gun every time it fired for the last three days. Somehow he and the corporal, by impressing any and all help they could get, had kept their 37 in the fight by dragging, hauling, heaving, and cussing it over the rocks and ridges and canyons and snowbanks of the damnedest piece of fighting ground a man ever saw. And he wanted to get a crack at that big Jap 77. They had been firing off and on at Jap machine guns and had even sniped successfully a time or two at particularly offensive Jap riflemen, but what they wanted, what they had slaved for, was a crack at the "big boy." They had the gun set up in a fine position in the rear of our left flank and they hung onto it through a thorough peppering from the Jap line, which showed no sign of letting up even now. And while Flyingnice was cussing the Jap 77, the little brothers were bouncing an occasional bullet off the shield of the 37 just for luck. The insolent little bastards!

Flyingnice was studying the shelling as he did every day. The Japs would fire perhaps three rounds, then for a long time, sometimes an hour, they would remain silent, waiting. Then they'd fire three more and wait again. The thing that was driving Flyingnice slowly batty was that not once could they get even a hint of the position of the 77 itself. Not a single time in all the days the gun had fired had they been able to figure out where it was located. Flyingnice and the corporal had covered every inch of the Jap ridge time and time again with their field glasses, only to be mocked by a new burst of shells at the fringe of the big snowbank where our mortars were located. Flyingnice swore again as a big black splotch smeared across the edge of the snowbank in front of the mortars, knocking down three men. Then he swung his glasses back to the Jap ridge. He stared straight ahead for a long time. Then he crawled quietly over to his gun. Very deliberately he adjusted on a large clump of rocks shaped roughly like a three-sided fort with pinnacles that stuck up like saw teeth all around. Flyingnice and the corporal were all that were left of the gun crew, and they had worked so much together that the regular organization of various duties of the crew members had deteriorated to simply two guys shooting at 37. The corporal asked him what he was doing and Flyingnice replied with Chippewa humor, "I'm gonna play games with the Japs." What he had in mind was like the bizarre game of "Cuckoo." It is done roughly as follows: One man who is blindfolded perches on a table and is equipped with a cudgel. Its weight and solidity depend on the participants' enthusiasm. The other player gets on hands and knees under the table. At any time the latter player chooses he sticks his head out from under the table, shouts "Cuckoo" and ducks, whereupon the player on top of the table attempts to brain him with the cudgel. A nice friendly game of Cuckoo was what Flyingnice intended to play, with the Japs under the table.

The corporal said, "I don't get it." But Flyingnice was adamant. He lay behind the 37 which pointed with deadly patience at the rock 800 yards away. Half an hour passed slowly, with Flyingnice never taking his binoculars down, watching the rock and waiting. Suddenly he dropped his glasses and checked the sights. The corporal glanced at the Indian boy and then looked at the rock. He could see nothing but rocks. Bam! the little 37 slammed out hard. Flyingnice smiled innocently as the shell burst at the foot of the rock fort. Then the corporal saw it too, the heavy muzzle of the Jap 77 and the square angle of the shield rapidly disappearing into the depths of the jagged rocks. "See what I mean?" asked Flyingnice, as he loaded the gun and made some adjustments on the sights. Now they both settled down with field glasses for another wait. Flyingnice was grinning now and confident that his patience was going to be rewarded.

Another long half hour passed. Then they saw it. The stubby muzzle was sliding forward again out of the rocks. The corporal was as excited as a bride at a stag party. But Flyingnice waited until the square shoulder of the shield hunched out of the rock. Then he pressed the trigger. Chunks of rock flew as the shell burst just above the shield of the Jap. The corporal made a quick adjustment as Flyingnice slapped another round into the chamber. The 37 barked again but the Jap muzzle was just disappearing into the rocks.

The Japs were silent for a long time. The two men were happy as children. Company D was getting well set up, relieved of the shelling of the 77, and as the evening wore on the troops began to advance again. The mortars at the edge of the snowbank began a barrage on the Jap ridge, blasting away at the Japs in their rocky nests, silencing their deadly chatter.

Flyingnice was waiting again. As long as the 77 could be fired, the Japs would use it and use it soon. They couldn't tolerate the pounding our mortars were dishing out for long without trying to neutralize them. He hadn't long to wait as they were already wheeling out their cannon. Its nose was sticking out tentatively like a curious puppy that has been nipped by a snake. "C'mon, push it out there." Flyingnice was mocking them. The Japs were finally getting a dose of their own medicine. They couldn't see our 37 and it had them plenty buffaloed. Still Flyingnice waited. The Jap gun was plainly visible now. He made a minute adjustment. Even two members of the gun crew were exposed now. In another instant they would be firing. Flyingnice pressed the trigger.

The flash of the heavy explosive took the Jap between the barrel and the shield, a direct hit. Flyingnice adjusted again and the corporal flipped open the breech and loaded again. Flyingnice shouted happily as he pressed the trigger. When the smoke cleared from the second round the Jap gun was still sticking out of the rocks, silent and battered. A little pile of tan marked the body of one of the crew. They fired again, hit again, and fired again.

They watched the battered 77 off and on until it got dark. It never moved. During the night the attack had pushed over the Jap ridge and early the next morning the mortars were firing on the new Jap position. Flyingnice and the corporal borrowed a crew of helpers and were dragging, hauling, heaving and cussing their gun over the rocks and gullies and snow. "Hell, this is like hunting gophers after you've just shot an elk," Flyingnice was complaining, but the corporal was happy.

Personally, I'd as soon play squat tag in a cactus patch as play games with Flyingnice.

The Taking of Vanderlaan Peak

Staff Sergeant Charles H. Roberts, Company I, 17th Infantry

Vanderlaan Peak? I'll say I remember it. It was cold up there. That's where one of our machine guns froze up, the night of the 28th. *Sergeant Roberts was talking:*

Vanderlaan Peak is the high point inland from Middle Peak on the right side of Jim Fish Valley. Company I had moved up there to relieve Company L on the 26th. During the afternoon of the first day on the mountain the Japs holding the high ground ahead had peeked over at the newcomers, holding their fire, and then their buddies behind would fire when the Americans raised up. They tried that gag once too often, and a Jap rolled spectacularly down the nearly vertical snow. The first afternoon was quiet, but that night the Japs attacked—about 16 of them. Ben Martin, our sentry, warned us; and the melee was hot and heavy for a few minutes. The Japs were right in with us, jabbering and throwing grenades, and then they withdrew. No one was hurt, not even a Jap unless some of them had rolled down the mountain. Martin had ducked just as a grenade landed at the edge of his hole, and it blew the bayonet off his gun and probably ruined his zero, but didn't even scratch him.

The next day we were ordered to advance along the ridge and take the high ground. We moved out before daylight with the 3d Platoon leading. We surprised the Japs on the top of the hill and the scouts killed four of them with grenades. The ridge ran fairly straight and level, and the Japs had dug in on a line vertically down the side, on the right. We brought up our machine guns and BARs and rifles and eventually knocked the Japs out of the holes. We passed through the dead Japs and headed for the point of the ridge where we were going to hold that night. A detail went back to the Jap holes to throw the dead occupants out, so some of us could use the holes that night while the 3d Platoon dug in around the point. They had thrown about eight or ten dead Japs over the hill and Corporal Lyle C. Blow had rolled over the last one. He had rolled down maybe a hundred yards when he stopped rolling, jumped up and started to run. Blow stared unbelieving while the rest of the detail banged away at the fleeing Jap. When he came under fire he ducked into a hole in the tundra, and a patrol started down after him. The patrol got almost to the Jap; then he blew himself up.

That night the 1st Platoon was sent back along the ridge. The 2d Platoon stayed in the Jap holes and the 3d Platoon guarded the point. Two Jap scouts came up to the point. One got away. Nothing much happened the next day, and that night the 1st Platoon went out to relieve the 3d. We put two BARs out on the point and dug little shelter boxes into the snow trench. Half of the men were to guard one hour, then the other half were to guard another hour, using the "buddy system." Half of the platoon remained out with the BARs and half came back along the mountain to guard the rear and flanks.

It was about 0300 when the Japs began moving in. They hit our flank and the point at about the same time. I was back with the flank guard, and the first thing we knew of Japs coming was that mortar shells whistled over our heads and fell on the other side of the mountain below us. Then Earle E. Gaule, our light machine gunner, began popping away with his carbine. I thought he was trigger-happy and went back to check. Down below, along a line of rocks, were some shadows moving about. One of them broke from the rocks and ran toward the right flank. It was a Jap all right, so we got everybody up and opened fire.

The fight out on the point was getting under way, too. Private Raymond V. Braun, who had just been relieved from guard, heard his buddy, Clarence J. Steinbach, holler "Halt!" and then "Who's there?" A voice out in front hollered back, "Friend," in good English. So Steinbach says "Little . . ." and the voice replied "Little what?" Braun still thought it was an American patrol after Steinbach had fired twice. Steinbach ran back to Braun's hole and said, "There are Japs out there!" They got up and waited but nothing happened. The Japs were getting set. Braun was just getting ready to crawl into his hole when Corporal Alvy Morgado came up and was getting everybody out. "Aw hell, Steinbach was just shooting up our own patrol," Braun grumbled. The corporal told him to get out and stay out and then the first Jap raised up. Morgado said, "Look out, there's one!" And as the Jap raised his rifle Morgado shot him and he fell.

Then it started. The Japs came up the hill toward the point shouting in English and Japanese. Braun got mad and between rounds he hollered to an English-speaking Jap to "Blow it, you little bastard!" The Jap hollered back, "Brow it yourself!" And Braun got madder and said, "Stick your head up, ya sonuvabitch, and I'll blow it for ya!" About that time Braun caught a bullet in his helmet which grazed his skull and knocked him out of his head. He went wandering back along the line saying, "I'm hit in the head, I'm hit right in the head." All the boys were busy firing at the Japs. Morgado looked at him between rounds and said, "Well, take your pills, damn it, take your pills," and as though that settled the whole thing he began firing again.

The Japs had begun moving up the hill toward the flank guard, and the heavy machine gunners got a line on them. They fired one round and the bolt stuck. The Prestone in the water jacket had been weakened by firing previously, and the water was frozen up. They fired several rounds single shot, and then picked up carbines and pistols.

A light machine gun began to bark down below, and in a moment the bullets were cracking right over our heads. They had our hole zeroed. Sergeant Jonathan H. Albright was in it with me and as he raised up to fire, a burst caught him. I staved down in the hole and tossed my grenades out at the Japs; the bullets from the Jap gun were coming so close you could feel them go by. Gaule finally got our light machine gun going on the Jap and quieted him down.

We had been fighting about an hour and the ammunition situation was very bad. Corporal Charles E. McKay had come up from the point for more ammunition and he saw the Japs trying to come up the mountain between the 1st and 2d Platoons. We sent two men back to block the gap and sent a runner to the 2d Platoon after more ammunition. Before long a squad from the 2d Platoon moved in with us with plenty of ammunition; and after another hour the Japs were about gone. We watched a wounded Jap roll down the snow to the bottom of the hill and crawl into a little aid station the Japs had set up. Later we found him dead there.

There was very little resistance after that. The Japs blew themselves up whenever we got them cornered.

The final tally around the point and the flank showed 19 dead Japs. We had lost two others besides Albright; Steinbach, the guard, and Louis J. Marcinek were dead.

IV: COUNTERATTACK AND CLEANUP

By May 28 the Japanese garrison was desperate. Only three moves were possible—surrender, death on the beach of Chichagof Harbor, or a desperate suicidal counterattack. Colonel Yasuyo Yamasaki chose the last course and issued a field order as follows (in part):

Order of Second Sector
May 29, 1943   123
Chichagof Harbor

1. By the fierce attack of the combined sea, land, and air units, the battalions on the front lines of the land front have almost been annihilated but the morale of officers and men of this sector is excellent and they are still holding some important parts. We are successfully planning an annihilation of the enemy troops. (Detailed instructions to follow.)

. . . .

14. I, in the advance for the attack, will advance in the center rear of the front lines.

YASUYO YAMASAKI,
Colonel, Infantry.

That order sealed the fate of the Attu garrison.

The Breakthrough — 1

Captain Albert L. Pence, Jr., Sergeant Robert Gonzales,
Private First Class Anthony Krsinich,
Company B, 32d Infantry

Company B, 32d Infantry, was ordered to move down Jim Fish Valley, pass through a gap between Companies K and L of the 17th Infantry, and establish a line across the valley at the near end of Lake Cories.

Captain Albert L. Pence, Jr., was leading the 3d Platoon and the attack was going beautifully. They were almost to their objective when the 1st Platoon ran into trouble. They were close to the Japs before the Japs opened fire on them. Then they were pinned down, and hard. Captain Victor A. Fenner was with the 1st Platoon and he couldn't even wiggle, so Captain Pence moved his 3d Platoon around to the right flank in an effort to unpin the 1st Platoon. They still hadn't spotted the exact source of the fire and suddenly they surprised the Japs and the Japs surprised them. They were 50 yards from the line held by the Japs who, for a change, had poor positions protected by foxholes. Captain Pence left the body of the platoon to cover him and he and Sergeant Fred S. Bogdanoff and two men crawled into a gulch that ran past the Jap positions. They wormed along to within grenade range and had blasted the first Jap position when a Jap jumped up to run and Pence shot him. Sergeant Bogdanoff hollered, "Nice shooting, Captain," and he raised up to move and caught a bullet which killed him on the spot. Pence saw the Jap that had fired and brought him down with three quick shots from the hip. The Jap was only 15 yards from Pence. The men crawled down the draw a few feet more and a Jap jumped up squarely in front of Pence who lunged at him with a perfect long thrust. The bayonet jammed hard against the Jap's back but it didn't penetrate his clothing. Instead it bent over near the handle. Pence swore as the Jap stumbled. Then he pulled the trigger and the Jap fell on his face.

The platoons had advanced on a run, moving the Japs back all across the valley. The attack had gone fast—too fast—and the men were very tired. The main body of the company was farther back. Captain Pence and three or four men had crawled up to a little hill and were lying behind it getting ready to move back to join the rest of the company. Fire was still falling all around them and it was getting dark. Pence nudged the man on his left to tell him to move back. The man was dead. It shocked Pence. He had heard no shot strike the man, and he had made no sound. He picked up the limp wrist and felt for a pulse. The man was dead. "Let's get out of here," he hollered to Johnson, the man on his right. Johnson hollered "OK" and as he raised up to move, thoomp! a bullet hit him in the chest. Captain Pence crawled over and half dragged, half carried the boy back toward the main body of the company. He was groaning. He was hit hard. Pence stopped and gave him a shot of morphine. Johnson began to talk about his wife and child back in the States. He was nearly dead when they got to the company. He could recognize only Pence. He begged him not to leave. Pence was undecided. He knew or felt that Johnson was about gone, but there was so much to do that had to be done soon. Pence held the boy's hand for a short moment while he talked about his wife. He was silent then and shortly after he died.

Meanwhile the company had received orders to withdraw. The order was being passed around more like a rumor than an order. It seemed strange. The whole night seemed strange. From somewhere down the valley flares were being fired into the sky, glowing red against the fog. Edmund E. Caraway and Donald R. Turner, a BAR team, had been advancing to the right, coming over with the rest of the company. Fire was still falling about and they were crawling up a small draw to the high ground. Caraway thought he saw a Jap move somewhere over on the right flank, and he tugged at the pants leg of the man crawling in front of him. He wanted to warn Turner of the Jap. The man turned around. Staring at Caraway was a big Jap who had gotten in between the two men by accident. Caraway shot the Jap with two of the quickest shots he ever fired in his life. Then, to hell with the fire! He bolted for the rest of the company.

The company had started to withdraw. The wounded men were a problem to move. Some of them were hit hard and were litter cases, and there were no litters available. Captain Pence and several of the men improvised litters from shelter halves and Jap blankets and rifles, and moved some of the more seriously wounded to the aid station near the CP of the 3d Battalion, 17th Infantry, before the rest of the company moved out.

The first hint of serious trouble appeared when Staff Sergeant Harold J.

Hunter spotted a column of several men moving to the rear. The way they walked, with short steps in single file, made Sergeant Hunter suspicious. He challenged them and the last man in the column turned and walked toward Hunter. Sergeant Hunter called "Little," and the man continued to walk toward him. He called "Halt!" and the man stopped. Again Hunter called "Little." The man stood there in the fog for a moment and Hunter moved toward him. Suddenly the man fell down with his hands over his head. For a moment he lay on the ground as though he expected to be shot. Sergeant Hunter still could not be sure whether the man was American or Japanese in the darkness and fog. Then the man leaped to his feet and began to run. Sergeant Hunter fired and the man fell. "Dammit, he should have talked," Hunter said as he returned to the others. The weird night continued, the red fire of the flares casting a strange glow over the valley. The company was moving out. Two platoons had moved back and the weapons were on their way to the rear. A flare lit the sky again and the men in Sergeant Hunter's platoon froze. Suddenly, Sergeant Hunter grabbed a rifle with a bayonet and jumped over a bank into the darkness. Gonzales hollered, "Hunter, Hunter, what's wrong?" Sergeant Hunter answered, "Something's fishy, look what I've got." He had bayoneted a Jap under the bank a few feet below them.

Then hell broke loose. Grenades began to burst in the valley ahead of them, and machine guns opened up. Japs, lots of them, began appearing through the fog in the strange glow of the red flares. They charged through the disorganized company, reducing it to little pockets of fiercely resisting men who shot down column after column, and still they came. The scattered pockets of men began falling back.

Sergeant Hunter and a few men found Alvin C. Roth who had tried to carry his mortar to the rear as the Japs swarmed over them. He had a saber sticking through him. He was suffering terribly as he was carried back toward the CP of the 3d Battalion, 17th Infantry. Another small group found Corporal Rudolf P. Bodane. He had been shot and they helped him back. Others were falling. The firing was becoming terrible, transforming the valley into a nightmare of flashes and noise and scampering shadows and death. Gonzales had given his rifle to a man while he helped carry Bodane, and as Bodane was laid in a foxhole Gonzales asked for his rifle. The Japs were nearly on them. The man repeated over and over, "I don't remember what I did with it." He was dazed. Gonzales was furious, but as he started to walk away he almost tripped over a loaded M1. He picked it up and started to work.

Captain Pence had moved to the rear with the first party of wounded that had been taken back. He reported to the 3d Battalion CP tent to Major Lee Wallace, who had received a message warning against a Jap counterattack as Company B began moving back. The CP tent was full of exhausted officers lying on the floor sleeping. Pence had reported that Company B was moving back when sounds of faint firing rose above the creaking and slapping of the tent in the wind. Major Wallace sent Captain Pence to investigate the shooting. Pence had just stooped over to go out of the tent and had pushed the flaps back as a man barefooted and without his jacket, dashed into the CP shouting,

"The Japs are here! They've broken through." Then they heard it. A horde of Japs burst onto the CP screaming and shouting. The wind had deadened the sound and then its full volume suddenly burst on them with blood-chilling, savage intensity. Pence shouted a warning and jumped out of the tent into the Japs. They were yelling and shooting, bayoneting, grenading—utterly destroying everything in their way.

For the next hour everything was a blur of shouts and explosions and screams and running figures. Pence pulled the pin and threw a grenade into a group of closely packed Japs. Then he grabbed one right in front of him with both arms and pulled his knife. He plunged it into the Jap's back, again and again. He lost his head in the viciousness of the fight. After a second, when he began to think again, he realized that he was beating the already dead Jap's back with the handle of the knife. The blade had broken off with the first plunge. He dropped the Jap and rolled over a small bank and began to work his way to the rear.

All over the valley sounds of fighting and streaks of tracers and cries and flashes of grenades marked other bitter, orgiastic battles being fought. Other Americans separated in the darkness from their outfits were moving back, alone or in pairs, looking for spots where the lines had held, forming new pockets of resistance, joining scattered forces.

It began to get gray in the fog over the mountains. It was a bloody morning, May 29.

The Breakthrough — 2

Corporal Lawrence R. Kelley, Company B, 32d Infantry

It was May 28. Everything seemed haywire that night. It was a bad night. First we got an order to advance to the lake, which was a hell of a job in itself; and then we were ordered to withdraw after we got there. The order withdrawing us was being passed around more like a rumor than a real order, probably because no one could understand it. It seemed like a Jap trick. But there were screwy things going on—flares being fired and footsteps.

Captain Victor A. Fenner ordered my squad to furnish rear-guard action and cover the withdrawal. The company had just started moving back when the Japs struck first. The attack lasted only a moment, but it was a holocaust. The Japs charged with bayonets and we fired frantically and drove them back. The confusion was terrible. Fights were breaking out all across the valley and up on the mountainsides.

The Japs began firing at us, and our men began to fall back. Finally the BAR man and I jumped up and ran back, too. We stopped in a ditch where we found four other members of the squad. Captain Fenner joined us from somewhere, and we moved out of the ditch again to find the rest of the platoon. When we got back to where the platoon had been we were hit by the Japs again. We used grenades and the BAR to try to stop them, but we fell back again to the ditch. The Japs crept up to within range and began tossing grenades into the ditch at us. One landed near Captain Fenner and he jumped over a little rise in the ground putting it between him and the grenade. Then they tossed one at him again, and he jumped back over the rise. I pulled the pin on a grenade and was just ready to throw when a Jap grenade landed right beside me. I jumped to the side and landed against a rock. It knocked the wind out of me and hurt my side, but I had to hang on to the grenade in my hand. I threw it just as two Japs jumped into the ditch with us. Rafael Luccio, on my left, fired twice at the two in the ditch and swung around and fired again just over my head and caught a third in midair, in just a matter of seconds.

Captain Fenner was separated from us. We thought he had been killed so we began moving back. The BAR man was badly wounded; we tried to move him but he didn't want to move; and we found that two others had been shot in the legs, and one boy had shrapnel scattered over his back. The BAR man died just as we were leaving, but the three wounded struggled along with us. We were crawling right down the icy water in a creek bed. I wanted to work over to the nearest place where I last remembered there were friendly troops.

The sky was blazing with tracers crisscrossing in every direction, and occasionally the vivid brilliance of a flare would make us all freeze motionless.

We headed toward the area behind Company L, 17th Infantry, which was masked by a small hill. We hoped we'd find some shelter and some security there. But as we came into view of the place where Company L had been there was a constant stream of caliber .30 tracers streaking back toward Engineer Hill, and occasionally a big ball of red fire from a 37 tracer hurtled across the valley toward Engineer Hill. The Japs had captured the area where Company L had been and were firing our weapons from there.

We stopped and watched from the creek bed. Figures were still running across the valley, Japs and Americans alike, all mixed up, grotesquely silhouetted for an instant by a gun flash.

We thought about crossing the valley to the other side—to Company K's side— but the Company K area was alive with tracers and flashes of grenades.

We moved on farther down the creek, heading for Engineer Hill. The wounded boys were having a hard time and my side hurt like hell. Our feet and legs were numb from the icy water, but to expose ourselves for long out of the ditch was deadly. My corporal was killed, struck in the side of the head with a bullet that could have come from anywhere. We waited . . . but we had not been seen so we moved along the creek again.

It began to get light. We had traveled about 400 yards down the creek in all that time. Engineer Hill still a mile away was a shadow through the dark mist. We stopped to rest and talk over the situation. We were in a bad spot. We were sure that there were Japs around us and we had no idea where friendly forces had held and where they had broken. The death of the corporal had demoralized the men. The man with the BAR was sick with fear and his foot was hurting. Russell C. Henderson and I were the only two that could fight, and my side was getting worse as time passed. It was getting quite light now, and we were undecided as to our course of action. We had just decided to move along the creek again when we spotted an American walking toward us across the open ground. It was Alvin A. Mahaffey and he wore a tight grin as he walked straight toward us. We hollered for him to get down but he kept walking. We heard a bullet crack over our heads and Mahaffey fell about twenty feet from us. He began to swear, and in a few minutes he rolled into the creek with blood running out of a gash in his arm. He had been playing dead in a hole out in the valley all night with Japs running over him every few minutes. He had been kicked and rolled over by three different groups of Japs, but miraculously none of them had jammed a bayonet into him. He had heard us talking and decided the only place for him was with Americans, wherever they were. He acted as though his worries were over when he joined us, but even seeing him as happy as he was didn't relieve our minds a bit.

We moved along the creek again and about 100 yards farther down we found a sheltered wash where we decided to stop. The wounded men were exhausted, and my side was aching and breathing was very difficult. Here we held another council of war; some of the men wanted to stay in the wash and wait until the situation cleared up; others were afraid that the Japs would spot us and close in. We decided that we'd leave the BAR with the wounded men, and Russell Henderson and I would work our way over the hill where we could see some troops moving and perhaps get some help. The hill was several hundred yards behind Company L's position and while we couldn't be sure they were not Japs, there was only one way to find out. So we started. Progress was slow and tricky and fights were flaring up all over the valley. Sudden bursts of fire would throw us to the ground breathless. We started up the hill in a little gorge and the going was very tough. My side ached something fierce and I was almost ready to quit. I had fallen behind Henderson after we had been pinned down by some firing that came our way, and I was sure we had been seen and were drawing fire ourselves. Henderson wouldn't believe me when I told him a burst of machine-gun fire had hit in the gorge behind and between us. I was lying down trying to breathe and holding my side, when Henderson sat on a rock and looked down at me. He began to swear. He swore slowly and deliberately and called me things that, if I hadn't been too sick I would have killed him for. But he got what he wanted. I was so damned mad that I started up the hill and reached the top ahead of him.

The troops on the hill saw us as we neared the top, and Captain Fenner, of all people, was there. He asked me what had happened and we told him the story. From somewhere up there a machine gun was brought over and set up, with several riflemen helping, and all during that afternoon this machine gun fired keeping groups of Japs pinned down and away from the little wash where our wounded boys were.

During the night they were moved to an improvised aid station which had been salvaged from the wreckage of the 2d Battalion supply dump and kitchens, and a day later the Japs were cleaned out, so at last they could be evacuated to the beach hospital.

Henderson apologized for the vile things he had called me while climbing the hill. "But hell," he said, "I didn't know you had a broken rib, and I sure didn't want to be traveling alone that day."

The Story of a Clearing Station

Captain George S. Buehler, Company C, 7th Medical Battalion

"I will never forget it." Captain George S. Buehler was not speaking idly. He meant it. He had finished telling his story of playing dead in his clearing station full of wounded men for a day and a half while the Japs slaughtered everything in sight around him in a futile but furious climax to a bitterly fought battle.

A set of fortunate circumstances, the meddling fingers of Fate, and the doing and not doing of just the right thing at the right time, make this story possible, as indeed they make any story possible when it must be told by one who lives the story and lives to tell it.

The clearing station had been set up at the foot of Engineer Hill. It was near the big draw that cuts deeply into Clevesy Pass. Captain Buehler and Captain James W. Bryce operated the station with seven aid men, all but one of whom had spent the entire day working patients up the hill on the sled. The sleds were tricky. They were arranged on each end of a cable and when supplies were sent down the slide, patients were sent up. The two sleds counterbalanced each other. The aid men walked beside the sled going up because sometimes the cable broke and the sled had to be held on the hill or it would slide down the steep wall and crash to the disaster of the patients on it.

The station itself was set in close to the bottom of the hill and it could not be seen from the top. It consisted simply of a double tent pitched with one door opening out the side of the tent nearer the slide. A stove was set up in the tent with a door. During the course of the station's operation, 25 or 30 rifles and some ammunition had accumulated around the tent. These had been stacked outside the door, along with probably 15 hand grenades. A system of operation had evolved around the station whereby one man would stay awake all night to be CQ[9] and guard, and if anything came up between 0200 and 0400 Captain Buehler would be awakened; after four Captain Bryce would take care of it. Since they seldom went to bed before 0200, this system would insure some hours of uninterrupted sleep for them each night.

The evening of May 28 was much like any other battle evening. The aid men had evacuated several casualties up the hill by means of the slide, had heard firing down the valley, and had eaten half-warmed C rations—there was nothing unusual except that American forces were closing in on the Japs from all sides and the pressure was increasing. The thought of a counterattack, a breakthrough, was in the air, but the station was a long way behind the lines.

Seven patients were still at the station and could not be evacuated until morning. Four were litter cases and three were ambulatory but painful. They had been arranged in a row across where the two tents were joined. Captain Bryce and Captain Buehler slept behind the patients away from the door. A medical sergeant who was sick with diarrhea, and two medics whose shelters had been torn down, were also arranging to sleep in the aid tent. One of the litter patients was a serious exposure case. He had been stripped, wrapped in blankets, and was

---

[9]In Charge of Quarters.

sleeping near the stove with his head at the door. Two of the medics were sleeping outside in a pup tent, and the CQ was standing guard.

It had gotten quite dark outside. The tent was as black as a cave, with the one small door tied shut except for the bottom flaps. The men talked for a while, looked after small needs of the patients, and made them as comfortable as the limited facilities of an aid station would permit. Captain Buehler had fallen asleep, and Captain Bryce was fumbling in the blackness for his sleeping bag. The sound of a cat motor roared behind Engineer Hill somewhere.

It must have been several hours later when Captain Bryce woke up. The CQ had come into the tent. Firing from somewhere down the valley was popping faintly. The tent flap had dropped back behind the CQ and it was coal black in the tent. Bryce whispered, "Who's there?"

"It's the CQ, sir. Something's wrong down in the valley. There's a lot of shooting." The distant popping had increased in intensity. It seemed a long way off. "I brought a couple of rifles," the CQ said as he crawled through the tent flap.

Bryce dozed off. He was sure he had slept only a moment. It was after four, the CQ was bending over him whispering loudly, "Wake up, Captain, the Japs are coming!" Japs! Coming clear back here? It was fantastic. The sounds of shouting were rising from the valley and the shooting was much closer than it had been before. Bryce grabbed for his boots and slipped them on. Then the first bullet ripped through the tent. All doubts vanished from Bryce's mind. The CQ was at the door again. "What shall I do, Captain?"

"Wake the others up, quick."

Shots were flying fast now. The stovepipe was hit with a crash. Bryce was on his stomach crawling over to Captain Buehler. The two aid men woke up, startled, full of questions. One moved toward the door. Thud! a bullet hit him, and he dropped with a gasp. The shouting was all around now, and a stream of running feet pounding the tundra passed the door. Bryce was shaking Buehler, "Wake up, the Japs are here!"

Buehler mumbled and turned over. "Too early to pull that stuff, Bryce."

The tent flapped open and the CQ dove into the tent. Rifles were banging away on all sides, punctuating the bedlam of confused shouts and running footsteps. "Wake up, Buehler, the Japs! Goddammit, can't you hear them shouting?" Buehler woke up, startled as consciousness swept back over him. The stove clanged as a bullet crashed through it. The patients were asking, "What are you going to do with us?" "What's going to happen?" The CQ told them it was all right; they had weapons.

Buehler was on his side pulling on his boots; Bryce was lying with his head against the tent, his eye at a bullet hole. With a loud rrrip, one bullet furrowed through his jacket across his back, and he cried out as another streaked over his eyebrow. What a nightmare, a madness of noise and confusion and deadliness. What had happened? What was happening? Buehler's sleep-fogged mind could find no rational answer. He only knew that death was zipping through the tent just over his head. One of the patients groaned loudly. He was hit again. Buehler fumbled for his carbine.

He was wide awake now, and grimly aware of the Japs all around outside. There must have been a hundred or so of them in the immediate vicinity of the aid station, and all chattering like monkeys. Escape flashed through his mind first, but with the Japs milling around outside in the first faint glimmer of dawn and the tent full of patients, the thought vanished as soon as it appeared. It was too late to even try to get out. The patients were asking again, "What are you going to do with us?" and Buehler told them all to be quiet, to lie down, low, and not to shoot under any circumstances. "Play dead, lie still and play dead."

The Japs were chattering outside and occasionally an English word would appear in the midst of all the Japanese. This added to the confusion of the puzzled minds in the tent. What had happened? What was happening? The name "George" was repeated several times just beyond the canvas wall. It was getting lighter rapidly. The riddled tent walls began to show spots of light, and the men inside could see the shapes of their fellows. Then the Japs found the stack of rifles and ammunition at the door. They fell upon the stack, rattling the guns and chattering excitedly. The stack had been formed between the guy ropes on the tent, and in moving the rifles the Japs stumbled against the tent, and each time the wall bulged with the shape of the Jap's body. Several times Japs tripped over the guy ropes and the whole tent lurched, as though it might collapse and outline the forms within for the Japs' bayonets.

The Japs were chattering outside and occasionally the flap of the tent would fly open in a little breeze, and each time it opened the men inside the tent caught glimpses of the Japs moving about outside. The wounded men had two rifles near them, and the thought of what might happen if one of the none-too-rational casualties fired at the Japs prompted Captain Buehler to crawl over and remove the rifles to his own corner of the tent.

It was light enough now for the eyes accustomed to the darkness inside the tent to distinguish more than just lumps and shadows. The tent was a mess. It had been riddled by bullets and the stove and stovepipe were full of holes. Of the thirteen men in the tent, four were still able to move about. Captain Buehler had miraculously escaped being hit at all. Captain Bryce had been creased across his eyebrows. The CQ was intact and one aid man who had been sleeping outside had somehow managed to get inside the tent without being seen or hit. The exposure case, who had been stripped and was sleeping near the stove, had been killed on the stretcher. The top of his head was a mess where a bullet had ripped into his skull, his face was bloody and brain tissue was spattered over the litter. The boy who had been hit trying to get out of the tent was moaning, "I'm hit in the heart. . . . I can't last long!" and Sergeant Lester L. Onken, who had been hit in the leg, was trying desperately to quiet him. They were both in the end of the tent near the stove. The rest of the men were in the other end of the tent. It was darker there, away from the flapping doorway.

The Japs outside seemed to have thinned out, their chatter had subsided. Apparently many of them had moved on up the draw toward Clevesy Pass. But there were still many of them around the tent. Captain Bryce crawled to the dead man on the litter. Cautiously he moved him toward the door. The tactics were simple—the aid station had escaped complete annihilation by a miracle.

By a miracle twelve men were still living, only one was dead. And twelve were playing dead. Bryce pulled the mutilated man halfway off the stretcher and left him sprawled face up in the doorway so that curious Japs who peered inside would see this first and perhaps only this, and accept the grisly testimony at its dead face value. Bryce had just completed setting the precarious stage and had crawled back from the doorway when the effectiveness of his work proved itself. A Jap pulled back the flap of the door and peered in. He just glanced at the dead man's head and withdrew, satisfied that the destruction inside had been complete. He will never be cited for valor, but the mutilated, dead soldier held his position against the door of the tent more valiantly and more effectively than he could have in life, and to the twelve live men in the tent he was a hero. Five times during the morning Japs pulled back the tent flap and looked in and each time they were driven back. The sight of the dead boy convinced them.

Later in the morning after the frenzy of the early morning fighting had subsided one Jap, perhaps in search of food, stuck his head into the tent and looked all around. He stepped over the body of the dead man in the door and stood up inside the tent. He had a rifle with a bayonet fixed. He blinked in the darkness of the tent's interior for a second. From deep inside the dark end of the tent Captain Buehler slowly raised his carbine and pushed off the safety realizing fully that a shot coming from inside the tent would bring the whole horde in on them. Either way it was suicide. At least he would take one of the bastards along. The Jap was looking down at the two wounded men. They were lying face down on the grassy floor. If Buehler stuck his bayonet into the man he would scream and the whole show would be lost. The Jap took a tentative step toward Sergeant Onken; Buehler's finger tightened on the trigger. Then suddenly, in response to a shout from outside, the Jap turned and ducked out through the doorway.

After this crisis the twelve men lay as though paralyzed for a long, long time. No one even hoped to get out alive during the long minutes that followed. Miracles were too flimsy to count on, and luck had already been pushed to a ridiculous extreme. The medic who had been hit in the chest was the first to break the long silence. He had been quieted by Sergeant Onken at first but once more he began moaning, "I'm hit in the heart, I won't last long. I must take the sulfadiazine pills." The sergeant hushed him again, but this time the man was insistent. He was following the pattern the doctors had drilled into his head: "Take the sulfadiazines immediately, all of them if the wound is serious." And his wound was serious. The other wounded men were stirring too, and the doctors were afraid their mumbled groans and sighs would give them all away. They got out the morphine and crawling carefully among the patients, gave them all shots to keep them quiet. To move inside the tent was extremely hazardous. If a Jap had looked in while they were moving, or if their movements were heard, the end would be certain. The morphine quieted the patients for awhile. Some of them fell sound asleep. But the doctors' relief was shortlived. The tired fighters began sleeping the complete relaxed sleep of exhausted men. And they snored! In an anguish of frustration the doctors and the two aid men woke them up again, turned them over, pleaded with them in urgent whispers to be quiet.

The hours dragged slowly along. There was nothing to do but wait, *wait*, and think in the distracted disconnected way of all nightmares, "What had happened?" The answers were a variety of pessimistic conjectures. The Japs had landed a strong force at Sarana Bay. . . . Maybe it was only a raiding party that had pushed into our lines. . . . None of the cats was operating. . . . The Japs had pushed clear into Massacre and the Americans had gotten on ships and pulled out. . . . There was still a lot of fighting going on around. . . . Maybe we'd get help. . . . Maybe the Japs had had strong reinforcements from Kiska and they had pushed the whole line back. . . . Maybe the Americans would counterattack again and we'd get help. . . . Nothing to do but wait. They thought of the phone, but Bryce had tried it. It was dead.

Captain Buehler rolled over and looked out through a low bullet hole in the tent wall. The little ragged hole framed a Jap. He was staring right back at the tent, not moving. The skin on Buehler's neck crawled. Had the Jap seen his eye at the hole? The Jap continued to stare; then deliberately he took a grenade out of his pocket and pulled the pin. Buehler wanted to move away from the hole, but he was fascinated by what the Jap was doing. He was raising the grenade up to ignite the fuze by tapping it on his helmet, when another Jap came into the scene. The newcomer was apparently a noncom. He held the first Jap's arm, restrained him from igniting the grenade. They talked a moment and from the gestures Buehler deduced that the noncom was telling the first man not to throw a grenade so close to the others who were apparently still around the tent. Buehler rolled back from the side of the tent. How could such miracles continue? Twice now the lives of twelve men had hung on a thread as fine as the split-second timing of a purely chance remark.

As hours slowly followed hours without actually precipitating death for the men in the tent, their courage rose. The doctors dressed the wounds of the men who had been hit in the early morning hours, moving through the tent cautiously, aware of their peril, like a man will move on a high scaffold after he has become accustomed to the height, aware of the possibility of a fall. Buehler looked at his watch. It was well into the afternoon, way past lunch time. He thought of food only from the habit of the hour, and not because he was hungry. No one was hungry or thirsty. The three boxes of K rations and two gallons of water, which would have been slim indeed normally were more than ample under the present strained circumstances. The normal processes of elimination, however, continued unabated; and relief was obtained only at great wear and tear on the nerve of the others in the tent and with a definite sacrifice to the normal attempts at immaculateness of an aid station, with the one exception that each small excavation was marked with a peg.

The sounds outside the tent had dropped to a few scattered shots from time to time, and little snatches of Japanese phrases. Captain Buehler crawled to the edge of the tent and peeked out again. He saw a Jap in a foxhole about seventy-five feet from the tent and up the hill. The Jap had his back to the tent and as Buehler watched he raised up and fired up the hill, then squatted back into the hole. Buehler watched the back of his helmet as the Jap looked from side to side. The helmet disappeared for a moment into the hole. Then, when it bobbed back up the Jap had a cigarette. From the opposite side of the tent two Japs were talking in low voices, close to the tent. Buehler rolled back from the tent wall.

The silence inside the tent, and the straining for silence, set everyone's nerves on edge. The simple clearing of the throat seemed to crash through the tent like a clap of thunder, and Captain Buehler noticed he was thinking with scientific interest of the hundreds of times the normal man coughs during the course of a day. None of the stretcher cases had been able to see outside, to realize how close the Japs were around them, and it was hard to convince them of the precariousness of their situation. Often they would cough in the open instead of covering their heads with their sleeping bags and smothering the cough with their arms.

A wind had come up and it began to rain lightly on the tent. The men inside felt more secure against random sounds giving them away; they counted on the rain and wind to muffle their sounds. Captain Bryce thought a small prayer to himself that the Japs would not seek shelter inside the tent, a prayer that continued all through the endless afternoon.

It was evening before the doctors gave much thought to actively trying to get help. It was Bryce's idea first that as soon as it got dark he would start out and move toward Massacre Valley after help. Sergeant Chester L. Gleffe, who had been sick with diarrhea but was feeling much better, volunteered to start out also, only he wanted to go in the opposite direction, toward where the advance station had been. The CQ, obviously nervous about staying longer in the aid station, was anxious to get out under the cover of darkness and be on his own again, so he, too, volunteered to go for help. Captain Bryce and Captain Buehler talked the situation over carefully and decided that Sergeant Gleffe should start first, about midnight, and that Bryce should follow in about half an hour. It was decided that Arthur D. Englert, the CQ, and Captain Buehler would remain behind with the patients.

The light of the long day persisted faintly. In the dimness the lone Jap in the foxhole on the hill was still visible, his helmet moving slightly as he looked from side to side. Buehler and Bryce crawled into the corner of the tent away from the Jap in the hole. They listened for a long time and looked out through the bullet holes in the tent. As far as their limited vision would permit, they studied the ground around this corner of the tent. The coast was apparently clear. Slowly and carefully they pulled the loops from the stakes in the corner and untied the lashing on the corner pole.

As soon as darkness came, Sergeant Gleffe crawled out through the low opening under the bottom of the tent and, sliding on his belly, very slowly, he disappeared. The men in the tent waited. Ten minutes passed, and nothing happened. The men relaxed from their tense waiting. Their hopes that Gleffe would get away and bring help had become almost a certainty, when the Jap who had been sitting in the foxhole fired ten shots in rapid succession. This outburst stiffened the men in the tent with apprehension. If Gleffe had been spotted close to the tent and had been shot, certainly the Jap would realize that live Americans were left in the tent. Once again there was a long wait filled with apprehension. For nearly an hour no one spoke or moved. Finally Bryce crawled over to Captain Buehler. He wanted Buehler's opinion as to whether he should try to get out or not. They discussed the idea again, assuming that Gleffe had been killed. The Jap would certainly be on the alert for further attempts by the Americans to get help, even if he didn't realize where Gleffe had come from.

Bryce raised up the bottom of the tent and peered out into the night. It was near 0100, but the high fog which normally blacked out even the stars' faint light was not there and even the contours of the tundra were visible. From way down in Jim Fish Valley flares were being fired into the sky. This hazard, added to the other difficulties of the undertaking, made the situation impossible; so, for another hour, Bryce waited inside the tent.

No flares had been fired for a long time. Bryce, who had been watching the ground of the valley from under the bottom of the tent was convinced he could leave now and with luck get through to help. But the nearest help was a long way off, of that much they were sure; and the early Aleutian dawn was only a matter of a couple of hours away. Finally Captain Buehler ordered Bryce to remain in the tent. It was not worth it, after all, he thought, to attempt to get help. They would try to hold out another day inside the tent; and the next night, if no help had come, they would try something. Bryce, who had prepared himself for the dangerous trip across the valley, was let down by the order to remain and tried to argue with the captain's decision, even though he realized, in his own mind, that it was wiser to be caught by the dawn in the tent than out in the coverless valley.

Morning came without incident, slowly; apparently nothing had changed during the night to alter the situation. There had been scattered fights across the valley and on the hill in rear of the station, recognized by the men in the tent only as scattered shooting and the occasional harsh explosion of a grenade. Several times they felt the dull rumble of artillery falling far down Jim Fish Valley, probably in conjunction with the flares. The Jap in the foxhole was still there, his helmet moving from time to time. And Sergeant Gleffe was gone. Otherwise the situation was unchanged.

It was 0800 when a cat motor roared on the hill behind the tent. Bryce was pessimistic and insisted that the Japs had captured the machines and were operating them. It was hard to believe that the Americans had suffered that much of a setback, and the fact that the lone Jap had not moved during the night somehow encouraged Captain Buehler.

For a long moment everything was still—the cat motor had been shut off, the faint breeze died completely out, the whole valley was silent—then someone far up on Engineer Hill called out in unmistakable English, "Hey George, look here a minute!" That instant was the turning point for the stranded men in the tent. That vague sentence, faint but unmistakable, answered every dreadful question and dissipated every dreadful fear that had been gnawing in the minds of the men since they had first heard the Japs' "Banzai!" twenty-eight long hours before.

The wounded men were enthusiastic, almost to the point of folly. They insisted that Captain Buehler go outside at once and signal the owner of the voice which had shouted the sentence. But Captain Buehler well realized that actually their condition had been little improved. True, Americans still held Engineer Hill, or most of it, and the breakthrough could not have been a complete tragedy for the American forces; but the situation of the aid station was still very critical, and the Japs, armed and deadly, were still in the immediate vicinity. It would be a terrible thing for them to give away the whole show now, with help so close. They must be patient, and cautious. If the Americans still held Engineer Hill, surely they would send patrols down into the valley; that would be the time to signal.

The morning hours wore on. It was just a matter of time, now, everyone was sure, until a patrol would come down the hillside and drive out the Japs. Fights were breaking out all over the valley, and there was a lot of firing on the hills on both sides and to the rear. Many times during the morning both Bryce and Buehler thought of shooting the Jap in the foxhole but always decided it would be better to stand pat, and wait the situation out, rather than to attract attention to the tent that so far had successfully sheltered the live corpses. Other Japs were likely to be in this area. Once they heard American voices again, apparently coming down the hill behind the tent, and there was a lot of firing close by. Buehler gave the wounded men their rifles, and told them that they would fight the Japs now if any of them attempted to come into the tent. The firing around the station came closer and closer, and the shouting voices were American, without a doubt. Once again the wounded men insisted that Buehler try to attract their attention, but though the men inside looked out of the tent in every direction, they could not actually see the attackers, so Buehler again told them it was better to wait. The Jap in the foxhole had not moved. Finally the firing stopped and the voices faded away. The effect on the wounded men was very definite. They felt that Captain Buehler had muffed their great opportunity. Buehler himself felt very badly as hour followed hour and nothing happened. He tried to reassure the men and himself that the Americans would come again, and he tried to explain that if he had gone outside or fired, or shouted, the Americans could not have known he was not a Jap, even if they could have heard him. And besides the menace of the Japs themselves was still a very real one.

It was after two in the afternoon when another fight started near enough to the aid station to be interesting to the isolated men inside. It started up the blind alley to the left of the tent and was moving down the valley. This time the Japs were retreating before the advancing Americans and the men in the tent were lying on the floor, their weapons ready, as they heard the Japs running by outside, trying vainly to return the American fire. Bryce looked for the Jap in the foxhole, but he was gone. This time the men were sure they would be released. In just a matter of moments after Bryce had announced that the Jap who kept his unknowing vigil over them for a day and a half had gone, they heard American voices. This time the voices were close enough so that they could hear spoken sentences. Americans! They were right outside the tent. The men had played dead for nearly two days, practically between the Japs' legs; now, here were Americans, right outside the tent. Before anyone could shout a greeting or make a signal of any kind one of the voices outside said, "We'd better toss a grenade in there!" For a terrible instant no one spoke. Then Captain Buehler blurted, "American wounded in here!"

The voice outside said, "It's a Jap trick."

But Captain Buehler hardly heard him. He was already moving toward the door. "It's not a trick. I'll come out."

The voice outside said, "OK, come on out but no funny stuff."

Captain Buehler ducked under the door flaps and stepped out. As he raised up he was staring down the muzzle of twelve M1 rifles. It was the most beautiful sight he had ever seen.

The dénouement was simple. The walking wounded, including two of the men who had been litter cases two nights before, and the aid men, moved up Engineer Hill to the hot coffee and slum of the rear clearing station. Captain Buehler and Captain Bryce stayed with the litter cases until the road opened up later in the afternoon. Sergeant Gleffe, who had started out for help the night before, had been caught by daylight out in the open and had lain in a foxhole and watched the Japs bayonet and grenade what was left of the aid station he had tried to reach during the night. It was late in the afternoon before he was picked up by another American patrol working down the valley.

It is hard to say, when so much depends on such little things and when pure "pot luck" figures so strongly in the outcome, just how much what one does or does not do at just the right times contributes to the final result. Bryce thinks that they might have spared themselves one discomfort during the dangerously adventurous thirty-eight or so hours spent playing dead in their canvas tomb. The thing that got him down, really, was that they didn't smoke all the time they were there for fear the odor of good old American cigarettes would give them away. "We may have overdone it, but, brother, we just were not in the chance-taking mood."

The Story of a Supply Dump

Private First Class Thomas Allen Sexton,
Headquarters Company, 32d Infantry

The boys in the company used to kid Sexton and call him "Old Tom." I guess because his hair is just a bit threadbare on top and he is such a mild-mannered, wise fellow that he seems to possess the mellowness of old age. Tom is really in his early thirties, I think, and before he came in the Army he worked in a bank. However, if it is possible to have years scared off your life, Old Tom is living on borrowed time right now. Sexton was the assistant company clerk for Company F and in the battle days every available man had been used to push ammunition and rations to the front-line boys. The 2d Battalion of the 32d had established a forward supply dump and set up kitchens in a gorge at the foot of the first steep rise down Jim Fish Valley and over near the left side of the valley. The battle was going along pretty well and it was in the final stages. The Japs had been squeezed into a small area, and the pressure on them was increasing every hour. Everyone was nearing exhaustion from constant exposure to numbing cold and from constant driving. The haul up the mountain from the supply dump to the front lines was a five-hour backbreaker, and Sexton had returned at

0100 May 29, from lugging a box of rations up the mountain and he was just about tuckered out. Staff Sergeant Joseph B. Orlow, the mess sergeant of Company F, and Corporal Wilson L. Johnson, the company clerk, had pitched a pup tent near the twenty-foot bank where the kitchens were set up. They got hold of Old Tom and the three of them crawled into their sacks with Sexton in the middle.

About 0430 Sexton woke up. There was firing up the valley. This was not unusual, so they stayed in their sacks and listened for a few minutes. The firing was increasing in intensity to such a degree that the men started to get out of their sacks. Suddenly the volume of firing, and, for the first time, shouting mushroomed into bedlam. The three men scrambled to get out of their sacks when the first grenade went off in the area.

Sexton was dazed. Just a few seconds after the grenades landed, one of the guards, a Mexican boy, shrieked. He had been bayoneted, and only then did Sexton realize that the Japs were actually upon them. A horde of screaming, chattering Japs poured down over the bank onto the sleeping or only half-awake men. They had rifles, grenades, machine guns, and bayonets tied on sticks. The bedlam was numbing. Johnson showed marvelous presence of mind. The three men were sitting up, still in their sacks, and in the tent. Johnson was firing his rifle toward the top of the bank. He emptied his clip and made a grab for his pistol, a pistol he had picked up the day before. One of the sentries had fallen back and was standing just outside the tent. He was firing frantically. Orlow kept repeating, "What will we do? What will we do?" The sentry outside bent over and shouted to him, "Give me your gun, mine's empty." Orlow handed his rifle out. Johnson fired twice with his pistol.

A Jap fell just outside the tent. Sexton heard a bullet whistle and thump into Johnson's body. Johnson gasped, but continued to fire his .45.

Then the Jap bayonets began plunging into the tent. Sexton felt Orlow lurch as a bayonet got him. Johnson fired again. Bayonets were ripping into the tent from all sides. Sexton had his carbine going and was firing through the tent at each bayonet thrust. Then Johnson got stabbed again. He and Orlow went down together. Sexton fell back with them. The Japs were screaming all around the tent. Sexton felt someone lift the tattered tent and heard a short Japanese phrase spoken over his head. Two English words were being repeated with frenzy outside, words he will never forget because they were so familiar and yet so alien that morning. The Japs were raiding the supply dump and repeated "grenades" and "cigarettes" over and over. The fight was over in a few minutes, and most of the Japs moved across the valley.

Sexton was unhurt. He lay motionless between his two dead friends until daybreak. The carnage around the camp was terrifying. Looking out of the torn tent Sexton could see the ground covered with bodies. Now and then a Jap would move across his line of vision. It was just getting light when the sentry who had grabbed Orlow's gun crawled into the tent. He had been shot and bayoneted so that he had thirteen wounds in his body. He was pulled into the tent by Sexton just seconds before a Jap walked by. The men were breathless while the Jap stood out twenty feet from the opening of the tent. The little Jap carried himself like a Prussian, straight and arrogant. He pushed several of the bodies with his feet. Sexton had his carbine lined on his back, against the possibility that he might turn around and discover them there and still alive. Finally he moved off. The wounded boy, Herbert Rines, began to moan. Sexton fed him his sulfa pills and he quieted for a while. All during the long day when he became restless Sexton would give him a pill and some water, the psychology of which worked well in keeping the boy quiet. In whispers Tom told him what a splendid fight he had put up, and marveled in his own mind at the wiry tenacity of the little man.

The day wore on very slowly; fights were springing up here and there, but the two men could not deduce from them where the Americans had held and where they had broken. They were convinced from scattered shots that cracked over them that there were Japs still in the immediate vicinity. The discouraging thing about the whole day was that none of the cats was operating on Engineer Hill. It was 1630 before Sexton saw anything that he recognized. An American patrol was moving across the valley floor from the right. He crawled out of the tent and looked for Japs. There were none that he could see, so he waved to the patrol. A lieutenant from the 17th Infantry was leading the patrol, and Sexton finally caught his eye. The patrol moved up slowly and carefully. They killed fifteen Japs before they got the area cleaned out enough to move Sexton and Rines out.

The hot slum and coffee that Sexton got at the 17th CP was as sumptuous as any feast he had ever had; and seeing live, moving Americans again made him change his mind from the decision he had made during the early morning hours to go to the beach and never leave it again. That night Sexton moved across Sarana Valley and up on Engineer Hill, where he found Paul Simpson, the company mechanic, and Henry W. Clark, the supply sergeant, and the next morning Old Tom was lugging chow up the mountain again.

The Engineers Fight as Infantry

First Sergeant Jessie H. Clonts, Jr., Company D, 50th Engineers

We had worked all night and up until noon of the 27th carrying supplies up to the front, then we slept four hours and worked almost all night again. We were so tired when we finally did get into our sacks that I didn't think anything could wake us up, but the 37mm. shell that smacked through the tent did it.

The shell was the first indication we had that the Japs had broken through. We had just gotten up before they hit us and things really began to pop. It was foggy and dark, which made it almost impossible to tell American from Jap during the early part of the fight. Lieutenant John H. Green saw a man walking out ahead of him, and he hollered for the guy to get the hell down in a hole; the fellow replied, "Me do, me do," but he didn't get down fast enough because Lieutenant Green shot him. They were right in with us. Lieutenant Jack J. Dillon and I were trying to establish a line and our best protection was to walk up straight. We decided we'd take a chance on stray bullets; both of us being over six feet tall was pretty good identification for us so our own boys wouldn't shoot us. The captain had a loud voice and all morning he shouted directions and pep talks that could be heard, even above the racket of the fight, all over the hill. We put two BARs in, one on each flank of our line, and they got in some good licks with tracer ammunition which marked our own line for our men, and also pointed out targets. I saw Sergeant Allstead right in the thick of things, and he is not the type of person you'd expect to find in the middle of a good fight. I asked him what he was doing up there and he said, "Goddammit! I've got as much right to be here as you have," just like it was a party or something.

The line we had established held, and very few Japs got through it. When daylight came we discovered a whole bunch of Japs pinned in a ditch in front of the road along which we had been fighting. While the boys kept firing to keep the Japs down, several others of us crawled up the bank and threw grenades into them. Helmets, rifles, and Japs flew out of the ditch. We were astonished at the mess of them. They had been lying three deep in the ditch trying to hide.

During the day, we fought back and forth every time a group of Japs were spotted. Lieutenant Dillon had a great time with his .30 and some long-range sniping, at which he is very good.

In the afternoon we were returning from a patrol up toward Cold Mountain when we spotted a Jap's head sticking out from the bottom of a big bank of snow. We shot him and saw another one, who had jumped up and tried to run to a kind of cave farther around the snow. We went down to investigate and discovered that the big snowbank was honeycombed with caves formed as the snow melted and the water ran off underneath. There were lots of tracks and other marks that indicated the Japs had been crawling in and out of this snow cave; and we had seen one other, besides the two we had killed, crawl into a cave a short distance away. We tried to fire into the snow and tried grenades too, but neither would work. This, apparently, was a job for the powder men. A few pounds of "persuader" on the snowbank would likely get the desired results. The TNT was brought up; we set a charge off on the snow. Nothing much happened, so we systematically punched deep holes into the right-foot snow roof of the cave and charged the holes. When we set her off this time, the whole center of the snowbank caved in. If the concussion didn't get the Japs, the few tons of closely packed snow and ice certainly did. We repeated this process with other suspicious snowbanks in the draw until we had enough crushed ice for a Legion Convention. Unorthodox tactics, maybe, but it turned live Japs into good ones, and packed them on ice.

A Day in Hiding

Corporal Virgil F. Montgomery, 1st Platoon, 14th Field Hospital

The 1st Platoon of the 14th Field Hospital had been used almost entirely for evacuation, because that was the big problem—moving the wounded men back from the front over the steep mountains and the slippery tundra filled with deep, treacherous holes.

The front lines were down Jim Fish Valley quite a ways so we had set up an advance aid station across Sarana Valley from Engineer Hill, and for three days we had used it as a sort of combination aid tent and collecting station. Major

Robert J. Kamish was working the station and there were seventeen men from our platoon with him. We had foxholes dug around the tent and pup tents had been pitched over many of them.

The night of May 28, Brown, my buddy, and I were sleeping together a short distance from the aid tent in our shelter. The 2d Battalion of the 32d Infantry had established a kitchen and a supply dump in a draw to the left of our draw maybe 400 yards, and the first we heard of anything wrong was a lot of shouting and some shooting coming from over there. I raised up to listen. It was about 0500 in the morning and still so dark that it was hard to distinguish objects. Firing from down the valley was the usual thing, but there had been comparatively little firing as far back as the supply dumps, so this sudden outburst worried me. I woke Cletus A. Brown up and we watched and listened. Then we saw six men moving out of the draw and coming our way. Although I could barely see them, something in the way they walked made me believe they were Japs. Others around us had heard the commotion and were getting up. We climbed out of our bags, and grabbed our boots and coats; the rest of our clothes were on; we had been sleeping in them right along. Other men had spotted the first group of Japs and had started to move out. We went toward the aid tent first, only to meet another column of Japs, who were running and chattering like monkeys, swinging in from the right. Brown was ahead of me and he started to run, shouting, "Up here!" We ran along the only route open to us, right up the hill between our draw and the draw the 2d Battalion's kitchens were in. As we broke to run, the Japs spotted us and began firing. We ran frantically until we got into a small nook on the hill. Brown stopped, breathless, and I caught up with him. We were panting from the hard run. The shouting and chattering and firing of the melee behind us was terrible. Brown was looking back down the hill, "Hell, here they come!" he said, and he turned and started on up the hill. I took a quick look and six or seven Japs had just come into view over the crest of the little flat we were on. They began firing again. I ran a few feet and hit dirt. Brown kept running ahead. I had made three or four dashes, the bullets whistling around me, and I hit the dirt again; this time my left leg had gone into a hole in the tundra clear up to my hip. Brown was shouting at me. I looked up. He was skylined at the crest of the hill. While I looked he let out a cry and fell. He had been hit.

I could see the Japs faintly, behind me, still coming. As I tried to work my left leg out of the hole, I discovered that the hole was wide at the bottom. My lungs were burning from the run, I dreaded to run again . . . I was desperate. I pushed myself down into the narrow slit until I was lying flat on my back. My shoulders were wedged tightly against the muddy sides. There was just room for my legs to be almost straight in one end of the hole; and my head was in the opening of a little underground passage in the other end. There was about six inches of icy water flowing through the hole, which issued from the bank in little trickles where my ears were. I lay very still for a long time. I wasn't sure at all that the Japs had not seen me. About three feet over my eyes I watched the slit of light sky showing through the opening, expecting any second to see the face of a Jap leer down at me. I held my breath once when the tundra shook with the footsteps of someone running by outside. The firing and shouting sounded faint to me. I began to study the leaves of grass that were springing one at a time back to their normal bend from which I had pressed them in squeezing down into the hole.

I had almost made up my mind to sneak a look. It was quite light now. I began to squirm in the hole; it was getting cold, and I wanted to see more about where I was. Then I stopped moving and listened. I had felt the ground tremble again. Someone was walking nearby. Then I heard voices, the chatter of Japanese. There seemed to be seven or eight of them, and they were close. One voice was dominating, giving orders. There was a lot of scurrying around right over my head. One Jap stepped over the hole. I remember the blur, the little hobnails and the light-yellow flannel pants. They were working all around the hole, chattering short sentences. I shrank down into the water in the hole. I had given up . . . I almost wished the earth would close over me and be done with it. I wondered what the Japs were doing just outside the hole. A heel was sticking out over the edge of the opening. Had they seen? Suddenly a machine gun fired right over me. Two or three voices chattered exictedly. The machine gun fired again; this time several hot cartridges fell into the hole and splashed beside my neck. The voices chattered again, and then seemed to move away. The heel vanished.

There was no sound. . . . Then the gun fired again and I felt the tundra tremble as someone moved above. But there was no talking. Apparently the Japs had left one man to fire the machine gun.

The gun fired sporadically all through the endless morning. From time to time the heel would stick over the edge of the opening, Christ! if that foot ever slipped. . . . My legs were numb from the cold water and my hips and knees ached. Sometimes I would be seized with a fit of shivering . . . and then I was afraid the Jap would feel the shake. Once I heard a funny sharp tuck! tuck! tuck! through the ground. I thought a BAR was firing at the Jap gun. The Jap replied with long rapid bursts, and the "tuck" sounds came no more.

It must have been well into the afternoon. The Jap had been firing just off and on in short bursts. Then the ground shook with a heavy explosion. And another. "My God," I thought, "they're firing artillery at this damned Jap gun." The tundra would leap and shake, then I could hear the heavy explosion, muffled, but powerful. At first I was sickened with the thought of an artillery shell dropping into the hole. The Jap's foot dangled into the opening, and I prayed that he would not be hit; even though he was responsible for my predicament. The ground lurched violently, and a huge explosion pushed on my ears. Pieces of shrapnel fell into the hole. The Jap's foot moved away, but he had not moved his body I was sure, neither had he been hit. He had not made a human sound that I could remember, only the firing of his gun. To hell with him! "We'll go out together, you little bastard." Again the ground shook.

For a long time nothing happened. My back was aching, my whole body was getting numb. "How will this end . . . how will this end?" The thought kept going over in my head. The Jap gun was firing almost constantly now, I realized. From time to time hot cartridges poured into my hole, onto my chest and neck. It was late again I thought. The sky was getting blue and losing the brilliant whiteness it had had a few hours before. I must have passed out, or maybe even dozed. The Jap was firing frantically—I realized I was strangly glad to hear it . . . I must have felt that a crisis was here . . . that it was over.

Between bursts of the Jap gun I was sure I felt or heard again the tuck! tuck! tuck! of bullets striking the ground around the hole. The Jap was burning up his gun. His foot stuck over the edge of my hole again for an instant and then disappeared. He had ceased firing. I heard the tuck! tuck! again. Bullets were striking all around now I was sure. Then an explosion roared over my hole. But it was different from the artillery or mortar that had landed before. The tundra did not shake so violently, and the explosion was lighter. Then another explosion went off. Grenades! I thought. Hand grenades. It never occurred to me to worry about a grenade falling into the hole. I was tickled, I was crazy happy. Then I heard the voices . . . I couldn't make out the words, but they were American voices, and coming closer. Then in good clear English words, someone up above me said, "Any more down there?" I raised up and hollered as loud as I could "Here's one. I'm here." I squeezed my head out of the hole. I was looking up to where I had seen my buddy, Brown, go down, it seemed like a week ago. . . . A man stood there with a grenade all drawn back over his head, ready to throw. There were four men with rifles pointed at me too, I saw, in a quick sweep of my eyes. The man with the grenade hollered "Hold it! He's one of our men." They came down and pulled me out of the hole. My legs wouldn't hold me up. They were completely numb. I saw the Jap gun, and the Jap about fifteen feet away, sprawled on his face.

I don't remember much of what followed. I think I passed out again. I remember telling about how I had lain in the hole and watched the Jap heel and heard the machine gun firing over my head. I remember getting dry clothes. I remember a cup of coffee and a strange walk across the valley and up onto Engineer Hill . . . and a sleeping bag.

Rear Clearing Station

Captain Lawrence L. Hick, Company D, 7th Medical Battalion

"Hey! Wake up and get the hell out of here! The Japs have broken through!" The sentry shouted his warning and dashed off to alert men in other tents. Grenades were bursting on Engineer Hill and machine guns sputtered; the clamor of the fight rose like a tide as the screaming Japs burst out of the fog and darkness onto the dazed rear echelon.

The four patients who had spent the night in the rear clearing station, set up in Clevesy Pass, were gotten up and told to clear out. Captain Lawrence L. Hick and Staff Sergeant Roger E. Williams waited until everyone had left, then they moved back toward the Hogback. They had no concept of the size of the counterattack. They thought that perhaps a small patrol of five or six Japs had moved into the area and were being cornered somewhere. But the furious firing and shouting continued; then half-dressed soldiers began to move to the rear, some with bayonet wounds and stories of Japs in numbers of forty and fifty. The impact of learning the size of the attack stunned the doctor. He and the sergeant went back to the station. It was getting light and several of the technicians were already there giving aid to the wounded men. Tec 5 Chester R. French had gone almost to the beach, decided he might be needed up front, and come back.

The clearing station was right in the front lines now. Japs were in a draw to the left front of the station. The two doctors, Captain Hick and Captain Abraham R. Koransky, built a barricade out of medical chests around the side of the tent from which the Jap bullets came and continued to work over the wounded men until the Jap fire pinned them to the floor of the tent.

As the day wore on, they heard Japs in a tent over on the left, but none apparently had gotten into the kitchen tent on the right. Some of the men crawled over and got canteens of coffee from a big 20-gallon pot that the cooks had left.

One of the patients had been bayoneted through the buttocks. He was in a sleeping bag just outside the tent. He had been afraid to stay inside, feeling sure that it would be grenaded; but it got so cold outside that the bottom of the tent was pulled up and he was moved back in. Just before they dropped the tent back down a bullet hit the man in the arm.

The Japs in the tent to the left could see a narrow strip of terrain out through a rip in the canvas. That strip was deadly, because they covered it with fire. A wounded soldier was lying in the mud about halfway across the strip, and Tec 5 Warren A. Lewis crawled out to get him and was shot himself. French dragged Lewis out of danger and dressed him. The ground was a quagmire where hundreds of grinding tractor treads had ripped off the tundra and churned the soft black dirt and melting snow and rain into a deep bog. Tec 5 Jack S. Bottema threw a rope out to the wounded man and sank in mud up to his hips dragging him out of the Jap fire.

There were many seriously wounded men on Engineer Hill, and time after time litter teams moved across the mud and onto the hill bringing the men down to the station. Two of the litter men had been wounded themselves carrying casualties down.

Bullets cracked through the littered tent all during the hectic day. Most of the time the doctors kept the fighting soldiers away from the station because they invariably drew a volley of fire. Private Norman F. Elliott was shot in the back when he tried to carry a wounded engineer down the hill and was lying exposed with Japs on a little rise just above him. Three infantrymen covered the rise with bullets while other aid men ran out and brought Elliott back. Sergeant Williams had been hit, and Bruce C. Heagney, dressing a bayonet wound inside the station, slumped over his patient, a casualty himself.

The wild day was almost over. The engineers had gotten organized resistance against the Japs and were busy cornering them in ravines and creek beds.

Several of the exhausted men in the aid station went to the now tattered kitchen tent for more of the coffee but a bullet had gone through the bottom of the big pot.

The sound of additional litter squads coming up from Massacre was wonderful. Everyone who could move in the station worked to evacuate the many wounded men in the fast-waning light. The fear that Japs might come back and grenade the tent in the dark was foremost in everyone's mind. The long job of removing the wounded was accomplished by midnight, and the ragged tent was deserted. Captain Hick looked around it quickly before he left. The barricade of medical chests was riddled with bullet holes, and the tent top itself hung in tatters, torn by bullets that had cracked crazily through it all day. The floor was scattered with bloody swabs and bandages. He let the flap drop back. He was tired. He stepped around a Jap body sprawled in the mud, one of 113 in the pass, and walked down the hill behind the last of the litter squads.

Little Flower

Technician Fifth Grade Ray Gonzales, Company C, 32d Infantry

Cooks during the battle used to carry canned rations and ammunition as an occupation, and cook slum and coffee for a pastime. We didn't think that we would ever actually need to fight, although we did carry our weapons and usually some grenades.

We had been working like horses for over two weeks and we were dirty and tired, but the fight seemed to be going in good shape; the enemy was pretty well cornered, according to rumors, and we thought we could see the end in sight. We had set up our kitchen about fifty feet from Company D's on Bagdad Hill, and the front lines were over a mile ahead in Jim Fish Valley. There were twelve of us, the kitchen crew, supply force, the clerk, and the artificer, and some others who planned to sleep in the kitchen; and, for the first time in a week for some of us, we undressed, and crawled into sleeping bags. It actually seemed peaceful as we began to fall asleep, and even the password seemed quiet and dainty—"Little Flower." We had slept perhaps two hours when the sentry woke us up saying that there was a lot of firing going on down in the valley. Someone said, "Well, let 'em fire, dammit, and let us sleep." I started to doze uneasily again when a shout crashed in on us, "The Japs broke through. They're coming this way!"

Everyone began to move in the maddest confusion of shoes and helmets and weapons. Corporal Kenneth G. Ramsay, the clerk, moved slowly and deliberately. He laced his shoes and lit a cigarette, I remember, while everyone else was scrambling and shouting. We rushed out into the night, as dark as the inside of a cow, and men were running in every direction, some dressed only in their underwear and shoes. The first of the retreating Americans and the first of the attacking Japs reached us about the same time. The Japs were yipping like Indians, and shouts of "We die, you die" were heard jumbled together with "Little Flower! I'm an American." I looked at the kitchen tent and Ramsay was just coming out. He stood up in the door and then spun around and fell. The firing and shouting and grenading was all around and the confusion was maddening. I jumped into a hole and saw three Japs in a hole near me. I fired over their heads once and they ducked, and then one raised up and I fired again . . . this went on for perhaps ten minutes—one would raise up and I'd fire at him. Then suddenly the hole the Japs were in exploded. I still remember the arms and legs flailing, silhouetted in the flash.

It began to be light finally and some of the men tried to get organized. We discovered seven Japs in Company D's kitchen. They were eating anything they could find. We threw some grenades, which broke up the meal, and a BAR man finished the Japs off—and also some of Company D's kitchen equipment that was left.

It was still very misty and it was hard to tell friend from enemy when we spotted two Jap officers (since found to be a major and a captain). I fired at one and the round was a tracer. It disappeared right into his chest. The other Jap ducked behind a cat. Tony, who was with me, was having trouble keeping his helmet on, since he had grabbed the wrong one in the scramble. But he had spotted the Jap so he crept forward to a small rise in the ground and took a careful bead; then the helmet flopped down over his eyes. He jerked it back and aimed again, when a BAR chattered over on the left, and Tony began to swear, ". . . damned BAR beat me to the draw."

With the coming of broad daylight everything calmed down quite a bit, but the fighting continued all through the day whenever isolated parties of Japs were spotted. A captain came over and told us to return to the kitchen and try to get some coffee made, so we crawled out of our holes and by short rushes returned to the kitchen. We had been gone about ten minutes when this same captain was wounded. All day long until late in the afternoon bullets continued ripping through the tent, but we got the coffee made and had started to cook some slum when a bullet went through the air tank on the stove. We later counted 47 dead Japs within fifty yards of the kitchen.

It was two weeks after that before I stopped taking the morning shift at the stove at sling arms with a round in the chamber. And the sound of the peaceful words "Little Flower" still sends shivers up my back.

Doctors and Wounded

Captain Charles H. Yellin, 7th Medical Battalion

"I recalled that I had been unusually lucky all my life; that the breaks always came at the right time; that—well—it was about time it changed, and here it was. Also, strangely enough, I was grateful for my insurance." That was Captain Charles Yellin's thought as the Japs swarmed around outside the aid station on the morning of May 29.

The day before, the advance clearing station had been moved across Sarana Valley to a position about 200 yards behind the CP of the 3d Battalion, 17th Infantry. On the evening of the 28th the Japs dumped several large shells in the area around the station. They were after a nest of 37s that were set up on the hill to the right, and they were missing. After the excitement of the shelling had subsided, Lieutenant Herbert Friedberg, assisting Captain Yellin in the station, began talking. He had a premonition, a feeling that something was going to happen to him. He was a fine chap, new in the company before the outfit moved out, and he was always very cheerful and coöperative. He was a dentist and there was comparatively little he could do in the field. He felt badly about this and was always delighted when he got tasks to perform, such as giving plasma. The two officers talked about their homes and compared pictures. Friedberg spoke of his wife and their child.

Casualties were lying along one side of the tent. They could not be moved over Engineer Hill until morning and were spending the night in the station. Before long other casualties began to arrive. The sounds of fighting up the valley echoed into the tent. By 0300 there were 15 casualties lined up on the floor of the clearing station. Captain Yellin and Lieutenant Friedberg worked among the men with no thought of sleep.

The sound of fighting was rising. The two officers thought it was the result of an organized Jap counterattack. Soon they realized the fight was moving close.

There was no question of what to do. The casualties pleaded with the doctors not to leave them alone. There was no time or equipment to move them. The two officers quieted the men, assured them they would not be left alone.

Chaplain Turner had come over to the station earlier in the evening to talk and catch some sleep. He had a sleeping bag and a tent and was sleeping outside near the station.

Suddenly the Japs struck. Noise and confusion and death crashed over the tent like an avalanche. The turmoil that followed garbled the sequence of brutal happenings into a maddening jumble of flashes and explosions, screams, and flying steel. "Banzai! We die, you die!" the Japs screamed, as they ripped and slaughtered and smashed everything in their path. The back of the tent was riddled with machine-gun bullets. A bayonet slashed into the canvas, tearing a great rip through which four grenades were thrown onto the men lying inside. Another Jap thrust the muzzle of an automatic rifle into the hole and sprayed bullets through the tent. Then they discovered the kitchen and stormed it.

The first orgy was over. The men alive inside the tent were helpless. They had few weapons and outside they could hear many Jap voices jabbering deliriously and much running back and fourth around the riddled tent. Several of the casualties moaned, and Captain Yellin gave morphine to all he could reach, then passed the syringe over to his sergeant, who injected the others.

As the slow coming of daylight gradually brought shadowy forms into sharper relief, the scene of carnage was shocking. Every man in the tent had been hit by a bullet or a fragment. Lieutenant Friedberg was hit in the head with a grenade fragment. His premonition had been right. He was dead. One of the casualties had been hit by the automatic rifle.

Chaplain Turner had come into the tent as the Japs struck. He crawled among the men, his presence and good spirits comforting them.

The Japs were all around outside. One wounded Jap, lying just beyond the tent, was struggling to reach his rifle, which had dropped into the tent as he fell. One of the wounded men who could move reached another Jap gun with a bayonet on it and stabbed him. On a rise in the ground a few yards behind the station a Jap had set up a machine gun and all through the long, seemingly endless morning he fired short bursts over the tattered clearing station at troops moving in the valley below. He was picked up by American mortar men, and soon the heavy shells began bursting around the gun, within a few yards of the tent, hurling fragments of steel that ripped additional holes in the canvas, no square foot of which did not already have a bullet hole in it.

In the early afternoon the Americans had organized resistance around their positions, and grim patrols moved over the hills and across the valleys pocketing the scattered Japanese into draws and destroying them. It was not long after noon that the Japs were driven away from the battered clearing station, and the men inside rescued. The casualties were moved to the security of the 3d Battalion CP there to wait until the way was cleared for evacuation.

The next night one of the last groups of Japs still not wiped out passed over the deserted station again and completed the job of destruction, utterly ripping to pieces every piece of equipment in the place before they were cornered and killed. It was a miserable anticlimax to the night before, a fiasco.

Flanking Fire

Sergeant John J. Sullivan, Company M, 17th Infantry

Sergeant John J. Sullivan was with a section of heavy machine guns attached to Company L, 17th Infantry, when they were up on the table on the left of Jim Fish Valley the night the Japs broke through. May 28 had been foggy and cold and during the night the fog had settled down in the valley, confining the horizon to the edge of the table where the guns were.

Early on the morning of the 29th the noise of fighting in the valley rose up through the fog and darkness in a confused bedlam, but the guns on the table were powerless to help.

When daylight finally came the curtain of fog rose, displaying the valley like a stage below them. The tents and camps established in the draws were a shambles and corpses were scattered in irregular circles around them. Everything was in amazing disorder. Communication wires had been cut, lines had broken and Japs had poured through, leaving isolated little islands of resistance. From time to time small groups of men crawled across the valley, but no one could tell if they were friends or Japanese. Sometimes a weapon would be used that could be identified, and then the heavy .30s were set to work. But most of the morning they sat idle, their potential fury held back, waiting for identification of the target.

Toward noon the lines were being reëstablished and some communication had been set up. A captain had asked for fire power to be directed across the valley. Lieutenant Stephen McIntyre was studying the situation with his glasses. Far across the valley where Company M, the gunner's buddies, had their CP Japs were moving behind a hill. There were 26 of them. At the top of the little hill Company M men crawled out, then ducked back, then appeared at the side of the hill, and ducked back. Lieutenant McIntyre talked to the gunners. He pointed out a little tan line of Japs along the foot of the hill and the Americans at the top of the hill. They determined the range at 1,800 yards. When all the Americans were out of sight for an instant both guns opened up. Two streams of tracer leaped from the muzzles of the guns and flew across the valley into the tiny tan line. One gun was right on the target, the other perhaps two mils off.

The guns fired several long bursts and the yellow line crumpled and portions of it trickled toward a thin, green creek bed below the hill. One of the guns adjusted on the creek bed and fired. The other continued to pour bullets into the foot of the hill.

The gunners ceased fire and Lieutenant McIntyre watched with glasses. The Americans on top of the little hill waved their arms. Some of them stayed on the hilltop while others worked around the side. Soon there were flashes of grenades going off and, after a few more minutes, the Americans moved back off the hill and down the valley. Lieutenant McIntyre counted 26 bundles of tan at the foot of the hill and in the creek bed.

Mopping Up

Private First Class Antonio Aguilar, Company A, 4th Infantry

As I had originally heard the story, this man Aguilar was a fighting tornado who had grabbed a Japanese officer's saber, wrenched it out of his hand, and run him through with it. And if it were my purpose or my desire to vaunt the glory and the swashbuckling invincibility of warriors I should have been sorely disappointed in learning what actually happened. As it is, however, I heard another now familiar story of the thinking courage of a boy fighting an enemy who can and will kill him, unless he kills first, and who represents vaguely a menace to his right to go to a dance or eat hot dogs on Sunday if he wants to.

Antonio Aguilar was a soft-spoken young man, obviously ill at ease as he said, "I don't see why you want my story. It is just what anybody else would have done." I told him that that was the reason I wanted his story, but he didn't understand. So I asked him to tell me what had happened.

"Well, sir, we were on a patrol, moving down Jim Fish Valley about a mile inland from Chichagof Valley on May 30. Four of us were working together and I was acting as scout. I was out in front of the others maybe 150 yards when I spotted some holes. I kept moving until I was sure they were Jap holes. Then I called back for the others to come up. As they topped a little rise in the ground so that they could see the holes too, I moved on down knowing that they would cover me. Two of the holes were covered with blankets and mats and I was sure there were Japs in them. As I moved over toward the first hole I guess the Japs must have heard me coming because one stuck his head up out of the hole. I shot him, firing three times; then another one raised up out of the same hole so I emptied my clip into them. Before I had time to reload I saw a Jap officer getting up out of a hole. He couldn't have been over ten feet from me. He jumped up suddenly and was fumbling with his sword trying to get it free of the scabbard. I was scared of that sword. I had seen some of them before and I knew how long and sharp they are. Without even thinking I guess, I jumped into the hole with the Jap and grabbed him, trying to keep him from drawing the sword. We were floundering around in the hole. He had the saber about halfway out of the scabbard and I had grabbed onto it when my buddies, Private Antonio G. Maquinalez and Private Frank N. Ochoa, came running up with Sergeant Archie L. Bundy. They shot the Jap."

The cut across the inside of his fingers was almost healed when he told me the story. "Is that all, sir," Aguilar asked. "Yes, thanks a lot, Aguilar," I said. He got up, embarrassed over the lack of heroics in his incident. "It's not much of a story, I guess," he said. We saluted and he left. I wish I had been able to do something about his soft-voiced embarrassment. True, he is not a hero. But these are not the stories of heroes; these are just the stories of guys who win wars and carry the scars on their hands.

The Taking of Chichagof Village

Sergeant Carmen J. Calabrese, Company L, 17th Infantry

It's a very rough soirée that we got ourselves into on the evening of May 30. The Japs are all over since we have never completely straightened things out from the breakthrough on the morning of the 29th. It all starts when our 1st Platoon gets way out ahead on the left flank and leaves the rest of us on a little ridge overlooking the Jap village in Chichagof Harbor.

Our left flank is wide open and the Japs start working through the gap. Lieutenant Russell W. Beegle comes up and decides, quite rightly, that we should withdraw, since our flank is apt to get rolled up like a carpet at any minute. There is nothing Sergeant Arthur H. Thomas can do but pull his 3d Platoon back also.

We spot some good ground over to our right rear and head for it. During the move, of course, we lose some of our control and the men are more or less on their own. They are just straggling up on the high ground as the Japs open up. Lieutenant Beegle, Albert Bianchi, Sergeant Thomas, and myself are up on this high ground already so we start firing back. Then we get an order to move to our left rear toward some higher ground, and the first thing I know Thomas, over on my left, is dead, shot through the mouth. On the right I see Lieutenant Beegle go down from a wound in his shoulder, and then Bianchi topples over a little cliff from a bullet in his shoulder, which is his second wound.

I hit the ground and begin crawling off that hill. Captain Mervin A. Elliot comes over to me, as a couple of our machine guns begin firing to our rear, and tells me the little draw up ahead is full of Japs. I get a couple of boys to go with me, and while the machine guns fire we crawl up to the draw and dump a bunch of grenades in on the Japs.

The fire is falling thick and fast around us, but we get reorganized and start back toward the ridge overlooking the village again. The snipers on the hills in back of the village have telescope sights, and they give us a fit for quite some time; but we manage to get up on the ridge again, and I see the Japs in the village start to move out. I send a runner back to hustle up the 3d Platoon but he never gets back. The captain sees some trouble over on our left again and wants a machine gun, so I send Louis S. Drozinski back to bring up Corporal Frank R. Burnes and a machine gun. The gun fires maybe five or six bursts, then both Drozinski and Burnes are wounded, Burnes in the throat. In the village and on across the valley there are little groups of Japs running around, all totaled up probably 130 or 140. We get an order to move back to our swamp by Lake Cories and bivouac. On the way back Major Lee Wallace, using his carbine for a cane, limps along with another officer for a ways. He is hit pretty hard in the legs. We are just getting nicely settled in the mud about 1230 when we get an order to move out again and attack the village. It is very dark by now, and we have a time getting things squared off. Sergeant Reid Clayson is going to lead off with about eight men. They are supposed to crawl up on the knoll above the village, and fire to beat hell for a while, and then pull back; while the rest of the company moves around for the right flank.

Sergeant Lester B. Thistle and I are staying in the rear as a rear guard, while the company moves out. The company has just gone over a little rise and we are following along when we spot this wounded Jap. While Thistle covers me, I go down to investigate. The guy is unconscious and I am taking a good look when five Japs pop up from some place and begin throwing grenades. Thistle and I duck while the grenades go off, then we raise up and fire into the Japs. We knock off all five and are starting out after the company. We can hear Clayson's squad banging away into the village, and before long they come back. Things have gotten mixed up again so it is decided that we will wait until morning before we go into the village.

The next morning the fight is all gone out of the Japs. For the most part we just walk along flushing out the holes and killing the Japs that don't blow themselves up. Once in a while we have a lively little skirmish, but nothing much. We toss a grenade into a cave, and get two explosions. We wait a minute and toss in another grenade, and get two more explosions. It turns out that there are Japs in the cave and every time one of our grenades goes off, a Jap blows himself up with a grenade.

There are three Jap tents in the village when we get down to it, and there are Japs in them. We fire into a tent, holler for the Japs to come out, and try to throw grenades in but they bounce off. So we gather up some tar paper and rags and creep up and set the tent on fire. It burns for a while, getting pretty smoky and hot inside, and then we hear three explosions and a bunch of gear flies out of the tent as the Japs kill themselves. One single damn Jap surrenders later in the day.

Just as soon as the battle is over we start policing up, and what a mess that island is in. It disgusts me. I'm anxious to get back to New York and go back in the wholesale fruit business.

A GI, sprawled on a cot behind Calabrese looking up at the ceiling, drawled, "Well, don't count too much on apples, Cal. The market is liable to be flooded."

The Aftermath — 1

Captain Albert L. Pence, Jr., Company B, 32d Infantry

Early on the morning of May 30 the rear guard sounded an alarm. Company B, which was reduced to about 25 riflemen, was up on the front line across a nose in Jim Fish Valley, and Japs were approaching up a draw from the rear, apparently trying to get down the valley into Chichagof Harbor. Captain Albert

L. Pence, Jr. quickly organized a patrol of five men to move out and get them. They spotted the Japs at the head of the draw and opened fire. Sergeant Robert Gonzales, swinging around to the right to a little above the draw, got behind the Japs. He looked up and there were eight Jap backs in front of him; he raised his rifle and fired right down the line.

The little draw led into a larger one and the patrol moved forward to check it. The Japs at this stage of the fighting were easily cornered and most of them offered only slight resistance. Suddenly without warning a machine gun chattered from somewhere, and the patrol hit the ground as the bullets furrowed the tundra around them. Andrew Mezei was in the open and he jumped to run for the cover of a small rise in the ground. The gun chattered again and he fell with a bullet in his hip. The gun had surprised them utterly. They couldn't spot it. Pence was crawling under a little wrinkle in the tundra that led toward a small hill beyond which, he thought, the Japs were firing the gun. Staff Sergeant Harold J. Hunter jumped up and ran to join him. The gun spoke again and a bullet caught Hunter squarely in the forehead. Pence swore as Hunter fell. It made him sick; Hunter was a good man, a brave man . . . and this was just a mopping-up job.

Lieutenant Robert Engley had been watching the action from the CP of the 17th Infantry about 200 yards away, and he began bringing up men on the left. Pence had crawled up the hill about halfway. The machine gun was firing again. He was about 25 yards from a little pocket at the top. He pulled the pin on a grenade and tossed it, planning to use the tactics which had worked so well before of throwing a grenade and following it up with a quick bayonet rush. But as he threw the grenade the Japs threw a grenade also. It hit against Pence's side and rolled about five yards down the hill. Pence pushed his face into the tundra as the grenade went off. He turned his head to the side and saw another grenade coming. The Japs threw two more, one an American offensive, and Pence got nicked under the nose. He quickly decided that that particular spot was no place for him so he rolled down the hill and crawled into a Jap foxhole. He threw two fragmentation grenades from there up into the Japs. The grenades went off. After a moment there was a huge explosion at the top of the little knoll and helmets, boots, and arms and hands flew into the air in a horrible geyser. The Japs had killed themselves. Pence jumped up an ran up the hill to finish the job if it needed finishing. The little pocket was a ghastly mess. Mangled bodies lay strewn everywhere, some turning over slowly, others just quivering. There were thirty-six Japs in a twenty-yard diameter at the top of the little hill.

It was later in the day. Shooting had become sporadic. Pence had gotten well off to the flank and was climbing a very steep incline. Suddenly he was picking himself up, shaky and breathless. A bullet had hit his belt buckle and gear in the center of his stomach and had not penetrated. He was sitting up from where the bullet had knocked him down and was looking around to see where the shot had come from. A man about 75 feet from him was crouched in a hole and looking around, too. He had an American helmet on and an American rain jacket. Pence looked away to spot the Jap who had shot him. Then he was picking himself up again. His ears were ringing and his nose was starting to bleed. A bullet had ripped through his helmet and grazed his skull. His eyes were blurred and he was dizzy. He lay on the ground flat for a few minutes until his head cleared. Then cautiously he raised up. The American helmet was still visible on the man 75 feet away. He looked away, then snapped his head back. The man with the American helmet was pointing a rifle straight at him. Pence lunged for his own gun which he had dropped when the shot hit his helmet. The Jap fired and Pence's thumb went numb. He winced and almost dropped his gun again. Then he raised it and shot the Jap right through his American helmet. As the Jap slumped down in the hole out of sight, from several yards behind the Jap two explosions followed in quick succession. Two others had blown themselves up.

Major Lee Wallace, who had watched the first half of the episode, told Lieutenant Colonel Glen A. Nelson that they could send some men out to pick Captain Pence up after a while. He had seen him get hit twice, once in the stomach and once in the head.

When Pence walked into the CP to get his head and thumb patched up a few minutes later, Major Wallace felt like sitting down for a moment—before he fell down.

The Aftermath — 2

Sergeant Horace A. Lopez, Company C, 32d Infantry

After the orgiastic slaughterhouse fighting of the night of the 28th, the cleaning up the next day seemed quiet and deliberate. There were many Japs in the area pocketed up in little ditches and draws all over the valley, and I was operating with my squad mopping them up. We spotted some dugouts about halfway up a small hill built on a shelf overhung with rocks. We circled the hill and worked our way up to the high points overlooking the enemy positions. The dugouts were slit trenches covered with American shelter halves, but littered with Jap equipment, grenades, and pieces of their fur clothing.

We studied the setup for a few minutes. Then I shouted down there for anyone in the holes to come out. Nothing stirred. I fired twice at the farthest hole, then waited, but still nothing happened. Then we put several rounds into each of the covered slit trenches just to make sure. We were about 20 feet above the shelf and could see the whole thing except that part just directly below. We waited, but nothing moved on the little shelf.

Our position on the hill gave us a commanding view of a wide strip of the valley. The panorama below was dotted with the figures of soldiers moving, closing with little groups huddled in ravines, firing over the edges. We became fascinated by the progress of a squad across the valley, working on a group of Japs. Six of them were spread out firing at the draw, while two others worked in closer and closer from above. We had almost forgotten our own part in this play when a rock crashed into a cleft on our flank. We all jumped and looked. A Jap was crawling up through the rocks toward us.

My shot went wild, I think, but Sergeant Roger A. Carpentier fired too, from behind me, and the Jap slipped back and rolled down the rocks. We could just see his face and one hand between the rocks where he lay. He cried several times in English, "I'm going to die. . . . I'm going to die." Someone of the squad said, "Shoot him again, quick; shoot him." Carpentier fired fast and the bullet hit him across the nose. He rolled over and had his back to us but we could see one hand moving. Several times it moved down his back across the small part we could see. Someone shouted, "Are you alive? Hey! Are you alive?"

Then suddenly, as if in answer to the question, there was an explosion. When we looked again as the smoke cleared away we could see the ragged, burned edge of his shirt thrown back across his body and a strip of yellow skin ripped by a black wound.

Paper Bullets

Corporal George H. Starr, Service Company, 32d Infantry

I was bouncing beside Starr on the big D-6[10] when he told me the story.

"Nuts," I said. "Bull."

"It's the God's truth," he insisted, and handed me a little pink paper bullet to prove it. "Keep it," he said. "I've got two clips of the stuff."

It was like this: Just at daylight on May 29 Corporal George Starr and his buddy, John W. Moore, stopped the cat and jumped into the mud. Crack! Another Jap bullet zipped over the newly vacated seat.

"It's coming from over on the left," Starr said as they squirmed around in the mud between the heavy treads of the D-6.

"Yeah, near that draw," Johnny answered. The two men looked hard at the little draw and the rise behind it. Crack! Another shot ripped through the fog, the sound coming unmistakably from the little draw.

"I can't spot him, can you?" Johnny asked. They covered every inch of the area of the draw minutely, their rifles ready.

Other shots were being fired up on the high hill to the right, but they were not part of this little personal war. Crack! Another shot, coming from the left. "I'm damned if I can see him," Starr said. Moore was looking hard through the tread at the draw. Starr moved back in the mud and glanced at the hill on the right. A Jap was perched halfway up in plain sight with his rifle raised. While Starr watched the rifle popped and from the draw on the left came the sharp familiar crack.

Starr said, "Look!" and Moore swung around. He quickly fired and the Jap slumped over and slid a few feet down the hill.

"I'm going over there," Moore said. "You cover me."

Starr watched the hill and Moore crawled out from between the treads and disappeared into a small ravine between the cat and the hill. Suddenly, from the ravine, a rifle barked and Starr called out asking if Johnny was all right.

"Yeah," he answered. "Come here a second."

The two men examined the new Jap killed in the ravine. He had a grenade in each hand and had been crawling toward the cat. They moved up and looked at the Jap on the hill. His rifle still had two paper bullets in it and his ammunition pouch contained two clips of paper bullets and nothing else.

---

[10]Medium tractor.

Notches on the Rifle
Corporal William E. Smith, Company C, 4th Infantry

From somewhere I had picked up the information that Corporal Smith had an interesting story but that he was very reticent about his battle experiences. This wasn't unusual. Most soldiers who have really been in the thick of battle are reticent about the details. Maybe they can't believe the things they remember themselves, after the memories have grown cold. Anyway, I was given a hint as to a lead on Corporal Smith when someone told me that, "He wouldn't part with that M1 of his for anything in this world that I know of." And so I went to talk with Corporal Smith.

I was surprised when I saw him. His hair, which had been dark, was streaked with white all through, and over his temples it was solid white. He was a slight man and he moved with the grace of an athlete, in spite of his age. We talked a bit about generalities of the fighting, and he told me that this was his second war. He had been with the 11th Field Artillery in the last war and spent his time with the 155 howitzers.

"Well, how do you like the Infantry?" I asked him.

"Well, this was my first groundhog war," he replied, "and I sure never fought one like this before. I still can't figure those Japs."

"There are a lot of us in that boat, Sergeant [Smith had since been promoted.] They did some strange things."

His rifle was lying on the bunk and I asked, "Is that your gun?"

"Yes sir," he answered, picking it up. It was in immaculate condition, so polished and clean that it looked new. The respect for his gun, and the pride he had in it, was apparent in the way the old sergeant fondled the rifle.

"Is that the gun you had during the battle?" I asked him.

"Yes sir, it is."

"Well, it must have been quite a chore to keep it in that condition through all the wet and hard knocks that Attu gave it, wasn't it?"

"Yes, it was, sir, but it sure was worth it."

"Why?" I asked him. "Did you get some Japs with it?"

"A few," he said, then after a pause he started talking again.

"The first one was a setup. I saw a sniper up on Cold Mountain, the first Jap I had seen on the island. He was about 600 yards away, I think, and his head was outlined above a rock. I set my sight and squeezed her off, and down he went. We checked with glasses, and I got him all right."

"That must have been about May 20, wasn't it?" After a pause I added. "You said that was the first one, Sergeant. When did you get the others?"

"Well, let's see. One day I kind of got lost and wound up out ahead of Company B. The boys saw me and called up Company B on the phone and told them I was out there. I got two that day before I got back to my outfit. I kind of caught hell for going out there by myself. So the next day I stayed around pretty close. The Japs had set up a mortar and were pounding our positions with it to a helluva note. Finally our machine gunners spotted the mortar position and were getting set up to fire when they were ordered into position on the opposite flank. The doggone mortar was blasting away so I crawled out a ways where I could see a little better and opened up on them. I still can't figure out those Japs As soon as I fired on them they pulled out of their hole and, one at a time, began climbing up a steep rocky ridge behind their position. There were four of them and I just waited until each one got up in plain sight and then picked him off. It was just kid play, like shooting ducks at 900 yards, the way they were exposed.

"And then the next time you turn around they are pulling stuff like they did up on Brewer Ridge. I was up there when Lieutenant Luther G. Brewer, Jr. was killed. And the Japs had dug holes so that you had to pass over them before you could see them. The only field of fire those Japs had from these holes was up the hill, at their own troops. But they got us that way. We had passed over these holes and then the Japs raised up and fired into our backs. Luckily I was on the flank and when the Japs raised up we saw right away what was going on, and so four of them, I know, didn't do much good with that trick."

"Sergeant, your company was in on the Sarana Nose fight, too, wasn't it?" I prodded him, after a long pause.

"Yes sir, it was, and that was quite a fight, sir. The company, or what was left of it, got 59 Japs in one hole up there. We lost 5 of our own boys, too, that day. May 29, I think. Major John D. O'Reilly was in on that one in person and he had a hell of a fine time throwing grenades that morning. We were on opposite sides of a little ridge, the Japs and our company, and whoever stuck their heads up first were the first to get clipped. I guess we were more curious than the Japs because we lay there just long enough to begin to wonder just exactly what was on the other side, then over we went. Some of the boys got shot up pretty bad, but we wiped out the Japs.

"The next night I had a silly hunch that the Japs might come through again, so it was another night that I didn't do much sleeping. And that was the wind-up. When you shot you just couldn't miss. It was almost morning when we spotted about 150 or 200 Japs moving out of a draw.

"We had them in the neck of the bottle. I was running around waking up some of my buddies when the first sergeant told me I'd better get down in the hole and start shooting. About that time they were helping me into a hole. The fight didn't last long and soon they were evacuating those of us who had been wounded. I turned my rifle over to my buddy, Vernon R. Chitwood, to look after for me because the first sergeant told me that they take it away from you at the aid station; and I sure didn't want to lose my rifle. I found out later, though, that the Medics wanted us to have our rifles with us. 'They raid these places,' the medics told us."

Sergeant Smith was fondling his rifle and rubbing the stock with his thumb. Along the small of the stock were a series of little scratches that neatly marred the polish of the rest of the surface.

"How did those marks get on there, Sergeant?" I asked him.

Sergeant Smith seemed embarrassed. "Well, sir, every time I was sure this rifle had killed a Jap I made a little mark with a cartridge right there on the stock."

"May I see it, please?"

He handed the rifle over to me. I counted the little marks, and Smith was grinning at me. I don't doubt the old sergeant's veracity—although 35 is quite a sum.

Post-Battle Casualties

First Sergeant Thane S. Bertrand, Company M, 17th Infantry

Within two days after the end of the actual fighting every available man was walking across the battlefields, working at his share of the gigantic job of cleaning up the huge litter of battle. The men found foxholes filled with rags, scraps of hastily eaten rations, a shoe, a broken rifle, a body or a piece of one, a radio set with a bullet hole through it, an unexploded hand grenade. . . .

All over the island, on mountainsides, up into ravines, and across valleys—areas miles square—troops moved slowly and stiffly, picking up, policing up the unbelievable scattered junk, remnants of the fight. It was like housecleaning with a gigantic hang-over the morning after a huge drunken party.

Sergeant Bluford J. Head stooped over and picked up a mess kit from the bottom of a foxhole. Lying inside the bent and rusty mess kit was a Jap hand grenade, a dud that had failed to explode. He looked at it and then picked it out of the mess kit and set it up on the edge of the hole. Even before his fingers had completely released it, it exploded with a viciousness that tore his hand off.

The troops had worked out of Jim Fish Valley, where Sergeant Head had been injured and were working up Sarana Valley, policing up. Private First Class Hubert H. Somers had set fire to a pile of rubbish, and was warming C rations on the blaze with some others in the vicinity. He bent over the little fire to stir the rations, just as the fire exploded furiously. The force of the explosion knocked him backward away from the fire. In a few moments his body looked like a red sponge, arms, legs, and face severely lacerated and filled with hundreds of tiny shell fragments. Another man sitting near by had a broken eardrum from the concussion. A shell about the size of a 60mm. mortar had exploded in the fire.

To men who had gone completely through the life and blood of living battle, this was like being whipped by a shadow. To fall in the stagnant dregs of afterbattle was a tragic thing.

Prisoners of War

Private First Class Howard L. Sparrs, Private Emerson L. Burgett,
Private First Class Ira E. Patrick,
4th Infantry

We were on an OP out in the Klebnikoff Point area. It was about 2200 on June 8 when Lieutenant John D. Gillespie and Sparrs spotted the first Jap, outlined against the skyline in the fog like a ghost. They took out after him and alerted the rest of the OP. Lieutenant Gillespie waited just long enough to shout directions to the effect that we should split up into three groups and scour the ground from the water line to about 500 yards inland for other Japs. Then he started out after Sparrs, Burgett, the Medic, and Corporal Roscoe C. Campbell. The Jap was running toward the ocean as fast as he could go. He disappeared over the crest of a little hill with us hot on his tail, and as we topped the hill we found ourselves in a little rocky hollow bounded on three sides by small steep banks, and opening onto an arm of rocks that struck out into the ocean. Perhaps we surprised the Japs more than they surprised us. Anyway, in the next instant we were fighting like madmen. I saw Burgett bring down two of them, firing his rifle from his hip. Sergeant Campbell was firing like a demon in front. I shot one of them who had jumped up on my right and he fell on his face. I looked over to the left and Sparrs had just shot one, but there was a Jap right behind him not over ten feet away. He had a pistol leveled at Sparrs' back. I will never know how Sparrs got out of it, but suddenly, just as the Jap fired, Sparrs turned like a cat and ducked. The Jap missed him and Sparrs fired. The Jap went down and rolled over, still holding his pistol. He pointed it at Sparrs again, but Sparrs was right on him this time. He wrenched it out of the Jap's hand and fired three times into his chest. The whole fight was over in a matter of seconds, and a quick survey showed six dead Japs and none of us even scratched. The rest of the Japs had made a break for the arm of rocks sticking out down into the water.

There must have been four or more that ran out onto the arm of rocks in the ocean, so we decided to take cover in the hollow where we had had the fight and cover the arm of rocks. They couldn't get off it, but we didn't think we could go down there and do much good either, since there were probably more of them than there were of us. So Lieutenant Gillespie decided that I should go back and contact one of the other groups and get some help.

I had gone back along the slope of the hill toward the ocean maybe 400 yards when I spotted the boys. There was something cooking all right. Smith and William W. Lucas were lying right on the lip of a steep gorge that led down toward the water line, and Patrick was moving down the hill along the opposite side of the gorge. They were all intent on something inside the gorge. I moved up to where I could see the whole thing. Apparently they had been working along the water line and had moved up on the hill to get around a wall of rocks that jutted straight up from the water blocking their path on the opposite side of the gorge from where I was. I hollered over to Lucas and asked him what was going on. They told me they thought they had a Jap spotted. They had seen something move down in the gorge, and after they had looked closely for a while they had spotted a Jap blanket stretched across a crevice in the rocks in the bottom of the gorge. "It may have been just that old blanket flapping in the wind, but we're not taking any chances," Lucas hollered back. Patrick was well down inside the gorge now, and moving closer to the Jap blanket. Lucas and Smith had their guns trained on the blanketed opening. Patrick crouched behind a shoulder of rock about ten feet from the blanket. "Come out of there!" he hollered. Nothing happened. "Come out of there, damya!" he hollered again. Still nothing happened. Patrick moved out from behind the rock and crept toward the motionless blanket. Very gingerly with one hand he reached out and gave the blanket a tentative tug. The blanket tugged back, jerked out of his hand. Patrick looked back up at Lucas and Smith. He grabbed the blanket and pulled again. Again the blanket jerked out of his hand. Smith hollered, "Pull her again, Pat," and Patrick gave the blanket a mighty jerk. It flopped off the crevice revealing a packed tangle of heads and legs and coats and blankets, like a knot of snakes, and spitting flame and bullets. Patrick lunged backward away from the hole and fell behind the shoulder of some rocks, at the same time Lucas and Smith opened up. They each emptied their clips into the hole.

Patrick had escaped being hit by the skin of his teeth. He beat a hasty retreat up the wall of the gorge, while Smith and Lucas went down to meet him. A tally showed that five rifles and a light machine gun with a man for each weapon had holed up in the tiny crevice and tried to hide out behind a blanket. It was frightful to look at after the grenades, so we stayed just long enough to be sure our job was completed.

I told them about the Japs on the point of rocks and how we had them bottled up, and they said, "Let's go get 'em." So we started back toward the little hollow where Burgett and Sergeant Campbell were waiting with Lieutenant Gillespie.

As we topped the hill we realized that we had missed the fun. Sergeant Kenneth Nicolay and some others had come up before us and already there were two dead Japs sprawled out on the rocks, and Burgett and Sergeant Campbell each had a prisoner. The two Japs were nervous but quite docile, and Burgett was getting a great bang out of his prisoner. The little fellow was a Jap eight-ball if ever there was one. He had a motley uniform on, and a heavy fur-lined, blue navy overcoat over his tan uniform. His pockets were full of assorted junk that fascinated Burgett, who was thoroughly shaking him down as we came up. Our arrival unnerved the little fat Jap even more and he tugged nervously at Burgett's pants leg when he saw our rifles pointing at him. Burgett was emptying his pockets into the ocean. The little Jap's pantomime was eloquent and he nodded a definite affirmation about getting rid of the grenades. Then Burgett pulled out a fistful of Jap paper money which he likewise tossed into the sea. The little Jap screwed up his face in agonized displeasure and pressed his palms together, finger tips under his chin, and bobbed up and down in little hops like a musical-comedy funny man, while he chattered frantically in Japanese. Then Burgett pulled out a Jap battle flag which he held up in front of the little fellow. The Jap shook his head violently in the negative and gestured so not a doubt remained—"Take it away!" The inner pockets of his coat revealed an assorted, and incidentally excellent, collection of divers pornography, consisting mainly of quaint, tinted pictures, neat and lewd, on silk handkerchiefs. The little Jap smiled innocently as Burgett gazed appraisingly over the collection (which, by the way, he pocketed).

The rest of us moved out onto the point of rocks to scour it and make sure we had missed nothing, leaving Burgett to guard the prisoners. Burgett and the Jap were smiling at each other, and Burgett grinning at the funny little fellow said, "Smile, you little bastard, but make one funny move and I'll blow your brains out." The Jap grinned toothfully in reply and sat down.

We checked the rock pile thoroughly and found nothing. We returned to Burgett and the prisoners and started back toward camp. On the way we picked up driftwood along the water to warm our C rations with when we got back.

Burgett piled the little Jap's arms full. Burgett marched behind his prisoner and when the little man straggled going up a hill he would work the bolt on his rifle and the Jap would shift into second and take off.

The Japs were in good shape all right, but they were hungry and Smith had caused the little eight-ball another seige of agony before we left the beach. He had kicked the big fish that the little guy was cooking back into the ocean. So, when we got back to camp and had our hash cooked up we offered some to the prisoners. Burgett had diligently carved an acceptable pair of chopsticks out of a board for the eight-ball, and with great ceremony he offered them to the Jap. The Jap looked puzzled for a second. Then grinning broadly reached into his boot and pulled out a GI spoon.

The other prisoner was morose, but we discovered he could speak English. He had actually surrendered, shouting, "No gun, no shoot," as Sergeant Campbell closed with him. On the way back to camp Campbell tried to get him to talk but he said very little. He did say, however, that his home was San Francisco, to which Sparrs replied wistfully, "Yeah, and you'll probably be there a helluva long time before I will."

This is a knocked-out war.

FINALE

On July Fourth, for those unable to cross the pass to the cemetery in Massacre Valley, a simple ceremony was held in camp.

The battalion was assembled. Major Charles G. Fredericks read the Roll Call of the men who had fallen. Lieutenant Colonel Glen A. Nelson spoke. A sergeant sang *My Buddy*. And Padre Habetz repeated a prayer.

After the volley, the last note of Taps echoed over the mountains. Then it was over.

Captain Robert C. Foulston said, "Forward . . ." but the "march" stuck in his throat. With chins clamped hard and wet eyes blinking, the silent fighting men marched off the field.

It had been paid for. Attu was ours.

INDEX OF UNITS

INDEX OF INDIVIDUALS

Photo by Signal Corps

Approaching Attu, 7th Division troops crowd the transport deck to get some fresh air or have a relaxing smoke. Fog and somber gray water surround the ship. Crowded conditions made it impossible to exercise aboard ship.

Photo by Signal Corps

Below decks every facility for shipboard training is utilized till the eleventh hour. These troops are seeing in miniature what their ship is carrying them toward—a model reproducing all of Attu except the Japs, whose rifles and machine guns were waiting along these snowbound crags. From the faces, it is evident that even a model of Attu had a sobering influence.

Photo by 11th Air Force

No model here—Attu itself, where the Southern Force landed on May 11, 1943. Massacre Valley, up which they advanced, stretches inland from Massacre Bay, its sides lined with towering snow-capped peaks. On the highest of these a Navy flyer crashed after strafing the fog-hung valley, thus giving his name to Henderson Ridge.

Photo by Signal Corps

The first wave of assault boats gropes its way through Aleutian fog toward the unknown Attu beach two miles ahead.

Artillerymen with their howitzer and 105mm. ammunition being transferred from transport to landing craft off the Attu beaches. Two leading boats of their wave, dimly seen in the background, are already half swallowed by the fog.

The Infantryman's foxhole view of Jarmin Pass, leading from Massacre Valley across to Holtz Bay. Jap trenches, sniper and machine-gun positions, cleverly camouflaged in the mottled tundra folds, swept the valley floor from the nose of Black Mountain and the low plateau (right center of photo) stretching across the mouth of Jarmin Pass. Mortars emplaced in low

Clevesy Pass, on the northeast side of upper Massacre Valley, led across to Sanara Valley and the distant heights of Prendergast and Fish Hook ridges. Strong Jap trenches, machine-gun and mortar emplacements held the slopes of Cold Mountain and the ridge leading up to Point A

Photo by Captain N. L. Drummond

ground behind the plateau pounded the Americans who were dug into the valley mud. Heavy continuous pressure by our forces compelled the Japs to abandon these positions the night of May 16. The following day the pass was occupied, thus joining the Northern and Southern landing forces and restricting the Jap garrison to the northeast corner of Attu.

Photo by Captain N. L. Drummond

(Point Able). Deadly fire swept the exposed slopes leading up to the pass. On May 19 the 2d Battalion of the 17th Infantry, and the 2d Battalion of the 32d Infantry, successfully assaulted these positions and opened the gate for a drive against Sarana Valley and the Chichagof heights.

Photo by Signal Corps

May 12—beachhead established. Since our landing caught the Japs off guard, no opposition developed and supplies could be rapidly brought ashore. In the background are transports and landing barges feeding troops and matériel into Massacre Beach. The banner between poles on the beach designates a dump for one type of supplies. In the foreground the tundra covered by coarse beach grass is used for a bivouac area.

Photo by Captain N. L. Drummond

The Southern Force advanced up Massacre Valley the evening of May 11. Their objective was the pass (Zwinge Pass) leading from the valley's upper end through the mountains to Holtz Bay. In the gathering darkness and fog which blanketed the mountains they finally met Japanese machine-gun, rifle, and mortar fire from strong positions surrounding the pass. The next morning fog still hid the heights of Henderson Ridge, stretching down from Zwinge Pass along their left flank. Jap snipers and machine gunners enfiladed the valley floor from high positions along the fog line. During the next few days small American patrols fought along these rugged slopes and gradually wiped out the Jap emplacements there. The photo was taken from the highest point (600 feet) on the Hogback, looking westward just to the left of Black Mountain.

Point A (Point Able) from which a determined platoon of Japanese enfiladed the Americans in the valley below. From their dominating height they beat back our first few attempts to climb the steep, slippery slopes and dislodge them. Finally, on May 21, Company E, 32d Infantry, scaled the top in the early morning darkness. The Japs' retreat was blocked by Company C, 32d Infantry, in positions along Gilbert Ridge. The Jap platoon chose to die to the last man. In the foreground is a heavily fortified American position on the Hogback overlooking Clevesy Pass and Point A.

Blue Beach, Massacre Bay, looking southwest. The typical fog line hides all but the lowest slopes of the 2,000-foot-high mountains in the background. In the foreground a "cat" with its trailer waits for supplies to haul up the valley. Tents and supply dumps line the beach now well established on May 16.

Colonel Wayne C. Zimmerman (now Brigadier General), commander of the Southern Force, and Lieutenant Winfield H. Mapes, 17th Infantry, in an OP on the north slope of the Hogback. Colonel Zimmerman is directing the Southern Force's attack against Clevesy Pass on May 19.

Men of the 4th Infantry move inland from the Massacre Bay beaches after landing on May 18 to reinforce the 7th Division. Note the churned-up tundra in the foreground and the mist in the background.

The first heavy-duty highway from Blue Beach, Massacre Bay. Tractors which often bogged down in the tundra used this gravelly stream bed entirely during the first week and partially thereafter. This "cat" with trailer is coming downstream empty for another load. To the men on the front lines flowed a real stream of supplies.

Manpower moved most of the front-line supplies and ammunition. Tractors were few on Attu and vulnerable to Jap fire. Here men of the 4th Infantry haul mortar ammunition and combat equipment up the Hogback.

Photo by 11th Air Force

Aerial view of northeast corner of Attu island. The Northern Force of the Attu invading troops landed on May 11 at Red Beach, extreme right center of photo. The landing was difficult but unopposed. They fought completely around Holtz Bay and then joined the Southern Force in the drive which ended at Chichagof Harbor.

Photo by 11th Air Force

Aerial view of Holtz Bay showing rock-infested approaches to Red Beach and the rolling snow-patched tundra terrain leading inland to Hill X (also known during the battle as Bloody Knob). Here the 1st Battalion of the 17th Infantry won its first major encounter with the Japs (May 12-13) and gained the high ground dominating the west arm, Holtz Bay Valley.

To Holtz Bay

To Massacre Valley

(L 5753) approx.

Route of travel

To Beach Scarlet

The independent Provisional Battalion, made up of the 7th Scout Company and the 7th Reconnaissance Troop, landed separately from submarines before daylight on May 11. Separated from the main Northern Force by four miles of jagged mountain peaks, they pushed up through the fog and snow to bivouac overnight on a snow-drifted pass. The next morning they attacked the rear of the Japanese positions in Holtz Bay, keeping up the pressure throughout four days.

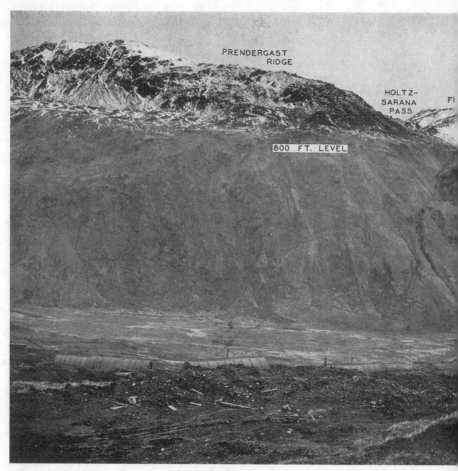

PRENDERGAST
RIDGE

HOLTZ-
SARANA
PASS

800 FT. LEVEL

The south side of Prendergast and Fish Hook ridges, looking northeast from the Sara
side of Clevesy Pass. Jim Fish Valley and Lake Cories lie to the right. In the Southe
Force's drive against the Chichagof area it was necessary to take these heights before progre
could be made along the valley floor. Two and a half hours were required to move a co
pany from the valley to 800-foot level. Japanese machine-gun and sniper nests studded t

POINT 3

RIDGE

POINT 4

BUFFALO
RIDGE

Photo by Captain N. L. Drummond

idge lines along which fog and snow squalls swept. The main enemy defensive system be-
ow Fish Hook Ridge guarded Clevesy Pass. The Fish Hook-Buffalo Ridge heights were the
inal iron ring of Jap defense for their Chichagof Harbor base. At any cost they had to hold
his line of crags and were willing to die in the attempt. Combined elements of the Northern
nd Southern Forces took the two passes and the southwest end of Fish Hook on May 25-26.

Photo by Signal Corps

Attu's northern coast line, a bleak, unfriendly jumble of empty crags, appeared through the lifting mists on May 12. Troops going in to Red Beach on the second day could see their objective five miles ahead, rising from the sullen waves.

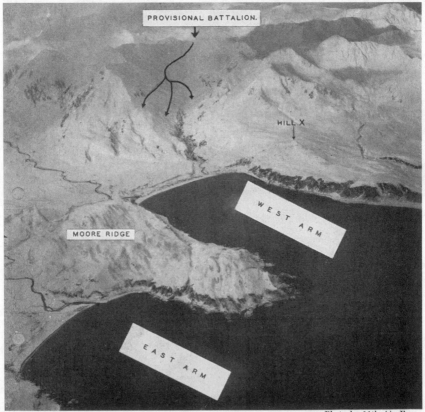

Photo by 11th Air Force

Aerial shot of Holtz Bay, February 1943, showing in graphic snow relief the junction area of the Provisional Battalion with the main Northern Force and the terrain features which were keys to the Holtz Bay battles.

Photo by Signal Corps

Close-up of Red Beach on May 12. Supplies and heavy equipment such as tractors and cannon had to be winched up the 200-foot escarpment which completely encircled the beach.

HILL X

Photo by Signal Corps

Beach area in the west arm of Holtz Bay on May 19 after its occupation by the Northern Force. Remains of the well camouflaged Jap supply camp and strong beach defenses are dimly visible. Five Jap dual-purpose AA guns, emplaced just back of the beach, heavily shelled our troops on the Hill X heights on May 12, 13, and 14. The Jap Zero on the beach was one of four destroyed by American P-38s a month before the battle. The photo was taken from Moore Ridge, which separates the two arms of Holtz Bay.

Photo by Signal Corps

Traffic problem—illustrating the difficulties of mechanized warfare on Attu. The sound of planes indicates to the man on the right the possibility of trouble overhead as well as underfoot.

HILL X

RED BEACH

WEST ARM BEACH

Photo by Captain N. L. Drummond

West arm of Holtz Bay Valley taken from positions along Moore Ridge which the Japs held after they were driven from the west arm. From these the enemy swept the valley floor with mortar and machine-gun fire. Detachments of Companies A and B, 17th Infantry, fought their way to the highest point on Moore Ridge and forced the Japs to withdraw to the heights between the east arm valley and Chichagof.

Photo by 11th Air Force

Aerial view of Holtz Bay valleys looking southeast, outlining the mass of mountainous terrain which separated the Northern and Southern Forces in their drive against Chichagof Harbor. Though the northeast part of Attu is clear, the typical overcast which rendered air support so difficult and uncertain throughout the battle blots out all of Massacre Valley.

Photo by Captain N. L. Drummond

The Bahai Bowl between Fish Hook and Prendergast ridges meant deadly fighting for the Northern Force on its way to Chichagof. The Jap forces withdrew from the East Arm valley in the middle foreground May 16-17, leaving rear-guard machine gunners and snipers along the rugged slopes. The main Jap positions were well constructed trench and tunnel systems just below the crests of Fish Hook and Prendergast ridges.

Buffalo Ridge, taken by the 32d Infantry, stretches down from the end of the Fish Hook to Lake Cories. From May 25 to May 30 the Southern Force attacked in this direction on three different levels—the crest line

LAKE CORIES

Photo by Captain N. L. Drummond

of Fish Hook Ridge; the 800-foot bench along which the camera looks; and in Jim Fish Valley below. The heights beyond Lake Cories figured only in the mopping-up after Chichagof Harbor was taken.

Photo by Signal Corps

Holtz Bay, swept by Japanese machine guns, against which the Northern Force fought on its way up to the Holtz-Chichagof Pass. The photo was taken from a Japanese position along the lower slopes leading up from the bay. The slopes are pock-marked with shell craters from our artillery across Holtz Bay. Troops are moving up to reinforce the Northern Force assault on Holtz-Chichagof Pass, May 25, 1943.

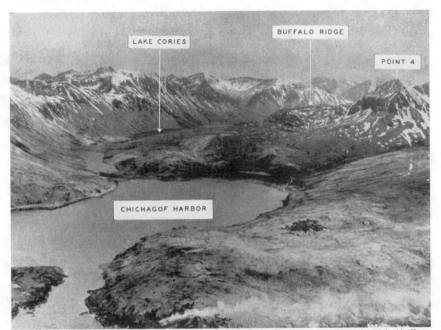

Like desperate cornered rats the remnants of the Jap force, crowded onto the low plateau between Buffalo Ridge and Chichagof Harbor, suddenly lashed out. Our forces were holding the entire Fish Hook, most of Buffalo Ridge and the Jim Fish Valley floor level with Lake Cories. The Jap night attack swept along this valley floor toward Clevesy Pass in a welter of blood and confusion.

Engineer Hill on the Sarana side of Clevesy Pass where the 7th

The jagged ridge line of the south part of the Fish Hook, photographed from just above the Holtz-Chichagof Pass looking northeast to Chichagof Harbor. These peaks, more than 2,000 feet high, and their precipitous slopes were strongly held by Jap infantry. From the pass northward the heights were taken by our 4th Infantry. This terrain was the key to the last Jap defenses. The only approach was

Photo by Captain N. L. Drummond

sion Engineers and 50th Engineers broke the Jap counterattack.

Photo by Captain N. L. Drummond

an icy knife-edged ridge leading out from the base of the Fish Hook to Point 3, then on 500 yards to Point 4. Along many sections one man at a time had to work ahead under covering fire to dislodge the Japs with rifle and grenade. A few feet to each side of him the ground dropped almost straight down for 200 feet. Heavy fog intermittently swept along the ridge, reducing visibility to a few yards.